The Best of
Reader's Digest
Timeless
Favorites

Reader's
Digest

New York / Montreal

A READER'S DIGEST BOOK

Copyright © 2021 Trusted Media Brands, Inc.
44 South Broadway
White Plains, NY 10601

The credits that appear on pages 312–314 are hereby made part of this copyright page.

ISBN 978-1-62145-589-9 (hardcover)
ISBN 978-1-62145-590-5 (paperback)
ISBN 978-1-62145-591-2 (e-pub)

Component number 116600105H

We are committed to both the quality of our products and the service we provide to our customers. We value your comments, so please feel free to contact us at TMBBookTeam@TrustedMediaBrands.com.

For more Reader's Digest products and information, visit our website:
        www.rd.com (in the United States)
        www.readersdigest.ca (in Canada)

Printed in the United States

10 9 8 7 6 5 4 3 2 1

Contents

Introduction

Whether the theme is Disney princesses, auctions, or college football, nothing is more American than the subjects and characters whose stories are told in *Reader's Digest*. For the past 100 years, we've been capturing in vivid detail the grand tapestry of life in the United States, from historic moments to childhood memories, life-altering events to simple pleasures.

In this volume, we've gathered some of our favorite narratives from the past century, full of chance encounters with celebrities, miraculous escapes from death, and hilarious accounts of all the little absurdities of life. You'll be fascinated by the behind-the-scenes report of how Ronald Reagan's famous exhortation to Mikhail Gorbachev to tear down the Berlin Wall was nearly cut from his speech; you'll be rooting for the blind duck that was a victim of an oil spill; and you'll laugh out loud at America's ten funniest jokes and the comics who chose them.

With stories about soldiers, criminals, and everyday heroes, *The Best of Reader's Digest: Timeless Favorites* has something for everyone, from humor to drama to heartwarming tales—each as funny, thrilling, and moving as when it was first printed in the pages of the magazine.

Happy reading!

—The Editors of *Reader's Digest*

Where Success Comes From

It is in the mind's eye—and the image of it, firmly held, can often help you to live up to your own best moments.

—

BY **ARTHUR GORDON**

Originally published in June 1960

ne of my most vivid and valuable memories goes back to a mild December afternoon in the Georgia low country. Vivid because I remember it so clearly. Valuable because, without fully understanding it, I was handed a remarkable bit of wisdom.

A single-barreled, 20-gauge shotgun, given to me for Christmas, had made me the proudest 13-year-old in Georgia. On my first hunt, moreover, by a lucky freak I had managed to hit the only bird I got a shot at. My heart almost burst with excitement and pride.

The second hunt was a different story. My companion was an elderly judge, a friend of my father's. He looked rather like a bloodhound, with a seamed brown face and hooded eyes and the easy tolerance that comes from knowing the worst about the human race but liking people just the same. I had some misgivings about hunting with the Judge because I stood in awe of him, and wanted mightily to please him. And I walked straight into humiliation.

We found plenty of birds, and the Judge knocked down one or two on every covey rise. I, on the other hand, didn't touch a feather. I tried everything: shooting over, under, soon, late. Nothing made any difference. And the more I missed, the tenser I got.

Then old Doc, the pointer, spotted a quail in a clump of palmetto. He froze, his long tail rigid. Something in me froze, too, because I knew I was facing one more disgrace.

This time, however, instead of motioning me forward, the Judge placed his gun carefully on the ground. "Let's set a minute," he suggested companionably. Whereupon he took out a pipe and loaded it with blunt fingers. Then, slowly, he said, "Your dad was telling me you hit the first quail you shot at the other day. That right?"

"Yes, sir," I said miserably. "Just luck, I guess."

"Maybe," said the Judge. "But that doesn't matter. Do you remember exactly how it happened? Can you close your eyes and see it all in your mind?"

I nodded, because it was true. I could summon up every detail: the bird exploding from under my feet, the gun seeming to point itself, the surge of elation, the warmth of the praise....

"Well, now," the Judge said easily, "you just sit here and relive that shot a couple of times. Then go over there and kick up that bird. Don't think about me or the dog or

> ### *"You've been focusing on failure. I want to leave you looking at the image of success," he said.*

anything else. Just think about that one good shot you made the other day—and sort of keep out of your own way."

When I did what he said, it was as if a new set of reflexes had come into play. Out flashed the quail. Up went the gun, smoothly and surely, as if it had life and purpose of its own. Seconds later, Doc was at my knee, offering the bird.

I was all for pressing on, but the Judge unloaded his gun. "That's all for today, son," he said. "You've been focusing on failure all afternoon. I want to leave you looking at the image of success."

There, complete in two sentences, was the best advice I'd ever had, or ever would have. Did I recognize it, seize upon it eagerly, act upon it fully? Of course not. I was just a child, delighted with a remarkable trick that somehow worked. I had no inkling of the tremendous psychological dynamics involved.

For a long time, with a child's faith in magic, I used the Judge's advice as a kind of hunting good luck charm. Later I found that the charm worked in other sports, too. In tennis, say, if at some crucial point you needed a service ace, it was uncanny how often your racket would deliver if you made yourself recall, vividly and distinctly, a previous ace that you had hammered past an opponent.

I know now why this is so. The human organism is a superb machine, engineered to solve fantastic problems. It is perfectly capable of blasting a tennis ball 70 feet onto an area the size of a handkerchief, or putting an ounce of shot traveling more than 100 feet per second exactly where it will intersect the path of a target moving 50 miles per hour. It can do far more difficult things than these— but only if it is not interfered with, if tension does not creep in to stiffen the muscles, dull the reflexes, and fog the marvelous computers in the brain.

And tension, which nine times out of ten is based on the memory of past failures, can be reduced or even eliminated by the memory of past success.

At first I applied this image-of-success technique only to athletics. Later I began to see that a similar principle operated for many of the successful career people whom I met through my work. These individuals varied enormously in background, in field of endeavor—even in brains. The one thing they all had in common was confidence.

One such man, a corporation president, reminisced to me about his first job. "I started my sales career," he said, "by selling pots and pans from door to door. The first day I made only one sale in 40 attempts. But I never forgot the face of that woman who finally bought something ... how it changed from suspicion and hostility to gradual interest and final acceptance. For years I used to recall her face as a kind of talisman when the going was rough." To this man, that housewife's face was a mirror that reflected the image of himself as a successful salesman.

There are times when even the brightest talent can be dimmed momentarily if this consciousness of competence is lost. Once I talked with Margaret Mitchell about the frame of mind in which she wrote *Gone With the Wind*. "It was going along pretty well," Miss Mitchell said, "until somebody sent me a new book called *John Brown's Body*, by Stephen Vincent Benét. When I finished reading that magnificent Civil War epic, I burst into tears and put my own manuscript away on a closet shelf. *John Brown's Body* gave me such a terrible case of the humbles that it

was months before I could find the necessary faith in myself and my book to go on."

A terrible case of the humbles. What a vivid way of saying that she lost her conviction of competence! And when she lost it, tension took over—and paralyzed her.

The truth is, all of us dread the hurt of failure, even in small things. And it starts young. Children face a world of constantly increasing demands. They need praise and reassurance and the repeated performance of tasks within their powers if the memory of past failures is to be crowded out by the memory of past successes. That was what the wise old judge did for me. When he saw that I was "focusing on failure," he made me turn around and stare at success.

Employing this stratagem is not just wishful thinking. The essence of the magic, it seems to me, is that you visualize something that actually did occur, and therefore can occur again. You brace yourself on a specific, concrete episode during which you functioned well.

Such episodes happen to all of us.

Initial failure, to be sure, is the price you pay for learning anything new. The first few times you try to water-ski, you may well topple in a heap. The first few times you try to make a speech or bake a cake, the results may leave much to be desired. But if you keep at it, sooner or later, by luck or the blessed law of averages, there will be a success.

This, then, is the image to fasten on the next time you approach the same problem. Nail it up in your mind like a horseshoe, and it will bring you something better than mere good luck.

An Electric Nightmare

Some violent, unseen force seemed to be stalking the whole family, reaching out, grabbing them.

——

BY **JOHN ROBBEN**

Originally published in June 1973

awoke that Saturday morning of August 28, 1971, knowing that something was wrong. Outside our house in Stamford, Connecticut, the woods were dripping from an all-night rain. But who, or what, had awakened and alerted me? I got out of bed to look around, feeling a chill on the back of my neck.

"Dad?" my eldest daughter, Sue, 16, called from her room. "Is something wrong?"

"Did you hear anything?" I asked.

"No. But something woke me up. I'm scared."

On the stair landing, I strained my ears but heard nothing. Perhaps something other than a noise had awakened me. A light? Yes, it had been a light, unusually and oddly white. Or had I only dreamed it?

Then I looked down the stairs, and noticed a tiny light flickering at the base of the double front doors. A firefly? At this time of morning? I went back to the bedroom, slipped on a pair of sneakers and went down to investigate. At the door, there were now *two* flickering lights.

As I leaned down to take a closer look, the two lights erupted into 10 or 12 and began to *bzzzz*. Electricity! What had awakened me was a flash of light.

I bolted back up the stairs, shouting, to arouse my wife and all five children. My first thought was to get everyone out of the house. I herded them all toward the back door. But as we came into the kitchen, a gurgling sound—like sloshing water—started up from the basement. I yanked open the cellar door, and was greeted with a cloud of blue smoke, shot through with orange and yellow flashes of light. Instinctively I turned on the light switch—and got a terrific shock.

"Don't touch anything!" I yelled. The children began to panic and cry. I slid open the back glass door leading onto the stoop. We stood there a moment, poised in fear. The woods were shrouded in mist, dripping with rain, and in the gray half-light of dawn looked eerie. It didn't seem any safer out there than inside. To run or stay?

Our large and willful dog made up our minds for us. Determined to get out, Trooper made a dash for the door. My wife grabbed him by the collar, but he pulled her out onto the landing.

"Hang onto him, Margie!" I shouted. How strong is habit, even in a crisis. I was worried about his running around, barking, and waking up the neighbors.

He bounded down the five wooden steps of the stoop, dragging Margie with him. He was pulling her off balance and I yelled at her to let him go. Too late! As the dog's paws touched the wet grass he yelped and leaped away, jerking my wife to the ground. Instantly she began screaming and thrashing convulsively on the grass. I ran down the steps.

"I'm being electrocuted!" she shouted. "Don't touch me!"

I froze.

"Oh, God!" she cried. "Save the children."

I saw what looked like a wire beneath her twisting body. If I touched her, I figured, I would be trapped and helpless as she was.

I don't know where I got the strength to leave her and return to the house, but there was no choice. I had to save the children first. They were gone from the kitchen. They'd fled back upstairs when their mother screamed. At my order, they came running down again.

"We've got to get out," I said. "Hurry!"

The walls were humming ominously now, the buzzing and sparking from the basement growing louder as I led the children out of the kitchen and down the steps. On the slate walk, single file, we went past Margie. She was still writhing on the grass, screaming for God's help—and for us not to touch her.

"Is Mom dying?" Sue cried.

"I don't know," I said.

The children wailed even louder. I took them down the walk and past the corner of the house, where the grounding rod for our house's wiring system was spluttering and shooting flames like a Roman candle. We ran across a bluestone driveway and through evergreen bushes onto our neighbors' property. Apparently awakened by my wife's screams, Stan and Rhoda Spiegelman were standing on their high porch. I saw terror in their eyes as they must have seen it in ours.

"Margie's being electrocuted. Our house is on fire!" I shouted. "Call the ambulance. Call the police!"

Then, pointing the children toward our neighbors' house, I started back for my wife. But I hadn't taken more than three steps

> ## *Suspended between wife and daughters, I stood paralyzed. Any moment I expected to be flung to the ground.*

when I heard the children begin to scream. Spinning around, I saw that while three of them had reached the safety of the porch, Sue and her youngest sister, Ellen, were down thrashing on the ground. For the first time I realized that the earth itself was electrified.

Suspended between wife and daughters, I stood paralyzed, unable to move in either direction. Any moment now I expected to be grabbed and flung to the ground myself. I could feel a tingling sensation through the soles of my sneakers.

Unlike my wife, whose entire body was pinned to the earth, the two trapped girls, crouched on hands and knees, were able somehow to crawl. Ellen inched toward Stan, my neighbor, who had started out to help her, felt a shock on his feet, and retreated to his wooden steps. His wife ran through her house, flung open a ground-level door and called to Sue from there. When I saw that the girls were going to make it, I started after Margie.

She was still thrashing on the ground. The wire I thought she was lying on was only a piece of rope. But when I bent over and touched her, a terrific shock slammed my arm. I let go. Then I grabbed an ankle and jerked her toward me, letting go as the shock struck again. I continued to grab and jerk, six or seven times, to get her away from the electric field to safer ground. On about the seventh pull I received no shock, and Margie lay still, sobbing.

After a moment she was able to raise her head off the ground. I lifted her and held her in my arms.

"The children?" she asked.

"They're OK."

She wept helplessly.

I helped her walk away from our house, past the now quiescent grounding rod and into our neighbors' backyard. There, waiting at the ground-floor door, were the children. They came running into our arms.

❖   ❖   ❖

The police arrived a short time later and drove Margie and Sue to the hospital. The firefighters came, but the fire was already out. Stan and I inspected the damage. It was remarkably little. The electricity was off, of course, and the clocks stopped at 6:10 a.m. The motor in the basement freezer was burned out. That was the extent of the fire. We opened the cellar windows to let the smoke out. There was no damage upstairs, but the nails in the cedar shingles on the front of the house had charred the wood.

Opening the front door, where I'd first spied the danger, I got a good look at what had happened. The broad trunk of a dead tree, its stability weakened by several days of wind and rain, lay sprawled across our driveway, about 150 feet from the house. It knocked down a cluster of wires, including—we were told later—a two-cable circuit that normally carried 13,200 volts. Ordinarily these two cables would have touched, short-circuited and blown a power-line fuse, cutting the current off. But for reasons still not entirely clear, this failed to happen. Instead, the electricity ran wild.

First it had gone into our well, burning out the pump. "But that didn't satisfy it," said the electrician who came to repair the damage the following day. "So it kept trying to find a ground for its force somewhere else." That's when it slithered into our house like some evil thing, into our food freezer and our wiring. The "fireflies" I had seen were actually droplets of rain that had become energized when they rolled onto the metal stripping at the base of the front door. And, in its relentless hunger, the electricity spread itself over a section of wet ground, creating an "energized field." *

It was probably the diffusion of its energy over this comparatively large area that saved my wife's life. Strong enough to cause her to lose muscular control and keep her pinned to the ground for seven agonizing minutes, the current wasn't concentrated enough to kill her. The doctor who examined her at the hospital that morning said she had suffered no heart damage. However, for months afterward she suffered recurring pains in her arms and legs. Meanwhile, repairs to our electrical system and freezer cost only $437.25.

For the next three nights we slept in the home of friends who were away on vacation. We each could have had a bedroom to ourselves, but instead we chose to sleep, side by side, on the floor of their playroom. Even together like that, we were uneasy, and we left the lights burning all night.

On the fourth day we returned to our own house, after an electrician had checked it out from top to bottom. The night there was eerie.

My wife turned in with some of the children and I with the others. Toward morning, I fell asleep, but awakened suddenly with a strange feeling. I looked at the clock and saw that it was 6:10—the precise moment when time had stopped for us four days earlier. At breakfast, when my wife proposed selling our house, I agreed immediately.

Apparently—as electrical engineer Bernard Schwartz explained later—the "hot" cable fell to the earth, while its companion "neutral" cable caught in a tree or on a nonconducting boulder. Thus, for the circuit to be completed, the current had to reach the nearest point where the neutral cable was grounded: at a transformer installation, two poles away. Under the given geology and ground conditions, the route lay through the Robbens' house and yard. As a result, there was a current flow—lasting about 10 minutes—that was finally sufficient to blow a line fuse.*

Anybody Want to Buy a $2,300 Dog?

There probably won't be any takers for Topper and, all things considered, it's probably just as well.

———

BY **ROBERT DE ROOS**

Originally published in October 1958

His name is Topper. He is a boxer with a fine tawny coat, a black muzzle, sharply chiseled ears and emotional brown eyes. There is not a mean bone in his body or a bad thought in his head. In fact there is no thought of any kind in his head.

He poses, stretched out on the steps like the marble lions in front of the New York Public Library, his stern gaze fixed on the middle distance. He is mighty handsome and he knows it. Man's Noble Friend, the watchdog, guarding the home.

A nice picture, but untrue. My dog is worthless as a watchdog. He lets anyone into the house. Milkmen, burglars, salesmen— they're all the same to him. The only thing he actually watches is me. I came in the other night at 3 a.m. and what happened? Good old Topper hollered until the whole house was awake.

This did not surprise me; Topper has been trying to get me for six years. When we bought him he weighed only ten pounds. He wore a puzzled look. "Oh, Daddy, don't you just love him?" cried the girls. "No," I replied. Everyone thought I was joking.

Today Topper weighs about 85 pounds and comes way up to here. He has consumed 4,380 cans of horse meat—$1,314. The girls laugh and call Topper "food's best friend." I do not laugh, but it is an accurate description. In six years I figure he has eaten 4⅓ horses. There is no indication that he will ever stop eating, and there is not a horse in the land that can be considered safe.

The girls blame me because Topper doesn't like me. "You teased him right from the start," they say.

I had been a little sarcastic, perhaps. "Boxer, huh?" I'd say. "Who'd you ever lick? You look like a palooka to me."

The fact is, I came to dogs late in life. But dogs came at me early; I was bitten five times before I was 12. This, I explain to people who adore dogs, is why I don't. It makes no impression. "It's all your fault," they say. "Dogs can smell your fear." When I grew up I married this girl, and the product of the union, as they say, was two more girls. That made me a minority of one. By and by, these girls began talking about getting a dog. So we went shopping.

Topper, the dog we bought, had practically no tail and his ears were long. He cost $50.

At first, that is. But everyone agreed I should pay for docking his tail, which set me back another $10. Right away he was a $60 dog. Then we had his ears shaped by a special veterinarian. "They send boxers all the way from Germany so he can dock their ears," everyone said. That was $25 more. Topper came home with his ears taped in two cones of adhesive that rose from his head like twin dunce caps. He looked pretty funny. But he was now an $85 dog.

The how-to-train-a-dog books cost $7.50. The training leash was $4; a steel-link collar $1.35. Topper liked to play with the rubber beach balls around a neighbor's swimming pool. He never meant to bite through them, of course; he always looked hurt when they collapsed. Replacing rubber balls over three seasons: about $25.

As he grew, he wandered through the backyard hedge and started making trouble next door. We then fenced in the back yard at a cost of $350.

I don't know what year we decided to get a new rug. The old rug showed every trace of mud Topper brought in, and the rug cleaner had told me, "Topper and this rug are going to see my children through college." The new rug is rather drab but doesn't show mud. It cost $400, but we thought that would be cheaper in the long run.

It has only been in the last year or so that Topper has learned how to go through a glass door. He doesn't actually go through the glass; he flings himself against the frame until its catch becomes loose. The glass breaks as the door hits the side of the house. But, as his mistress says, "He doesn't do it very often."

In an effort to avoid the shattering of glass we decided

to make Topper an outdoor dog. We bought a prefabricated doghouse, brightly painted and weather tight. Topper would have nothing to do with it. Then we installed on our house a special dog door, a thing with a plastic flap that allows the dog to go in and out. It works fine. That is, if everyone hollers, "Go to your door!" whenever he scratches on a forbidden portal. But even Topper knows the dog door leads only to the back yard, so he prefers to lunge against the front door.

Topper has lots of energy and he loves to get up a tremendous head of steam racing around the yard and then come straight at you, veering off only at the last second. This is not only disconcerting, it can be expensive. He made such a dash at his mistress just as she opened a door to go into the house. In the narrow quarters Topper miscalculated and slammed into her. It was not really a break, the doctor said, just a chip off a foot bone. The lady spent only two days in the hospital after the operation to remove the chip.

(X-rays, $30; operation, $100; hospital, $24. A total of $154 against Topper's account.)

We should have flung Topper out long ago. But his mistress is head over heels in love with him. And, though he doesn't know it, even I have a sneaking admiration for him.

So maybe we won't sell after all. Anyway, who'd pay the price—the cost of all the rugs, glass, books, rubber balls, horse meat, and so on? We added it all up not long ago and came to a pretty grand total of $2,363.35. Who'd be fool enough to pay that much for a dog?

Us, I guess.

Terror in the Night

"I'm a bloodhound," he told her.
"You can't get away from me."

———

Originally published in September 1991

For a Chicagoan like Tracy Andrews, camping near Arizona's Superstition Mountains promised the adventure of a lifetime. Jutting fiercely out of the desert east of Phoenix, the Superstitions offered the 19-year-old the appeal of a wilderness she had known only through books and movies.

Tracy and her boyfriend, Rick Brough, 24, drove a Ford pickup to the Burnt Corral campground and had just pitched their tent when Larry Pritchard, another camper, stopped by. The six-foot, 300-pound fount of friendliness had come to make sure the city slickers were settling in comfortably. Pritchard was something of an invalid, but he hobbled around with his cane and pet beagle, Molly.

Everyone seemed friendly, including the stranger in the blue Chevy pickup who ambled up as Rick and Tracy sat around their campfire the second night. "Knock, knock," he said with what sounded like a country twang. "My name's Robert, and this is my kid Mitchell." Tall, lean and carrying a drink, Robert Comer was slightly tipsy. "Your friend's up at our place partying," he continued. "Come on over."

Tracy and Rick declined the invitation, but welcomed Comer again when he and the eight-year-old boy returned later. "Mitchell

16

and I like to cut wood," Comer explained as he dropped a night's supply beside the fire. The daytime temperature was in the 60s, but the February nights were cold.

❖   ❖   ❖

"OK, everybody up!" Tracy and Rick sat bolt upright in their sleeping bags. The campsite was flooded by headlight beams; someone was screaming at them from outside the tent.

"Get out of there or I'll blow your heads off! This is Arizona Drug Enforcement. This is a bust!"

Confused, Rick and Tracy stumbled toward the bright lights. As Rick exited the tent, he was pushed face-first into the dirt. Tracy recognized the man: Robert Comer. Beside him stood a stocky woman, pointing a rifle at them.

"I'll blow you sky-high!" Comer shouted. "I'm your worst night-mare!" Turning to the woman, he shouted, "Get me the cuffs!"

Knowing they'd done no wrong, Rick and Tracy sat passively as Comer bound their wrists and ankles with industrial-sized garbage bag ties and duct tape, then wrapped more tape around their heads, partially covering their mouths. Comer shoved Rick and Tracy into the Ford, leaving the woman behind.

Down the road, Comer pulled into a dry creek bed. "It's a long way to the Phoenix lockup," he said. "If you've got to go to the bathroom, now's the time."

As Comer led Tracy from the truck, a new wave of panic struck her. Comer first lashed Rick to the truck's bumper. Then he drew a foot-long knife, slashed Tracy's long underwear, and raped her—inches from Rick.

Afterward, putting his .38-caliber pistol to Rick's head, Comer turned to Tracy and said, "You know I have to kill him."

"Please, don't do that!" Tracy pleaded. "He won't do anything." Comer put away his gun, hogtied Rick, covered him with a blanket and kicked him into the brush. "You try to rescue her and I'll kill her," he promised. Then he drove off with Tracy into the starless night. It was 2:30 a.m.

❖   ❖   ❖

Senseless violence had been a way of life for Comer. During a late-1970s spree, he had raped a young girl and less than 24 hours later stabbed a stranger in the back at a fast-food restaurant. His trip to the Burnt Corral campground had begun weeks before in Sacramento County, California, where authorities claim he murdered the owner of the Chevy pickup. Traveling east with his girlfriend, Juneva Willis, and her two small children—Mitchell and ten-year-old Sarah—Comer, 30, was suspected of pulling an armed robbery in Salt Lake City and breaking into cabins in Colorado to steal food and guns.

❖ ❖ ❖

Clad only in a sweat suit and socks, Rick lay beneath the blanket, shaking with cold and thinking, Can this really be happening? Rick's mind turned to his Catholic upbringing: the Hail Marys came quickly, followed by the Act of Contrition and the Lord's Prayer. *Our Father who art in heaven...*

As he prayed for a miracle, Rick squirmed uncomfortably: Comer had left him lying on top of a rock—one with a razor-sharp edge. Rick cut his bonds and began making his way toward what he thought was the road. Unable to see in the pitch blackness, he stepped into a mass of thorns. Wait until there's light, he thought, wrapping himself in the blanket.

❖ ❖ ❖

As the truck bounced up the steep mountain road, Tracy also prayed silently. Comer had ditched the Ford pickup and dragged Tracy into his Chevy, where Juneva Willis was waiting. Learning that Rick had been left alive, Willis asked Comer, "Why didn't you kill him?"

Tracy made two disturbing discoveries: Mitchell and Sarah were in the back of the truck, under a tarp. And on the floor of the cab was Molly, Larry Pritchard's dog. Only one thing could explain Molly's presence: Comer must have killed Pritchard.

Comer drove through the night, crossing into the rugged Mazatzal Mountains. Stopping occasionally, he warned Tracy, "Remember, city girl, if you try to get away, I'll shoot you in the kneecaps and leave you for the coyotes." To emphasize his point, Comer tossed a piece of moldy bologna in front of the truck, and when Molly dashed to retrieve it, he shot and killed her.

At the top of a peak, after five hours of driving, the truck ran out of gas. Comer forced Tracy into the woods and raped her again.

As the sun rose, Rick walked to the camp, where he met two trappers who drove him seven miles to a phone. At the campsite, officers discovered Larry Pritchard's body beneath a pile of firewood. He had been shot through the head, his throat cut. My God, Rick thought, Tracy is with a homicidal maniac.

Assisted by military helicopters, authorities began scouring the area. Their overriding fear: Tracy would not be found alive.

❖　❖　❖

Tracy wanted to make breakfast for the children. Looking at them broke her heart: dirty faces, matted hair, the girl with a large burn across her leg. But Comer ordered they were to have no breakfast.

Though terrified of Comer, the children quickly warmed to Tracy.

Now, they told her, she could live with them too. "Mother will make you moccasins like she will for us." Tracy looked down to see the children's toes sticking out of their ill-fitting shoes.

Even Willis had moments of seeming friendliness. Occasionally, she would touch Tracy's arm and whisper, "It's going to be OK."

Apparently believing he had intimidated Tracy into submission, Comer turned to chopping firewood. "If you're going to go," Willis confided to Tracy, "you better go now. This is the busiest he'll ever get, and he'll never let you go."

"I can't take you with me," Tracy said softly to the children. "But if he comes, don't tell him what direction I went in."

Tracy glanced at the clock in the truck. It was 7:59 a.m. Then she ran, with no idea where she was going, with no shoes, only socks, crashing through snow and rocks, cactuses and thorns. She gave herself a stern order: You will not feel the pain. You will not give up.

Only minutes later, Comer returned and noticed Tracy had

vanished. "Which way did she go?" he shouted. Willis pointed in the direction she had told Tracy to flee.

Grabbing his rifle, Comer fired several shots into the brush.

❖　❖　❖

The four peaks area of the Mazatzal Mountains is characterized by steep, soaring slopes and narrow valleys. Its desert plants are covered with thorns and spines. Tracy, praying the snow would numb her feet, was propelled by the fear that Comer was right behind her. "I'm a bloodhound," he had told her. "You can't get away from me."

As she ran, Tracy discovered strengths. For 13 years she had been a figure skater, and she was in excellent physical shape. Cutting through the savage brush, she calmed herself by recalling the music that had accompanied her across the ice: Ravel, Mozart, Tchaikovsky.

She also developed an alter ego modeled after her demanding Catholic schoolteachers. Whenever she slowed, this new, strong voice chided her: Get going, you wimp.

She reminded herself, as well, of her "three miracles." The first was being adopted by loving parents. The second was meeting Rick. The third was in the making: I will survive this.

As Tracy ran through the snow and cactuses, she thought, I have been visited by angels before. They will not abandon me now.

Before long, Tracy's feet were totally numb. Long spines from a barrel cactus drove deep into her thighs.

At midday she came upon a waterfall that blocked her escape. Could she double back? No, she might run into Comer. Edging her way out onto the slick rocks, Tracy lost her footing and dropped through the torrent, smashing her head on a rock and knocking herself unconscious. Mercifully, the shock of the freezing water quickly revived her, and she struggled to the bank.

Night brought another miracle: a sky full of stars. God is with me, she thought. He is lighting my way. However, the fear of Comer would not leave her, even as exhaustion demanded she stop and rest.

Comer wasn't the only wild animal that concerned her. Two

coyotes ventured within yards, showing an unnerving interest in her feet. In a nearby tree, she saw a mountain lion watching her.

As the sun burst across the desert, the new day brought welcome sounds: an orchestra of birds and later, in the distance, the most beautiful music of all —the sound of passing cars. Tracy staggered down the road, rejoicing, still running from Comer 24 hours after her escape.

"I've been raped and kidnapped!" she told Bob McCollum, the first driver who stopped. "And I can't feel my feet." Severely blistered, they were swollen to more than twice their normal size.

Word raced through the small town of Payson, Arizona, that a young woman had escaped shoeless through the mountains and was in the Lewis R. Pyle Memorial Hospital. Soon Tracy had a waiting room full of well-wishers.

Eight hours after Tracy's rescue, police discovered Comer's abandoned pickup truck. An hour later, they found Comer behind a bush. He had buried his pistol, but

he brandished his rifle at the approaching officers. He finally surrendered and was airlifted out of the mountains under heavy guard.

Comer was sentenced to a 353 years for armed robbery, kidnapping and sexual assault, among other charges. He was sentenced to death for the murder of Larry Pritchard. Says Maricopa County prosecutor K. C. Scull, "Robert Comer is one of the cruelest people I have ever encountered in my 28 years of law enforcement. He is truly a monster." Juneva Willis received 9½ years for kidnapping; her children are being raised by relatives.

Tracy and Rick were married after their ordeal, on July 14, 1990. Doctors had feared Tracy's feet might have to be amputated, but, surprisingly, they healed.

The nightmare failed to drive Tracy and Rick from the desert. Indeed, their favorite pastime remained camping in the mountains. As of the time of publication, they lived in Apache Junction, Arizona —30 miles from the penitentiary where Robert Comer sat on death row.

My Bad Genes

An actor tries out a genetic testing kit and finds himself caught in the shallow end of the pool.

BY **MICHAEL IAN BLACK**
FROM THE BOOK **NAVEL GAZING**
Originally published in February 2017

ne of the unfortunate byproducts of conducting genealogical research about yourself is cataloging all the various and sundry ways in which relatives met their ends. Here be congestive heart failure. Here be polio. Here be industrial accidents and lightning strikes and diseases of the spleen. Each ancestor's death is like a fun house mirror asking, "Will you, too, be felled by the French pox?"

Yes, medical advances have lessened my odds of contracting the plagues of yore, but I have been conditioned to accept the fact that my time here on earth is apt to be brief and horrid.

Because I have bad genes.

The poor quality of my family genes was an oft-discussed topic in our household while I was growing up. On what felt like a nightly basis, Mom would remind me and my brother, Eric, that our medical futures looked bleak, her words delivered with the weary resignation of a tarot reader who'd just flipped over the death card.

Cancer runs thick and greasy through my family blood. Mom had uterine cancer, which I think I am safe from due to my lack of a uterus. My family's real bogeyman is colon cancer. In a bit of grim familial symmetry, my father's mother and mother's father both died from it.

Yet despite Mom's relentless fearmongering, it never occurred to me to question whether my genes were, in fact, "bad." Until I ordered a genetic testing kit online.

The company I ordered my test from uses a process called genotyping, by which computers match your genome against a control genome. The discrepancies between the two are genetic abnormalities that can be linked to your specific health risks.

When the kit arrives, I assume there will be an assortment of science gizmos, including a hypodermic needle, a high-speed centrifuge, a DNA sequencer, safety goggles, and a tabletop laser. Not so. The box contains exactly one (1) plastic spittoon and one (1) mail-in envelope. Hmm. Shouldn't the process for untangling my personal double helix be a bit more Star Trek-y than filling a plastic cup with spit?

A few weeks after mailing off my spit, I receive an e-mail informing me that my results are ready for viewing. On the website, I find information broken down into four categories: "Health Risks," "Drug Response," "Inherited Conditions," and "Neanderthal Ancestry." Whoa, whoa, whoa. Neanderthal ancestry? Everything else would have to wait.

I am 2.9 percent Neanderthal. That may not sound like a lot, but it is a full .2 percent above the norm. In other words, I am nearly 10 percent more Neanderthal than the average person! This was the manliest thing that had happened to me since getting hit in the eye with a pitch during Little League. I rush to tell my wife the good news.

"I'm a Neanderthal!" I tell her, showing off my test results.

I expect her to whip off her clothes and make passionate love to me then and there.

"That explains why you look like that," she says.

"Like what?"

"You have a Neanderthal brow."

She's right. I do have a heavy brow. It overhangs the rest of my skull like a buzzard on a tree limb. How did she manage to transform my cool genetic idiosyncrasy into a jab about my physical appearance? Damn her and her more highly evolved *Homo sapiens* brain.

Deflated, I return to the website, turning to my lines of ancestry, which are a total letdown. I am exactly what I believed myself to be: 100 percent Ashkenazi Jew, which is characterized by European roots, a long history traced to the original Israeli tribes, and a love for NPR.

Next up, the subject I have been dreading: "Health Risks." I expect to find a giant blinking nuclear hazard symbol informing me that I am already dead. Instead, the page lists a long column of diseases, along with my approximate odds of contracting each.

The disease I am most likely to develop is not, as I believed, colon cancer, but something called atrial fibrillation, which I learn is basically an irregular heartbeat. I am also three times more likely than the general population to develop "venous thromboembolism," which is a fancy way of saying blood clots.

As it happens, I already knew this, because my aunt nearly died from a venous thromboembolism of her own. My doctor said there isn't much I can do about it other than take a daily baby aspirin, get exercise, and make sure I walk around when flying long distances, all of which I now do, except for the part about walking around when I fly long distances and exercising.

Whoa, whoa, Whoa. Neanderthal ancestry? Everything else would now have to wait.

Some other stuff I am at elevated risk for: gallstones, chronic kidney disease, rheumatoid arthritis, macular degeneration, and lung cancer.

Lung cancer??? My lung cancer number is legitimately scary: 11.6 percent. That's a lot of percent. How can it be that high? I have never used any tobacco products, although I do confess to thinking that hookahs look kind of cool.

Panicked, I take an online "lung cancer risk test" that asks me about my smoking history (none), whether I have ever worked with asbestos (no), and if any work I have done with mustard gas was performed with adequate protection (yes, all my mustard gas work was done with adequate protection). After I submit my answers, the test informs me I have a "much below average" risk of contracting lung cancer.

Phew. Mentally, I adjust my odds of getting lung cancer from the 11.6 percent figure to 0.0 percent, because of all the medical strategies known to humankind, denial is the most effective.

But wait—where is colon cancer? I'm supposed to get colon cancer. Mom said so. Nowhere on my "elevated health risk" list does it mention anything about colon cancer. So I jump to my "decreased risk" section, where I learn I am at lower risk than the general population for contracting prostate cancer. That's good news. After all, the prostate and the colon are physically very close to each other. They may even share a cubicle.

The last list is where I finally find my colon. It turns out I am almost exactly average in terms of risk for colorectal cancer. Average risk! This is a huge relief. My colon is run-of-the-mill. Boring, even. It's the kind of colon you wouldn't even look at twice if you passed it on the street.

I'm going to live forever! I celebrate my good news by not getting a colonoscopy.

A few months after receiving my test results, I read that the Food and Drug Administration has forbidden my genetic testing company from continuing to sell their product, expressing concerns about the "validity of their results." Maybe everything they told me is a lie. Maybe my genes really are bad.

Maybe, but I'm not going back to worrying about that stuff. I can't. It's too exhausting. I'll just do what I can do. I will get my colon checked out—soon, I promise. I will take my daily baby aspirin.

But I will no longer freak out over a future I cannot control. After all … I. Am. A. Ne-an-der-thal!

A Soldier's Story

Years later, a war photographer tracks down one of his earliest subjects.

— ▬ —

BY ROBERT HODIERNE

Originally published in May 2002

Maybe it was all the images of war that filled my TV and newspaper pages in the fall of 2001. But for some reason, for the first time in many months, I began staring at a photo that hangs on my office wall.

It was taken 35 years ago. In the picture, an Army sergeant is on his belly, pinned down by enemy fire, looking grim and determined. In the foreground is a dead GI, in the background, a seriously wounded one. The person behind the lens that day was me: a skinny young civilian war photographer experiencing his most terrifying day in Vietnam.

I have relived that firefight countless times. It wasn't my first battle experience, but that day, on the Bong Son plain in Vietnam's central lowlands, it felt as if the North Vietnamese were shooting at me. Burst after burst kicked sand in my face. I remember wondering what odds I had of living through it.

I remember also that sergeant crawling out into the killing zone, inching toward his dead comrade to retrieve his grenade launcher. Was he nuts? That's when I took the photo.

My notes from that Valentine's Day ambush in 1967 were long lost, along with the sergeant's name. I did remember the rueful, ain't-it-a-joke look on his face when he'd told me that until a few weeks earlier he'd been an Army cook. The poor bastard, I thought. One minute he's ladling out powdered eggs, the next he's alongside me in hell.

The photo has faded into the background—become like wallpaper—over the years, but I've always given it a prominent place in various offices and dens. If anyone asked why I had it on the wall, I'd joke: "To remind me that no matter how bad things get here, at least people aren't shooting at me."

When I began gazing again at the picture last fall, I started wondering about that hard-luck sergeant. How many more firefights had he endured? Did he even survive the war? Strange how one terrifying day could bond me to a virtual stranger, but it had. I decided to try to find him, to see how his life had turned out.

I posted my photos from that battle on the Internet, along with queries to Army alumni websites. Did anyone who was with the 1st Air Cavalry Division remember that Valentine's Day fight? I wrote. Did anybody recognize the soldiers I'd snapped that day at Bong Son?

Within days my phone rang and George Goswick was on the line. "Everyone called me Baby Huey," he said by way of introduction. Goswick, of Adairsville, Georgia, had been a radio operator in the 1st Cav. "I know who that sergeant is in your photo," he said. "That's Sergeant Rock. Joe Musial."

Goswick told me Musial had been well known by everyone.

Guys in other units would stare at Rock and ask, "Is what they say about him true?"

"He liked to fight with officers," Goswick said with a chuckle. Apparently Musial had been one of those peacetime garrison screwup types. By 1966, when he was shipped to Vietnam, he'd been in uniform for 12 years and was just a Specialist 4. Draftees with less than a year in the Army outranked him.

The next call told me that Musial's story didn't end on Bong

Son plain. Bret Barham, 54, is now an assistant district attorney in Jennings, Louisiana. But in 1968, Barham was a 21-year-old sergeant in the 1st Cav in Vietnam. "Rock was an absolute legend in our battalion," Barham told me. "I can remember guys in other units, when Rock walked around the perimeter, they'd stare and ask, 'Is what they say about him true?'"

And what they said about him, I learned, was that Joe Musial was the real deal. He was a hero.

Roger McDonald, 66, of Cartersville, Georgia, filled me in on the metamorphosis of Joe Musial. McDonald was a 1st Cav platoon sergeant and a buddy of Musial's from stateside. In 1966, McDonald was leading a reconnaissance platoon in Vietnam, 30 or 40 men who would be dropped by chopper deep in hostile territory. The sergeant sought out his old pal, Joe Musial. "He was handing out groceries in the chow line," McDonald recalled. "I said, 'You want to join recon?' He took his apron right off and left the mess hall."

The Valentine's Day battle I photographed was one of Musial's first. His bravery in that fight went pretty much unnoticed by the Army. There were no medals won that day. But Musial went on to serve two more tours in Vietnam, leading recon patrols and infantry platoons, and by the time it was all over, he wasn't Joe Musial anymore. He was Sergeant Rock.

Nobody could remember when he first got tagged with the name of the World War II comic book character. But everyone knew how he earned it.

❖　❖　❖

On August 23, 1968, Musial's troops were surprised by a far larger enemy force. North Vietnamese machine gunners began ripping rounds into their position. Musial didn't duck for cover. He charged forward under heavy fire, flinging grenades at the machine-gun nest, destroying it. That day Joe Musial earned his first Silver Star.

He was awarded a second Silver Star for his actions on March 21, 1969, defending an obscure little outpost called Landing Zone

White. North Vietnamese Army sappers—explosives experts—had broken through the perimeter and were throwing charges into bunkers crowded with GIs. Musial, out in the open helping wounded troops, spotted three sappers. Armed only with a pistol, Musial shot two before the third one tossed his charge. Bits of shrapnel tore into Musial's flesh, but he stood his ground and gunned down the third attacker.

His buddies came to revere him, yet knew all too well the pugnacious side of Rock that couldn't be suppressed. One night, away from the front, Musial got drunk and picked a fight—as usual, with someone who outranked him. That episode cost him a stripe. "We had this great fear he'd get busted again and we'd end up outranking him," Barham said. "We'd have followed him anywhere, but we knew he wouldn't follow us."

And follow Musial they did: into enemy villages erupting with rifle fire, down booby-trapped trails, into dark caves where Musial insisted on entering first, alone. By war's end, the screwup cook had amassed not just two Silver Stars, but three Bronze Stars and three Purple Hearts. Perhaps the greatest tribute, though, came from his 1st Cav comrades. It was the tradition in that division to name chopper landing zones and other outposts after men who'd died in combat. But they decided to name one after a living man: LZ Rock.

❖   ❖   ❖

A few of the veterans told me that if I wanted to meet Musial, I had better make it soon. The guy who'd survived so much in Vietnam was now in the VA hospital in Battle Creek, Michigan, dying of lung cancer. I called Musial, who said he'd be happy for the visit, so I made the ten-hour drive from my home in Washington, D.C.

When I walked into the hospice room, a 65-year-old man looked up at me, an oxygen bottle tethered to him. But there was a roguish twinkle in those sunken eyes, and I could see the ghost of that young sergeant.

"Oh, I remember you," he said immediately. "You were bored because there hadn't been any action." We both laughed.

I put before him my battle photos. "God, I was young," he said. "But I don't remember these other guys. There were so many."

His first major fight, he recalled, came on December 28, 1966. He'd led his platoon into the village of Gia Duc when Viet Cong opened fire. "That was a bad day," he said. He earned one of his Bronze Stars there, but that's not what pricks his memory. It's Skip Baumann, a 20-year-old private. "He kept getting up to see them and I said, 'Get down!' And God darn, he got hit. I got him and was holding him." Musial paused to use his oxygen. "The reason I remember him so well is his last question. 'Am I a good soldier?' he asks. I said, 'Hey, you're a great soldier, you're the top. You're airborne.' And, of course, he passed away."

We talked a bit about the Valentine's Day ambush and I told him that some of his men said he should have gotten the Medal of Honor for LZ White. Musial shrugged. He wasn't having any of the hero stuff.

I spent most of the day with Musial, during which he told me about his life after the war: how he went to work on oil rigs in the Gulf of Mexico; how he lost his right leg in an accident there; and how, with his Army pension and a settlement from the oil company, he'd bought a house on 35 rural acres in southwest Michigan. "That place was his paradise," his sister, Eugenia Zelas, told me later. "That's where he found peace."

Joe and I never talked about the fact that he was dying. When I shook his hand and left, we promised to meet at a 1st Cav reunion next June. We both knew he wouldn't make it.

On the drive home, I couldn't get out of my head something that Bret Barham had told me. "In Vietnam, Rock was doing what he was designed by God to do—be a warrior."

I put Joe's picture back up at home. Battles raged on the TV, while Rock's war—and mine—sat frozen in time in a small frame.

Then the call came on a chilly afternoon. Joe Musial, Sergeant Rock, died early on November 11, 2001. Veterans Day.

Tear Down This Wall

*President Reagan's speechwriter explains
how his famous line was almost deleted.*

—

BY **PETER ROBINSON**

FROM THE BOOK **HOW RONALD REAGAN CHANGED MY LIFE**

Originally published in February 2004

he call of a trumpet. Many of Ronald Reagan's speeches sounded that way to me. During his long political career he used simple, direct, forceful language to make his points. So when I joined his speech writing staff in 1983—at age 26, its youngest member—my goal was to help Reagan go on sounding like Reagan. One big challenge was the speech at the Berlin Wall, which Reagan would visit during a 1987 trip to Berlin to help commemorate the city's 750th anniversary. I was told only that he would speak at the wall, that he'd likely draw a crowd of about 10,000, and that, given the setting, he probably ought to talk about foreign policy.

One day in April 1987, I met the ranking American diplomat in Berlin, hoping to get some material. The diplomat knew what Reagan shouldn't say. Since West Berliners were intellectually and politically sophisticated, he would have to watch himself. So no chest-thumping. No Soviet bashing. And no inflammatory statements about the wall. People who lived here, he said, had long ago become used to the structure that encircled them.

After meeting the diplomat, I flew over Berlin in a U.S. Army helicopter. From the sky, the wall seemed less to cut Berlin in two than to separate two modes of existence. On one side I saw movement, color, crowded sidewalks. On the other, buildings were pockmarked from shelling during the war; pedestrians were poorly dressed. The East Berlin side was lined with guard posts, dog runs, rows of barbed wire.

That night, I went to a dinner party hosted by Dieter and Ingeborg Elz, native Germans who had retired to West Berlin after Dieter completed his career at the World Bank. We had friends in common, and they were hosting this party to help give me a feel for their city. They had invited Berliners of many walks of life—businessmen, academics, homemakers. We talked about the weather, about German wine. And then I related what the diplomat had told me. "Is it true?" I asked. "Have you gotten used to the wall?"

The Elzes and their guests glanced at one another uneasily. My heart sank. Had I come across as brash, tactless? Finally one man raised an arm and pointed. "My sister lives 20 miles in that direction," he explained. "I haven't seen her in more than two decades. Do you think I can ever get used to that?"

Another man spoke up. Each morning on his way to work, he said, he walked past a guard tower. Each morning, the same soldier gazed down at him through binoculars. "That soldier and I speak the same language," he said. "We share the same history. But one of us is a zookeeper and the other is an animal, and I'm never certain which one is which."

Our hostess now broke in. "If this man Gorbachev is serious with his talk of glasnost and perestroika," she said angrily, pounding her fist, "he can prove it. He can get rid of this wall."

❖ ❖ ❖

Back in Washington, I told Tony Dolan, who oversaw Presidential speechwriting, that I wanted to make Ingeborg Elz's comment the central passage in Reagan's speech. I thought the passion and decency it conveyed sounded a lot like Reagan—like that trumpet again. But when I sat down to write, the words didn't exactly flow.

In one draft I wrote, "Herr Gorbachev, bring down this wall," using "Herr" because I thought it would please the President's German audience, and "bring" because it was the only verb I could think of.

By week's end I'd produced a first draft that even I considered banal. I can still hear the clomp-clomp-clomp of Tony's cowboy boots as he walked down the hallway from his office to toss that draft onto my desk. "It's no good," he said.

"What's wrong with it?" I asked.

"I just told you. It's no good."

"Which paragraphs, Tony?"

"The whole thing is no good."

The next week I wrote another draft. This time I used stronger language, urging Gorbachev to "tear down the wall." On Friday, May 15, the speeches for the President's trip to Rome, Venice and Berlin were sent to him, and on Monday, May 18, the speechwriters joined him in the Oval Office. My speech was the last to be discussed. When Tom Griscom, the director of communications, asked Reagan for his comments, the President replied simply that he liked it.

"Mr. President," I said to him, "I learned that your speech will not only be heard in West Berlin but throughout East Germany." Radios might be able to pick up the speech as far east as Moscow. "Is there anything you'd like to say to people on the other side of the Berlin Wall?" I asked.

"Well, there's that passage about tearing down the wall," he replied. "That wall has to come down. That's what I'd like to say to them."

❖ ❖ ❖

With three weeks to go, the speech was circulated to the State Department and the National Security Council. Both tried to squelch it. The draft was naive, they said. It was clumsy. It was provocative. State and the NSC submitted their own drafts—no fewer than seven in all. In each, the call to "tear down the wall" was missing.

In principle, State and the NSC had no objection to a call for the wall's destruction. One draft, for example, contained the line "One day, this ugly wall will disappear." I looked at that for a while. "One day"? One day the lion would lie down with the lamb, too, but you wouldn't want to hold your breath. "This ugly wall will disappear" was another line. What did that mean? The wall would disappear only when the Soviets knocked it down.

A few days before the President was to leave for Europe, Tom Griscom got a call from the chief of staff, Howard Baker. Secretary of State George Shultz objected to the speech. "He said, 'I think that line about tearing down the wall is going to be an affront to Mr. Gorbachev.' I said, 'Mr. Secretary, the President has commented on this line. He's comfortable with it.'"

When the traveling party reached Italy, Shultz objected again, this time to deputy chief of staff Ken Duberstein. On June 5, Duberstein briefed Reagan on the objections and asked him to reread the speech's central passage. He did. Duberstein told Reagan that he thought the line about tearing down the wall sounded good. "Then," says Duberstein, "he got that wonderful, knowing smile on his face and said, 'Let's leave it in.'"

When Reagan arrived in Berlin, State and the NSC submitted another draft. Yet the President was determined to deliver the controversial line. "The boys at State are going to kill me," he told Duberstein, smiling, "but it's the right thing to do."

So at the end of this long, messy process—what? The President stood before the Berlin Wall on June 12, 1987, the Brandenburg Gate behind him, the crowd hanging on every word. Then came the line: "Mr. Gorbachev, tear down this wall." There it was. No euphemisms. No wishful thinking. The truth. Reagan sounding like Reagan.

After the President delivered the speech, people felt he'd been correct to do so. As Tom Griscom recalls, "The Secretary of State found me after the speech and said, 'You were right.'"

The Night I Met Einstein

A lesson in life—and music—from the most brilliant mind in the world.

—

BY **JEROME WEIDMAN**

Originally published in November 1955

When I was a young man, just beginning to make my way, I was invited to dine at the home of a distinguished New York philanthropist. After dinner, our hostess led us to an enormous drawing room. My eyes beheld two unnerving sights: Servants were arranging small gilt chairs in long, neat rows; and up front, leaning against the wall, were musical instruments.

Apparently I was in for an evening of chamber music.

❖ ❖ ❖

I use the phrase "in for" because music meant nothing to me. I am almost tone deaf—only with great effort can I carry the simplest tune, and serious music was to me no more than an arrangement of noises. So I did what I always did when trapped: I fixed my face in what I hoped was an expression of intelligent appreciation, closed my ears from the inside, and submerged myself in my own completely irrelevant thoughts.

Einstein started playing violin as a child.

After a while, becoming aware that the people around me were applauding, I concluded it was safe to unplug my ears. I heard a gentle but surprisingly penetrating voice on my right: "You are fond of Bach?"

I knew as much about Bach as I know about nuclear fission. But I did know one of the most famous faces in the world, with the renowned shock of untidy white hair and the ever-present pipe between the teeth. I was sitting next to Albert Einstein.

"Well," I said uncomfortably, and hesitated. I had been asked a casual question. All I had to do was be equally casual in my reply. But I could see from the look in my neighbor's extraordinary eyes that their owner was not merely going through the perfunctory duties of elementary politeness. Above all, I could feel that this was a man to whom you did not tell a lie, however small.

"I don't know anything about Bach," I said awkwardly. "I've never heard any of his music."

A look of perplexed astonishment washed across Einstein's face.

"You have never heard Bach?"

He made it sound as though I had said I'd never taken a bath.

"It isn't that I don't want to like Bach," I replied hastily. "It's just that I'm tone deaf, or almost tone deaf, and I've never really heard anybody's music."

A look of concern came into the old man's face. "Please," he said abruptly. "You will come with me?"

He stood up and took my arm. I stood up and as he led me across that crowded room, I kept my embarrassed glance fixed on the carpet. A rising murmur of puzzled speculation followed us out into the hall. Einstein paid no attention to it.

Resolutely, he led me upstairs. He obviously knew the house well. On the floor above, he opened the door into a book-lined study, drew me in, and shut the door.

"Now," he said with a small, troubled smile. "You will tell me, please, how long you have felt this way about music?"

"All my life," I said, feeling awful. "I wish you would go back and listen, Dr. Einstein. The fact that I don't enjoy it doesn't matter."

Einstein shook his head and scowled, as though I had introduced an irrelevance.

"Tell me, please," he said. "Is there any kind of music that you do like?"

"Well," I answered, "I like songs that have words, and the kind of music where I can follow the tune."

He smiled and nodded, obviously

> **"Now," he said with a small, troubled smile. "You will tell me, please, how long you have felt this way about music?"**
>
> ———

pleased. "You can give me an example, perhaps?"

"Well," I ventured, "almost anything by Bing Crosby."

He nodded again, briskly. "Good!"

❖ ❖ ❖

He went to a corner of the room, opened a phonograph, and started pulling out records. I watched him

uneasily. At last, he beamed. "Ah!" he said.

He put the record on, and in a moment, the study was filled with the relaxed, lilting strains of Bing Crosby's "When the Blue of the Night Meets the Gold of the Day." Einstein beamed at me and kept time with the stem of his pipe. After three or four phrases, he stopped the phonograph.

"Now," he said. "Will you tell me, please, what you have just heard?"

The simplest answer seemed to be to sing the lines. I did just that, trying desperately to stay in tune and keep my voice from cracking. The expression on Einstein's face was like the sunrise.

"You see!" he cried with delight. "You do have an ear!"

I mumbled something about this being one of my favorite songs, something I had heard hundreds of times so that it didn't really prove anything.

"Nonsense!" said Einstein. "It proves everything! Do you remember your first arithmetic lesson in school? Suppose, at your very first contact with numbers, your teacher had ordered you to work out a problem in, say, long division or fractions. Could you have done so?"

"No, of course not."

"Precisely!" Einstein made a triumphant wave with his pipe stem. "It would have been impossible, and you would have reacted in panic. You would have closed your mind to long division and fractions. As a result, because of that one small mistake by your teacher, it is possible your whole life you would be denied the beauty of long division and fractions."

The pipe stem went up and out in another wave. "But on your first day, no teacher would be so foolish. He would start you with more elementary things—then, when you had acquired skill with the simplest problems, he would lead you up to long division and to fractions.

"So it is with music." Einstein picked up the Bing Crosby record. "This charming little song is like simple addition or subtraction. You have mastered it. Now we go on to something more complicated."

❖ ❖ ❖

He found another record. The golden voice of John McCormack singing "The Trumpeter" filled the room. After a few lines, Einstein stopped the record.

"So!" he said. "You will sing that back to me, please?"

I did—with a good deal of self-consciousness but with, for me, a surprising degree of accuracy.

Einstein stared at me with a look

> *"Allow yourself to listen," he whispered. "That is all."*

on his face that I had seen only once before in my life: on the face of my father as he listened to me deliver the valedictory address at my high school graduation ceremony.

"Excellent!" Einstein remarked. "Wonderful! Now this!"

"This" turned out to be Caruso in what was to me a completely unrecognizable fragment from *Cavalleria Rusticana*, a one-act opera. Nevertheless, I managed to reproduce an approximation of the sounds the famous tenor had made. Einstein beamed his approval.

Caruso was followed by at least a dozen others. I could not shake my feeling of awe over the way this great man, into whose company I had been thrown by chance, was completely preoccupied by what we were doing, as though I were his sole concern.

We came at last to recordings of music without words, which I was instructed to reproduce by humming. When I reached for a high note, Einstein's mouth opened, and his head went back as if to help me attain what seemed unattainable. Evidently I came close enough, for he suddenly turned off the phonograph.

"Now, young man," he said, putting his arm through mine. "We are ready for Bach!"

As we returned to our seats in the drawing room, the players were tuning up again. Einstein gave me a reassuring pat on the knee.

"Just allow yourself to listen," he whispered. "That is all."

It wasn't really all, of course.

Without the effort he had just poured out for a total stranger I would never have heard, as I did that night for the first time in my life, Bach's "Sheep May Safely Graze." I have heard it many times since. I don't think I shall ever tire of it. Because I never listen to it alone. I am sitting beside a small, round man with a shock of untidy white hair and eyes that contain in their extraordinary warmth all the wonder of the world.

When the concert was finished, I added my genuine applause to that of the others.

Suddenly our hostess confronted us. "I'm so sorry, Dr. Einstein," she said with an icy glare at me, "that you missed so much of the performance."

"I am sorry too," he said. "My young friend here and I, however, were engaged in the greatest activity of which man is capable."

She looked puzzled. "Really?" she said. "And what is that?"

Einstein smiled and put his arm across my shoulders. "Opening up yet another fragment of the frontier of beauty."

Awake Through a Brain Operation

*The gripping story of a patient's faith—
and a surgeon's skill.*

BY **ANNETTE ANSELMO**

Originally published in July 1964

n the fall of 1953, Annette Anselmo of Salt Lake City, Utah, traveled to a well-known neurological institute to seek help from Dr. Jones (not his real name), a renowned brain surgeon. For 30 years, ever since the age of four, Annette had suffered epileptic seizures with devastating frequency. Anti-convulsant drugs and a brain operation performed by a Salt Lake City surgeon had banished the severest seizures. But she still had as many as 65 convulsions an hour.

Dr. Jones took brain X-rays and electroencephalograms, then gave his decision. "We believe an operation will help you," he said. "But I do not promise a complete cure. And you realize the risk: You may he paralyzed."

For Annette, the possibility was worth the risk. Here is her account of the operation.

❖ ❖ ❖

Early that morning a barber came into my room and shaved my head so that it resembled a large billiard ball. Then my bed was wheeled into the hall, where Dad and my sister kissed me, trying hard not to cry. "Don't worry," I said. "I'll be back." My feeling was "Today is the beginning of the end of my 30-year war against epilepsy."

In the X-ray room, a doctor said to me with a smile, "This is a big day for you." In one hand he had two wires, each about a yard long; in the other a glass of water. "I'm going to insert a wire in each of your nostrils," he said. "I want you to take a drink and swallow when I tell you to." The wires were to go down into my stomach. Each time the doctor said "Swallow," a few more inches would disappear, until only about a foot and a half remained in view. Then the doctor took an X-ray to see if the wires were in proper position. Three times they were not, and he would say, "Let's start over."

Finally the wires were in place. As he taped the ends to my chest, he explained that these electrodes would provide a reading of stomach movement—the sensation I had often experienced with the onset of an attack. When electrical stimulation of the brain came close to the point from which my attacks originated, the stomach sensation would be produced.

Now my bed was wheeled into the anesthesia room. I knew that I was to remain fully conscious throughout the operation so Dr. Jones could be guided by my reactions. The anesthetist was to give me injections to deaden the feeling in my face and scalp.

He asked me to open my mouth and, with his thumb, located the hinge bone connecting the upper and lower jaw. Into it he inserted a needle—so far upward that it seemed to reach my skull bone! I felt a searing pain. But these injections were the only way to deaden the feeling in my scalp and facial skin.

Dr. Jones now entered, and I could feel him tracing a design on my scalp. "This is the skull opening I want," he said to the doctors with him. One replied, "Yes, a full butterfly flap." The anesthetist said, "She is about ready for the operating room."

"I'm not afraid," I said, "but do me a favor. When my skull is about to be opened, will one of you tell me a joke?" I thought it would help to mask the moment of intense pain I anticipated.

Out in the hall the doors of the operating room opened to allow my bed to pass through. I had reached the point of no retreat.

Inside, I looked at the wall clock: 8:05. I could see the glassed-in gallery where doctors, nurses, and students were waiting to observe. Each of the six doctors who were to take part in the operation wore special glasses, for the room had ultraviolet lighting instead of glaring overhead bulbs. I heard one doctor say, "We'll be lucky if we get out of here by suppertime."

A doctor behind my head said, "This will sting. I'm going to paint your head with iodine." The anesthetist told me to lie flat on my back and turn my head to the left. Towels were placed around my neck to hold my head in place. They held it firmly but not uncomfortably. In fact, I hardly noticed them after a few minutes.

Now Dr. Jones was standing at my head, a tray of instruments beside him. With foot or hand controls he raised my head to the proper position. It was up to me not to move; no sandbags or straps restrained me, except one to keep me from falling off the table. He asked if I was comfortable. I said, "Yes, but I'm freezing." A blanket was tucked around me. Doubtless the impact of what was about to happen had given me chills.

"I'm going to inject several needles at the base of your skull, Annette," Dr. Jones said. "This will eliminate as much pain as possible, but I can't deaden it entirely."

He began inserting the needles. As he worked, Dr. Jones consulted his associates and dictated notes to a secretary in the gallery, through an intercom. He told the type and amount of medication in each injection, reviewed my case history, and explained what he believed to be the cause of my seizures: damage resulting from an interference with the circulation of oxygen-carrying blood to one side of my brain at the time of my birth.

Each needle felt as if it would come through my mouth. I finally lost count of the needles. "How many more?" I kept asking.

"Not many. Try to bear it a bit

longer," the doctor would answer.

I glanced at the clock. It seemed impossible, but it was already 11:30.

Now I felt the pressure of what I was certain was a scalpel against my scalp. No pain; just the sudden warmth of liquid trickling down my cheek. When I realized it was my own blood, I said, "I'm going to throw up." A pan was held close to my face. My mouth felt parched. A piece of ice was placed between my lips.

Dr. Jones said, "Annette, we are about to make a few holes in your skull." The drilling began. There was a period of dull pain, and a dull grinding sound. There were to be, I knew, five to seven fairly large burr holes.

After an interminable interval, everything was still—almost morbidly so. Then I heard the sawing of bone. I waited for the pain I so vividly remembered when the skull had been opened in my other operation 2½ years before. I asked how much longer it would be before they would break through my skull. Someone patted my hand

and said, "It's already done."

The clock showed noon. A nurse held a cup of something steaming—soup perhaps—and Dr. Jones drank it through a straw.

I heard, more than felt, the awful sensation of liquid being squirted over my brain. When the brain is exposed, the air dries its surface quickly, and it must be continuously moistened.

At 1:30, Dr. Jones said, "Turn the machine at this angle." I knew he was referring to the machine he would use to stimulate the electrical activity of my brain cells.

Pictures were taken, both in black and white and in color. Then Dr. Jones spoke to me quietly. "Annette, from here on I will need your full cooperation. We are going to stimulate your brain, and I want you to tell me exactly what you feel and where." Was I ready? I said I was.

A few seconds later I felt a light current go through my body. "I feel as though I am about to fall off the table to my left," I said. He answered, "That's fine. We'll try it again." This time the current was stronger. I said, "My left leg feels as though it is about to fall off the table." Moments later I felt someone lift my leg back onto the table. Then I heard the doctor say, "I want a few more color pictures, please."

More brain stimulation. "Doctor, that felt as though my left forefinger pointed inward." Dr. Jones repeated the experiment, then said, "Let me hear what Annette said during the stimulation." I heard my own voice and realized my words were being recorded. Immediately after, Dr. Jones said, "Annette, I am going to remove a small section of your brain that is causing some of your trouble."

Then I heard words that I shall never forget: "Annette, remember, just so much is in my hands."

A few minutes later came the clicking sound of metal as he put down the instrument he had used, and I knew the excision had taken place. I looked at the clock. It was 2:30. How much longer?

Dr. Jones said, "Annette, I'm going to stimulate again. Please tell me what you feel." I felt the current, and at that instant I felt

my left eye turn inward. It was repeated. Then Dr. Jones said, "I am going to remove another small piece of brain."

At that crucial point I said, "Doctor, I have a funny feeling I've never had before. I'm afraid I'm going to have a seizure." Metal clicked as he laid aside his instrument. A few moments later I had the seizure, a small one.

"What kind of reading did you record?" Dr. Jones asked an assistant. The answer came, in medical terms.

Once more I felt the stimulating current go through my body. And this time I had a familiar sickish feeling in the pit of my stomach.

Once again the doctor said, "Annette, I'm going to remove another affected bit of brain." And, speaking to his assistants, he explained how far into the brain he was going. He said that the Salt Lake City surgeon had excised at precisely the right spot, but had not gone this deep, fearing he would leave me paralyzed.

For the first time I felt true cutting pain momentarily. When it ceased I said, "If anybody ever says again there is no feeling inside the brain, Dr. Jones, don't believe him. I know better."

I kept saying, "I'm tired, Doctor. Please put me to sleep."

He answered, "I'll bet you a quarter you'll fall asleep within the hour, Annette."

Then he said that he was about to make his third excision, and now he would touch the section of the brain that controls vision. For the first time, I said a silent prayer, asking God to steady Dr. Jones's hand. Then I heard him put down his scalpel. I could still see the anesthetist clearly—and I thanked God!

Dr. Jones said, "Still awake? I guess I owe you a quarter." The recording shows that I replied weakly, "Deduct it from my bill."

I was so tired I could hardly hear the voices around me. After a while the doctors began testing the reflexes of my arms and legs. Dimly I heard them say, "All four extremities have good reflex actions. No paralysis."

The anesthetist spoke: "Hold your arm steady, Annette, while we locate a vein." It meant that the operation was over. Now they would put me to sleep to close my skull.

Exhausted, I glanced at the clock as I felt the needle going into my arm: 4:30 p.m. "No paralysis." All was well.

❖   ❖   ❖

The kind of surgery performed on Annette Anselmo is quite unusual, and is undertaken only in certain rare cases. For more than 99 percent of people with epilepsy, it would be neither applicable nor beneficial. It should also be noted that the techniques she describes have since changed.

On mild medication, Annette Anselmo now leads a full, active life with no restrictions on her activities. She still has seizures, usually mild and brief; they come at night, and only two or three times a year.

My Fight with Jack Dempsey

An enterprising writer launched a literary career—from a reclining position.

———

BY **PAUL GALLICO**

Originally published in July 1954

t was 1923 and I had been movie critic for the *New York Daily News* a scant six months when the publisher demanded that the smart aleck who kept denouncing the daily film fare be fired. This might have ended my newspaper career had not a friendly managing editor concealed me in the sports department, without benefit of byline.

I was assigned to Jack Dempsey's training camp at Saratoga Springs to write some color pieces on his preparations for the defense of his title against the massive Argentinean, Luis Angel Firpo, the "Wild Bull of the Pampas."

There was lots of color at Uncle Tom Luther's camp: the rough, tough Dempsey; Jack Kearns, his manager; the scented Beau Brummell; the bland Tex Rickard; famous sports writers; and all the rag, tag, and bobtail of the prize-fight world.

But there was also mystery there, at least for me. It was boxing itself.

I had attended a number of prize fights and watched boys tagged on the chin go rubbery at the knees, eyes glazing over. What worked this havoc with the human mechanism?

What was it like to be on the floor from a punch with nine seconds to rise? What thoughts pass through a man's head when he has bees in his brain, sickness gnawing at his middle, and molasses in his legs?

How could I write about these things graphically without having experienced them? I felt that I had to find out or I would never be any good at my job.

It was foolhardy for a chap who had never boxed in his life to want to climb into the ring with the man-destroyer Dempsey, yet I did just that. If ever a man began a literary career from the reclining position it was me.

I presented myself to Dempsey one August afternoon on the porch of his cottage at the camp and asked whether he would spar a round with me so that I might write a story on how it felt to be hit by an expert. Dempsey looked me up and down and then inquired in that curiously high-pitched voice of his, "What's the matter, son? Don't your editor like you no more?"

I explained that I expected to survive and said my only serious doubt was my ability to take it in the region of the stomach. I asked the great man if perchance he might confine his attentions to a less unhappy target.

Dempsey reflected and then replied, "I think I understand, son. You just want a good punch in the nose." He agreed to stage the affair the following Sunday. We shook hands and I departed well pleased.

Kearns was aghast when he learned what Dempsey had promised. It must be remembered that I was an unknown newcomer to the sports world; I was just under six feet three, weighed 190 pounds, and was still in superb condition after having captained the varsity crew at Columbia. When I removed my glasses and stripped down I looked as ugly and capable as any professional pug. Nobody would have guessed that within this menacing monster beat the heart of a rabbit.

Thoughts of the plots and machinations of his profession inflamed Kearns's brain. I might be what I said I was, or I might be a ringer from the Firpo camp sent to cut or otherwise injure Dempsey before the fight. His verdict to Dempsey was: "Don't take chances with this guy—nail him quick!"

Sunday was gala day at the camp and some 3,000 spectators were on hand. Hype Igoe, one of the leading sports writers of his time, said to me, "I understand you're fighting the champ this afternoon."

"Oh, not fighting," I said. "We're just going to fool around. Dempsey is going to take it easy."

Igoe gave me a pitying look and said, "Son, don't you know that man *can't* take it easy?"

I stood near the ring clad in swim trunks, boxing shoes, and boxing gloves. Dempsey, wearing a brown leather head-protector, was boxing with a middleweight to develop speed. In a clinch he cuffed the spar mate absently on the back of the neck with the side of his fist.

"What's that tapping on the back of the neck for?" I asked one of Jack's sparring partners.

The fighter replied, "Shakes you up. Here, I'll show you." Thereupon he hit me on the back of the neck with his gloved hand. My eyes

glazed, my knees began to give, and I nearly collapsed. I came close to being the first man ever to be knocked out *before* climbing into the ring.

Next Farmer Lodge, a huge heavyweight, entered the ring with Dempsey. He shuffled about for a few seconds; then there was a flurry and a hook accompanied by the sound of a steer being poleaxed. The farmer sank to the canvas and lay there. Four mates reverently removed him. Kearns came over and said, "OK, Gallico. You're next."

Kearns did up the introductions in style. "In this corner, the heavyweight champion of the world, Jack Dempsey!" The hills echoed the cheers of the spectators. Next: "In the opposite corner, Paul Gallico of the *Daily News*." From the 3,000 came only a clammy silence, except for one voice from the crowd that inquired mockingly, "Who?"

The bell rang. Reluctantly I left my corner. Dempsey danced over and touched my gloves perfunctorily, then went into his crouching weave

from which he could explode those lethal hooks. I assumed my own version of "Pose A" from the Boxer's Manual, left arm extended fully and all the rest of me removed as far from Jack as possible.

Dempsey pursued, weaving and bobbing. Gone was the friendly smile with which he had lulled me on the porch. With the broad leather headband across his brow, baleful eyes, and snarling lips, he resembled a tiger stalking his kill.

Someone in the crowd made a rude noise. Its result was to undo me by arousing the pride of the Gallicos. Tentatively I stuck out my left. Dempsey ran into it with his nose. Wow! A point for Gallico. Overwhelmed by what I had done, I poked out another left, and another, landing them all for the simple reason that Dempsey didn't bother to defend himself.

Three jabs landed! Why, this was fun. Fancy Dan Gallico, the Galloping Ghost of the Squared Circle. I'll just try another. I did.

"BOOOOOOOOOOOOM!"

I can remember seeing Dempsey's berry-brown arm flash for one instant before my eyes. Then there was this awful explosion within the confines of my skull, followed by a bright light, a tearing sensation, and then darkness.

Slowly it grew light again. I was sitting on the canvas with one leg folded under me, my mouth bleeding, grinning foolishly. The ring made a clockwise revolution, stopped, and then returned counterclockwise.

I heard Kearns counting over me. "Six—seven—eight—"

And, like an idiot, I got up!

I didn't have to. I had proved my point. I had gained the precious secret I had sought. But the posture on the deck was humiliating before all those people. And so with my head swimming and a roaring in my ears, I climbed to my feet on legs of soft rubber tubing.

Dempsey rushed over and pulled me into a clinch, dancing me around and at the same time holding me up. He had proved *his* point, namely, that I wasn't any ringer but just a bum fresh out of college who had never had a glove on. Even Kearns was laughing.

Dempsey whispered into my ear, "Hang on and we'll wrestle around until your head clears, son."

Mercy from the killer! I clutched him like a lost brother. We wrestled around a bit. Absently, Dempsey hit me with a half dozen of those affectionate taps on the back of my neck, and the next thing I remember was Kearns again counting over me. I would have been there still except they needed the premises for further exercises. They told me the affair lasted just one minute 37 seconds.

I was assisted from the enclosure and taken some place else to lie down until my addled wits collected themselves sufficiently for me to get to my typewriter. I had a splitting headache and was grateful to be alive.

My story was printed under my first sports byline. They say that the publisher of the *News* laughed his head off when he read it and saw the photograph of me stretched out colder than a mackerel. About a year later he made me sports editor.

So Long, Duck

The forlorn little seabird couldn't fly or fish or even float. And yet there was something about her that made her life worth fighting for.

BY **VIRGINIA BENNETT MOORE**

Originally published in April 1970

t first I thought it was a stone. But as the dog sniffed, it flung an uncertain head at her. It was a brown seabird, a duck most likely, huddled on the beach beside the water. The dog sniffed again. "Amber!" I shouted. Her intrusion had driven the bird to its feet. It struggled up on two shaky paddles and ran from Amber's nosing—straight into me. Baffled, it sank to the ground at my toes. I realized then it was blind.

A sightless bird is a wingless bird, no longer a bird at all. The duck seemed close to death. Would it be a kindness to walk on?

The January light was failing fast, and night was already sharpening its knives. Arctic winds crossing Long Island Sound would strip the breath from this small beached voyager. Well, at least we could give it a place to die: I stooped and picked it up. It barely squirmed, then fainted. We walked home up the cliff, with the walnut bird quiet in my hands. It was mostly feathers. Starving, probably. But why blind? Shot in the head? I remembered news the week before of a large oil slick leaking from a grounded barge.

Yet this was no pitiful tar-dipped body; the bird had only a black patch on its breast.

Home, I set the duck outside in a corner, sheltered from the winds by the arms of the house. My friend Terry was sympathetic. "You can't take a bird in to die without giving it a last meal," she said.

But what kind of meal? We looked at the glossy seal-brown head, the sculptured ebony bill with a slight hook on the tip, the strong wings and skin diver's feet, and consulted books. By its wing-patches we decided it must be a white-winged scoter; by its brown color, a female. Seafood, then, for this was a diving duck and a fisherman. Indoors, I proffered some canned tuna, but the starving bird flung it across the room. She must be past eating. There was only one way left. We mixed a thin gruel of tuna fish and wheat germ in some warmish milk. While I held the bill open, Terry dropped the soup down its throat with a poultry baster. The duck was too limp to care.

We tried to blot the oil patch off her breast, for we knew that without the dry, airy insulation of its feathers a duck soon dies of cold. I settled her outside on a blanket of dried marsh hay, and tacked chicken wire across her corner to protect against strange dogs. She sat there now in the night, a silent shape in her dark prison of frustration. Intermittently she shook her head, or rubbed her eyes hard against her

> *Her feedings became a contest. For a wild bird, it must have been a shocking humiliation.*

back to brush the darkness away. The rest of the time she sat not moving a muscle. Next morning she was still there.

Now her feedings became a contest. I wrapped a sling around her wings, using both hands to open the gullet while Terry squirted the baster. For a wild bird it must have been a shocking humiliation. She fainted between mouthfuls. Once, caught, she broke her wild thing's silence with a bleat of dismay. "You may kill her with your kindness," Terry said.

We tried putting a tray of water in her pen with slivers of fish and seaweed in it. Wayward as ever, the duck stumbled through the pan, at last drank some of the water, flung away whatever food she encountered, and waded in to take a bath. Then it began to rain. The drops, instead of rolling off, settled to stay. Though the duck tried to groom and fluff herself, she obviously found no oil in the preen gland near her tail: starvation must have used it up. Drenched, she huddled, and waited.

We brought the soaking creature inside then and dried her. For once she didn't fight us off. We smoothed lanolin lotion over her damp feathers and left her in a cozy spot. The icy little paddle feet grew warm; she closed her eyes, and gave a long sigh. When we looked again, she had tucked her bill under her wing in a room full of dogs and people.

And so she became a boarder in our kitchen. We made a nest of thick newspapers and marsh straw

for this duck with none of a duck's capacities: she couldn't see, couldn't fly, couldn't fish, couldn't float, couldn't even shed water to stay warm. And if she grew, well, what? But something about the way she sat there, and why she was there at all, made me feel she had to be fought for.

Each time I came in I'd say, "Hello, Duck," and talk to her. She seemed to find reassurance in my voice. As I left her, I'd add, "So long, Duck." A dozen times a day I chirped, "Hello, Duck." The third day, and thereafter, Duck answered. "Quonk," she said hoarsely.

She was improving. One day she was strong enough simply to close her throat against the insult that had kept her alive. Green gruel cascaded down her feathers, my fingers, and was spattered over the room. I felt the nip of despair. And a nip of another kind—she had clamped onto my gruel-coated finger. But instead of wrenching it, she tasted it. Quickly I dipped it back in the soup. Again she lapped it off with a flat pink tongue, and again.

Well fed, Duck stood and flapped her wings. Tentatively at first, to be sure of a clear swing. Then so vigorously that the roar filled the kitchen and the papers skidded. Her wings warmed up, Duck waddled a little way off from her nest and, taking blind aim, flew back to it and settled in. Then she ambled to her water tray, whose location she knew by now, and began to bathe, splashing in, slurping out, flapping, shaking, drying, splashing again.

In three days she stopped eating again. Again I despaired. It turned out now she simply wanted to drink for herself, but there began the agonizingly slow business of getting the bill to find the bowl. I would splat my finger in the mixture: sometimes Duck came, often she fled. Sometimes she landed in the bowl.

One morning when I'd filled it, adding her slivers of fish, she walked over and began a startling maneuver. Thrusting her bill in, she vibrated her head up and down and clapped her bill shut about six times a second, exactly as if she had turned on a little outboard motor. The force of it squirted a steady stream of liquid out the fine-toothed sides of her bill; a *scoter* ("shooter" in Scottish), I learned then, was named for this distinctive way of feeding. A technique marvelous to sieve out food while diving, you could see. Now she ate only this way, and only from her water tray, in which she had formerly spurned all food. Terry grinned wildly.

> ## Duck was one more victim of one more ecological outrage. Except that, unlike most, she was alive.

"She's going to live," she said.

But where? It was on Valentine's Day as I cleaned her corner that Duck pointed the way. Her papers were her home. She often lingered near while I changed them, waiting to bustle back in and do her wing exercises. This day I had set the water tray a few yards off, and was startled to see her walk over to it and take a drink. She waddled back with her sailor's gait, settled herself, and began imperturbably grooming. My hand was passing her left side with the filled tray of water and food when—whang!— she grabbed it. In disbelief, I put my hand back near her left eye. Whang! She got it again. *She could see.* Only a little, but what a Valentine gift!

Outside in her pen that day, she stared at the sun one moment and the next flew into the air. But the thin branches of a pear tree neatly hooked her and dropped her in the lilacs, where she sat stock still. She could see, but not enough.

Still puzzled by how she was blinded, I went to the library. I knew that swallowing oil depletes the body of vitamin A, part of the chemistry needed for sight. We had given Duck this fishy vitamin squirted first in her gruel and later on her breast feathers, where she cleaned it off like anything else. Like, say, tanker oil. I hadn't even reached the medical shelves when I noticed a book about the *Torrey Canyon*, the giant oil tanker that broke up off English beaches in 1967. Hundreds of seabirds were lost in that messy tragedy, the first big one of its kind, and hundreds more died later. Aftereffects, it was found, included liver and kidney damage, paralysis, and blindness.

Now I knew Duck's fate. Spotted by oil as she rode the waves, she tried to clean it off. How much of it she had to swallow we can't know, nor how long it took for her world to grow black. Duck was one more small victim of one more ecological outrage. Except that, unlike most, she was alive and recovering.

The days were growing longer now, and the air was filled with bird calls. The day before Easter, Duck, strolling in the yard, looked into the bright blank sky and flapped off in a roar toward the Sound. I ran after her as she lurched through the air, but she rose in a burst of willpower—straight for the trees. If she had been stronger, she might have made it to the open water. But I had seen that faltering, wind-hooked takeoff. After all these weeks, I could not bear to think she would ricochet from some treetop to hang up in a bramblebush, slowly dying.

I went to the woods and called, but all was quiet. Upset, she would be mute anyway. It began to rain. I went home, put on boots and slicker, sharpened a machete, and started out again. I laid out a systematic search course, and cut my way back and forth through thick briar. No Duck. From the woods I went to the Sound to scan

For a Duck grown stronger, it would be quite easy to fly up into the bright sky, and back to the water where she belonged.

———

the water, the beach, the cliffs. Suddenly six ducks appeared, flying north very fast and low over the water, wing beats in unison. White wing-patches flashed like flags— Duck! But no, she couldn't be among them, ever again, flying that fast and sure.

Easter dawned damp but turned

gold. That afternoon Terry and I walked down the beach with Amber. Half a mile from home, Terry saw a brown stone among the others. A small shape and familiar. "Duck?" she said.

"Quonk," came the hoarse reply. We carried her home and put her, shivering, in front of her favorite heater. She had sprained one leg: that was doubtless why she was beached again.

About a week later, Duck once again solved things herself. She spent the day in her pen, sunning. Visiting friends urged us to begin to leave her there during the balmy nights to harden her. Next morning dawned bright and warm, and I looked out to see how Duck was taking the weather.

She was gone! There were no feathers; no scuffle woke Amber. The wire of the pen was pulled down from the inside. I saw that for a Duck now grown stronger, it would be quite easy to fly up into the bright sky, and back beyond the beach where she had flown before, to the water where she belonged.

We like to think she made it...

And perhaps she did. In a few days, the neighbors who live above that beach reported that their two semi-tame gulls were joined for a while by a brown duck. "I thought it might be yours," one of them told us, "so I said, 'Hello, Duck, what are you doing there?' And the duck actually swam toward me and sat, listening."

Seeing our intense interest, she added, "It looked very happy out there."

So long, Duck.

The Case of the Swaggering Smuggler

Despite constant surveillance, Billy Greer had managed to stay one step ahead of the law. Now he was plotting his biggest deal ever.

BY **RICHARD & JOYCE WOLKOMIR**

Originally published in May 1994

ick Carter, a special agent of the U.S. Drug Enforcement Administration (DEA), sprawled in an icy Vermont meadow, peering through binoculars at the lighted window of a gray clapboard farmhouse. Inside, two men were talking in comfort. It was a freezing night in April 1991, and Carter's patience was thinning. For seven years he had secretly watched Billy Greer's house, tracing a spider web with Greer at the center. Moving endlessly along the

strands were drugs and money. Greer was aware he was under surveillance. He also knew Carter had no solid evidence. Sometimes when Carter was tailing him in an unmarked car, Greer would stop and wave, grinning insouciantly.

Investigating a man he had known all his life was difficult for Carter. His father had been chief of police in the small town of South Burlington, where the Greers were proprietors of a successful sporting goods store and a dry-cleaning business. The Carters and Greers had been friendly, but lived on

opposite sides of town: the Greers in a sprawling colonial home, the Carters in a small ranch house. Young Billy—charming, good looking, a high-school football star—won people over. Rick Carter, resentful at being a cop's son, got into frequent fights. He looked up to Billy Greer.

Carter joined the Vermont State Police in 1980. His first assignment was in tiny St. Johnsbury. There he made an ugly discovery: Virtually every crime he investigated in this picture-post-card hamlet was rooted in drugs.

In 1984, Carter became a member of the Special Investigations Unit, focusing on Burlington, the state's largest city. The informants he developed there were buzzing about Billy Greer. It seemed that Greer had become a key figure in the local drug trade.

By now Greer had married a girl from Rick's high-school class. But rumor had it that Greer had been taking drugs. On a whim, Carter heard, Greer would jet off to the Rockies on skiing trips or disappear for weeks in Europe.

Carter put Greer under surveillance and soon verified that he was growing marijuana in a greenhouse on a secluded farm. When Carter had enough evidence, he knocked on Greer's door with an arrest warrant. The police found 150 marijuana plants and starting planters for 2,000 more.

The fine, though, was only $500; the sentence just a few days in jail. Two years later, Maine issued a warrant for Greer's arrest on another marijuana charge, and Carter tracked him down and arrested him once more. "Plead guilty," Carter told him. "Put this behind you and start over." But Greer shook his head. In the end, he was acquitted. Carter was appalled.

In 1990 Carter fulfilled a longtime ambition and joined the DEA. At the top of his to-do list as a federal agent was Billy Greer.

In November of that year, Vermont State Trooper Jim Colgan spotted a trailer bearing two all-terrain vehicles, or ATVs. They were heavy-duty six-wheelers with cargo bays. Colgan recognized the driver: Billy Greer's partner, Stephen Hutchins. Colgan suspected that they were using the ATVs to sneak drugs across the Canadian border. With Rick Carter away, training for his new DEA job, Colgan called John Donnelly, a U.S. Customs special agent who had worked with Carter. The next day, the U.S. Border Patrol called to tell Donnelly there had been sightings of six-wheeled ATVs along the border.

Two days later, customs agent Mike Desjardins and a Border Patrol agent drove a cruiser up a one-lane dirt road that led to the border. It was 4 p.m. and the day was darkening. Just short of the border, the car turned around and stopped, blocking the narrow road. On one side were cedar woods; on the other, a steep drop-off to a field.

Meanwhile, a quarter-mile back, John Donnelly heard the ATVs and saw them speed by. He radioed

Desjardins and then pulled his pickup off the road. Donnelly and his partner would cut off the ATVs' retreat.

Moments later three ATVs—two big six-wheelers and one smaller four-wheeler—roared toward Desjardins, headed for Canada. Helmets hid the drivers' faces. When they reached the cruiser facing them, Desjardins jumped out of the car and held up his hand. "Stop, police!" he shouted.

But the drivers moved forward. The small four-wheeler squeezed past Desjardins, teetered at the edge of the drop-off, then escaped toward Canada. One of the six-wheelers became stuck in the brush, and the other turned back the way it had come. As the vehicle came at him, Donnelly yanked his wheel to the left, shutting off the road. He braced for a collision. But the ATV veered and disappeared into the woods.

Meanwhile, Desjardins and the Border Patrol agent, his service revolver pointed at the driver, approached the ATV stuck in the brush. "Turn off the engine!" the agent yelled. The driver put up his

hands, and the agents locked him in the cruiser's back seat. Then they searched the ATV's cargo compartment, where they found two duffel bags stuffed with money. It totaled $1.3 million.

Radio calls now had authorities busy on both sides of the border. The escaped six-wheeler was found crashed in the Vermont woods. The driver was gone.

Across the border, the Canadians were looking for the escaped four-wheeler. A homeowner told agents that about 5 p.m., a man in a four-wheel ATV had stopped to chat. The agents displayed photographs. "That's him!" the homeowner said. He was pointing to a picture of Billy Greer.

Later, the money taken from the first ATV went to the FBI for examination. On one manila envelope, in which $100,000 had been stuffed, the FBI found a palmprint and a fingerprint—Billy Greer's.

On the other side of the world in a harbor in Oman, in early 1991, a Panamanian tug towing a Dutch barge filled with empty blue barrels began a long journey. Off the coast of Pakistan, another vessel tied up to the barge, and hundreds of bulging sacks marked "Sugar," "Wheat," "Rice," and "Flour" were transferred to the barge's hold. After the two boats separated, the tug towed the barge around the southern tip of Africa and up into the Atlantic.

In June, on the Portuguese island of Madeira, three large rubber boats and outboard engines were loaded onto the barge. Then, once more, the tug towed the barge out to sea, now heading toward Canada. On the way, the crew loaded the 50 or so tons of "Rice," "Sugar," "Wheat," and "Flour" into the barrels.

As soon as Rick Carter returned from his DEA training in Quantico, Virginia, in January 1991, he checked in with his drug-world informants. The word was that the money seized from the ATV was part payment for a big hashish shipment coming in. Carter already knew that Greer had bought a fishing camp in Quebec, somewhere on the Gulf of St. Lawrence.

But the DEA's evidence against Greer might be too weak to stick in court, especially since the arrested ATV driver refused to talk. The agents, hoping for a break, stepped up surveillance of the gang.

The ring members all lived in small towns. To their neighbors, they seemed ordinary, like Stephen Hutchins. A clean-cut, trim man with glasses, he was a volunteer firefighter in suburban Colchester. But when police discreetly asked his neighbors what he did for a living, none could say.

Carter spent more uncomfortable nights in the meadow across the road from Billy Greer's house. As he peered through binoculars, he saw members of the gang coming and going more frequently, the meetings inside looking more intense.

But one day Carter sensed something wrong. Nobody was around. No cars were coming and going. He hadn't seen Greer once. The dog wasn't out. These were telltale breaks in routine.

Worried, Carter sped to Colchester to check on Hutchins. He was gone, too. DEA agents quickly drove by the houses of other ring members. Nobody was home.

On the evening of July 22, 1991, the tug and barge arrived in the Gulf of St. Lawrence, about 100 kilometers up the coast from Sept-Iles, Quebec. Three rubber boats dropped into the water. Crewmen then unloaded the water-tight barrels, tying them together into seven floating rafts of 45 barrels each for the boats to tow to land.

Men came out from the shore in a motorboat and boarded the rubber boats. Seconds later, the engines roared. But then came shouting and cursing. The tug's crew apparently had made the rafts too long for the underpowered rubber boats. They were foundering under the strain. The rafts began breaking loose, and the barrels floated away into the darkness.

Panicked, the men from the shore climbed back into their motorboat and sped off. The tug moved away, too, towing the now-empty barge while the abandoned boats and barrels floated in the Gulf.

Late the next morning, a biologist out for a day of whale watching spotted a rubber boat, empty and adrift. Curious, he boarded it and found expensive European diving equipment. Then he saw two more boats on the surface nearby. He radioed the Canadian Coast Guard.

Soon Quebec police boats fanned out in the Gulf. Besides the three abandoned boats, they eventually collected 273 floating barrels, each packed with about 180 bricks of hashish. With an estimated street value of almost $1 billion, it was the biggest drug bust in Canadian history, and one of the biggest by U.S. standards.

In Sept-Iles harbor they found an oceangoing barge with traces of hashish in its hold. On July 25, the tug that had towed the barge arrived in Montreal. Police arrested all 15 men on the tug.

Scouring the coastline for the hashish's intended landing site, the Quebec police turned up two adjacent waterside plots in the hamlet of Rivière-au-Tonnerre. Local records revealed that several Vermonters owned the land. One

was Stephen Hutchins. Another was "Thomas William Dodds." The names meant nothing to the Quebec police.

At the campsite, police found a pound of hashish and blue straps matching those that tied the barrels together. They also discovered a driver's license and other documents in the name of "Thomas William Dodds." Officers hid outside, keeping watch. Three days later, on July 27, a young man drove up and looked around nervously. Soon he was under arrest. His name: Michael Johnson.

In Vermont the next night, John Donnelly called Rick Carter to tell him the Quebec police were looking for William Greer, Stephen Hutchins and some other Vermonters. And they had arrested Michael Johnson, known to be one of Billy Greer's underlings. Weeks earlier, Carter had alerted the Canadians of his suspicion that Greer might move drugs through Canada. Now the Canadians wanted to know if Carter would come to Montreal to interrogate Johnson.

"You bet I would!" Carter said.

"He's cooperating," a Quebec police officer told the two American agents upon their arrival.

When Carter and Donnelly sat down across from Johnson, they found a worried and exhausted man. Slowly he told his story. Billy had hash coming in. He offered up to $25,000 per trip if Johnson would help smuggle the drugs.

Before the tug and barge were due, the gang members drove to the Gulf of St. Lawrence. Finally, night came and several of them headed into the Gulf in their motorboat.

Just before dawn, one of them returned to the group on shore. He was frantic. The crew of the tug had bungled the job, he said. Most of the gang went back to the United States, but Greer, Hutchins, another man and Johnson had stayed on in Canada. On July 26, Johnson told Carter, the four drove to Montreal, where they met with three Canadians.

Johnson did not know the Canadians. But Carter and investigators in several countries eventually pieced together evidence of an international drug-smuggling ring, headquartered in the Netherlands.

By now Quebec police had shown photos to the notary who had witnessed the purchase of the Gulf campsite. "That's Dodds," he had said, pointing to a picture of Billy Greer.

Seven years I've been watching Billy Greer, Carter thought. And now, for the first time, I've got solid evidence.

On July 29, Canadian arrest warrants were issued for the Greer gang. U.S. warrants were issued the next day. Within hours, Greer and all his cohorts were brought into custody.

At the DEA office in Williston, Vermont, agents ushered Greer in. He was wearing bathing trunks, a T-shirt and a baseball cap. Carter was face to face with the man he had been watching so long. "Let me talk to Greer alone for a minute," Carter told the other officers.

"This time you're really in hot water," Carter said. For once, Greer had lost his cockiness. Carter laid out what would now happen—extradition to Canada, the trial, jail. "Plead guilty, give us evidence, and maybe your sentence will be shorter. You're 42 years old. It's time to start fresh."

A guy with two little kids, Carter thought, staring at Greer. How could he have put his family into this situation?

But Greer shook his head. In 1986, Carter had given him much the same speech. That time, Greer won. And Greer had already telephoned an expensive New York City attorney. "I'll have to see how it turns out," he said.

That's it? Carter thought, as he stared disbelievingly at Billy Greer. As a child, he had looked up to him—the charismatic football star. Now he stifled an urge to punch the man in the face. "OK, Billy," Carter said. "That's your decision."

Outside the interrogation room, officers were waiting to transport Greer to jail. It was 5 a.m. when the last of the gang was processed. Documents littered Carter's desk—surveillance reports, arrest records, informants' statements. They represented seven years of lying in frozen meadows at night, maintaining surveillance on a criminal who had all the answers, or seemed to. Carter stuffed the documents into a file marked "Greer, Billy," closed it, and drove home to his wife and three children.

A Quebec court sentenced the Vermont drug gang to the Cowansville penitentiary in Quebec. Billy Greer and Stephen Hutchins received the harshest punishment— 8½ years.

Rick Carter, meanwhile, is still working on the case. When the gang gets out of jail in Canada, he expects that they will face trial again in the United States, with stiffer sentences to follow.

The Greatest Quotes Never Said

An author sets the record straight on famous misquotations.

—

BY **RALPH KEYES**

FROM THE BOOK **NICE GUYS FINISH SEVENTH**

Originally published in June 1993

The saying W. C. Fields is best remembered for is "Any man who hates dogs and children can't be all bad." But Fields didn't say it. These words were said *about* Fields by Leo Rosten, a young writer, as he paid tribute to the comedian at a Hollywood banquet in 1939—except that Rosten said "babies" instead of "children."

Later Rosten's line was picked up by the national press. Few people had heard of Leo Rosten. So, before long, a version of his words was put in Fields's mouth and has stayed there ever since.

But Rosten deserves credit for the line, right? Well, not exactly. In November 1937, more than a year before the banquet, *Harper's Monthly* ran a column quoting a *New York Times* reporter as saying, "No man who hates dogs and children can be all bad."

So reference books should attribute the quote to this *Times* reporter named Byron Darnton. Byron who? That's the point. Few remember his name, and most of us have heard of W. C. Fields. The better-known name gets the credit.

Such cases are common. Many of history's best-known quotes have been inaccurately recorded, attributed to the wrong person or both. For instance:

- "Winning isn't everything, it's the only thing" was the slogan of Vanderbilt University football coach Red Sanders before it was attributed to Vince Lombardi.

- "The opera ain't over till the fat lady sings" is popularly associated with basketball coach Dick Motta. He credits sportscaster and writer Dan Cook. Actually, it was adapted from an older saying: "Church ain't out till the fat lady sings."
- "Elementary, my dear Watson" does not appear in any of Arthur Conan Doyle's Sherlock Holmes books.
- Leo Durocher never said, "Nice guys finish last." What the Brooklyn Dodgers' manager said, before a 1946 game with the New York Giants, was: "The nice guys are over there—in seventh place."

It is a rare quote that can't be improved. As pressure mounted for him to become a presidential candidate in 1884, William Tecumseh Sherman wrote, "I will not accept if nominated and will not serve if elected." That response was pithy. But history's rewriters made the Civil War hero's statement even pithier: "If nominated, I will not run. If elected, I will not serve."

This is a recurring process. Quotations that start out too long or too clumsy end up shorter, more graceful and rhythmic. One of the most quoted lines of modern times is Pogo's "We have met the enemy, and he is us." The original expression of this thought, in Walt Kelly's 1953 introduction to his book *The Pogo Papers*, was "Resolve then that on this very ground, with small flags waving and tinny blasts on tiny trumpets, we shall meet the enemy, and not only may he be ours, he may be us."

In 1916, a year before America's entry into World War I, a *Chicago Tribune* reporter pressed Henry Ford for the historical context of his pro-disarmament views. "What do we care what they did 500 or 1,000 years ago? ... History is more or less bunk," Ford replied. "It's tradition. We don't want tradition. We want to live in the present, and the only history that is worth a tinker's damn is the history we make today."

Copy desks and the public mind telescoped the crusty automaker's remark into one that was terser, less equivocal, more like what we

> ## *The public mind telescoped his remark into what we imagined Henry Ford would say.*
> ———

imagined Henry Ford would say: "History is bunk."

That single colorful word "bunk" proved to be a powerful hook that fastened this sentence in our collective memory.

Sometimes the changing of a single word can make a big difference. Upon stepping to the surface of the moon on July 20, 1969, Neil Armstrong uttered the immortal phrase, "That's one small step for a man, one giant leap for mankind." At least that's what Armstrong meant to say. But he forgot the "a," and it came out "That's one small step for man, one giant leap for mankind." This didn't make much sense. NASA quickly explained that transmission problems clipped the "a" from the astronaut's words. Balderdash! Armstrong blew his line, pure and simple.

Another case of an added "a" involved writer Gertrude Stein, whose most famous line is "A rose is a rose is a rose." What she actually wrote, in her poem "Sacred Emily," was "Rose is a rose is a rose is a rose." Was she referring to a flower or to someone named Rose? To make the words more coherent, we added an "a" to the beginning and pruned a blossom from the end. Eventually, the poet herself seems to have adopted the popular version of her line.

Most people have heard Willie Sutton's explanation of why he robbed banks: "Because that's where the money is." But in his autobiography, Sutton denied ever saying the words.

"The credit belongs to some enterprising reporter who apparently felt a need to fill out his copy," Sutton explained. "I can't even remember when I first read it. It just seemed to appear one day, and then it was everywhere."

Some quotations benefit from a little syntax straightening. While

> ## The aphorism floats around like a dandelion seed waiting for a famous name to land on.

managing the inept New York Mets, an exasperated Casey Stengel once said, "Can't *anybody* play this here game?" After reporters cleaned up his grammar, "Can't anybody here play this game?" became one of Stengel's most famous lines.

Sometimes famous quotes have perfectly good grammar. They just need famous mouths. An often repeated adage is "No one on his deathbed ever said 'I wish I had spent more time on my business.'" The comment was widely quoted after former U.S. Senator Paul Tsongas included it in a 1984 book, crediting his friend Arnold Zack.

Still, these words are hardly ever attributed to Zack, because most people don't know who he is. Mostly the aphorism just floats around like a dandelion seed waiting for a famous name to land on. Tsongas himself sometimes gets credit for the quote.

By one popular account, former Indiana Congressman Richard Thompson dropped in on John Babsone Lane Soule, the young editor of the Terre Haute *Express,* in 1851. Thompson had just returned from a trip to Kansas and was impressed with prospects west of the Mississippi. He suggested that the editor write an editorial recommending that readers go west and grow up with the country— a sentiment being pushed by *New York Tribune* editor Horace Greeley.

Soon Soule wrote an editorial

declaring that Horace Greeley himself could not give a young man better advice than to "Go West, young man." Before long this admonition was credited to Greeley.

Though he agreed with the sentiment, Greeley spent years disavowing authorship of the line. Eventually he gave up, realizing no one was interested. The quote demanded a marquee name and Greeley's was it.

In some cases, who you think said something may depend on where you live. U.S. Supreme Court Justice Oliver Wendell Holmes Jr. is famous for saying "Oh, to be 70 again" when he saw a comely woman on his 90th birthday in 1931. A British quote collection credits French Premier Georges Clemenceau with saying the same thing on his 80th birthday in 1921. And Prussian Field Marshal Count Friedrich Heinrich Ernst von Wrangel is remembered in Germany for saying in his 90s, "If only one were 80!"

Even within a country, the credit for familiar quotations can vary depending on whom you ask. In the world of sports, Yogi Berra gets credit for saying, "If people don't want to come to the ballpark, how are you gonna stop them?" In theater circles, producer Sol Hurok was renowned for observing, "If people don't want to come, nothing will stop them."

With so many streams of miswording and misattribution out there, we can be sure of only one thing: As long as there are quotes, there will be misquotes. And you can quote me on that.

My Father's Music

In that odd and dreaded instrument was the gift of a lifetime.

BY **WAYNE KALYN**

Originally published in August 1991

remember the day Dad first lugged the heavy accordion up our front stoop, taxing his small frame. He called my mother and me to the living room and opened the case as if it were a treasure chest.

"Here it is," he said. "Once you learn to play, it'll stay with you for life." If my thin smile didn't match his full-fledged grin, it was because I had prayed for a guitar or a piano. It was 1960, and I was glued to my AM radio, listening to Del Shannon and Chubby Checker. Accordions were nowhere on my hit parade. As I looked at the shiny white keys and cream-colored bellows, I could already hear my friends' jokes about the squeezebox.

For the next two weeks the accordion was stored in the hall closet. Then one evening Dad announced that I would start lessons the following week. In disbelief I shot my eyes toward Mom for support. The firm set of her jaw told me I was out of luck.

Spending $300 for an accordion and $5 per lesson was out of character for my father. He was practical—something he learned growing up on a Pennsylvania farm. Clothes, heat, and sometimes even food had been scarce.

Before I was born, he and my mother moved into her parents' two-story home in Jersey City, New Jersey. I grew up there on the second floor; my grandparents lived downstairs. Each weekday Dad made the three-hour commute to and from Long Island, where he was a supervisor in a company that serviced jet engines. Weekends, he tinkered in the cellar, turning scraps of plywood into a utility cabinet or fixing a broken toy. Quiet and shy, he was never more comfortable than when he was at his workbench.

Only music carried Dad away from his world of tools and projects. On a Sunday drive, he turned the radio on immediately. At red lights, I'd notice his foot tapping in time. He seemed to hang on every note.

Still, I wasn't prepared when, rummaging in a closet, I found a case that looked to me like a tiny guitar's. Opening it, I saw the polished glow of a beautiful violin.

"It's your father's," Mom said. "His parents bought it for him. I guess he got too busy on the farm to ever learn to play it." I tried to imagine Dad's rough hands on this delicate instrument—and couldn't.

Shortly after, my lessons began with Mr. Zelli at the Allegro Accordion School, tucked between an old movie theater and a pizza parlor. On my first day, with straps straining my shoulders, I felt clumsy in every way. "How did he do?" my father asked when it was over. "Fine for the first lesson," said Mr. Zelli. Dad glowed with hope.

I was ordered to practice half an hour every day, and every day I tried to get out of it. My future seemed to be outside playing ball, not in the house mastering songs I would soon forget. But my parents hounded me.

Gradually, to my surprise, I was able to string notes together and coordinate my hands to play simple songs. Often, after supper, my father would request a tune or two. As he sat in his easy chair, I would fumble through "Lady of Spain" and "Beer Barrel Polka."

"Very nice," he'd say. Then I would segue into a medley of his favorites, "Red River Valley" and "Home on the Range," and he would drift off to sleep, the evening paper folded on his lap. I took it as a compliment that he could relax under the spell of my playing.

One July evening I was giving an almost flawless rendition of "Come Back to Sorrento," and my parents called me to an open window. An elderly neighbor, rarely seen outside her house, was leaning against our car humming dreamily to the tune. When I finished, she smiled broadly and called out, "I remember that song as a child in Italy. Beautiful, just beautiful."

Throughout the summer, Mr. Zelli's lessons grew more difficult. It took me a week and a half to master them now. All the while I could hear my buddies outside playing heated games of stickball. I'd also hear an occasional taunt: "Hey, where's your monkey and cup?"

Such humiliation paled, though, beside the impending fall recital. I would have to play a solo on the stage of a local movie theater and I wanted to skip the whole thing. Emotions boiled over in the car one Sunday afternoon.

"I don't want to play a solo," I said.

"You have to," replied my father.

"Why?" I shouted. "Because you didn't get to play your violin when you were a kid? Why should I have to play this stupid instrument when you never had to play yours?"

Dad pulled the car over. "Because you can bring people joy. You can touch their hearts. That's a gift I won't let you throw away." He added softly, "Someday you'll have the chance I never had. You'll play beautiful music for your family and you'll understand why you've worked so hard."

I was speechless. I had rarely heard Dad speak with such feeling about anything, much less the accordion. From then on, I practiced without my parents making me.

The evening of the concert Mom wore glittery earrings and more makeup than I could remember. Dad got out of work early, put on a suit and tie, and slicked down his hair with Vitalis. They were ready an hour early, so we sat in the living room chatting nervously. I got the unspoken message that playing this song was their dream come true.

At the theater, nervousness overtook me as I realized how much I wanted to make my parents proud. Finally, it was my turn. I walked to the lone chair and performed "Are You Lonesome Tonight?" without a mistake. The applause spilled out.

I was lightheaded, glad that my ordeal was over.

After the concert Mom and Dad came backstage. The way they walked—heads high, faces flushed—I knew they were pleased. My mother gave me a big hug. Dad slipped an arm around me and held me close. "You were just great," he said. Then he shook my hand and was slow to let it go.

As the years went by, Dad asked me to play at family occasions, but the lessons ended. When I went to college, the accordion stayed in the hall closet next to my father's violin.

A year after my graduation, my parents moved to a house in a nearby town. Dad, at 51, finally owned his own home. On moving day, I didn't have the heart to tell him he could dispose of the accordion, so I brought it to my own home and put it in the attic.

There it remained, a dusty memory, until one afternoon several years later when my two children discovered it by accident. Scott thought it was a secret treasure; Holly thought a ghost lived inside. They were both right.

When I opened the case, they laughed and said, "Play it, play it." Reluctantly, I strapped on the accordion and played some simple songs. Soon the kids were dancing in circles and giggling. Even my wife, Terri, was laughing and clapping to the beat. I was amazed at their unbridled glee.

My father's words came back to me: "Someday you'll have the chance I never had. Then you'll understand." I finally knew what it meant to work hard and sacrifice for others. Dad had been right all along: The most precious gift is to touch the hearts of those you love.

Later I phoned Dad to tell him that, at long last, I understood. I thanked him for the legacy it took almost 30 years to discover. "You're welcome," he said, his voice choked with emotion.

Dad never learned to coax sweet sounds from his violin. Yet he was wrong to think he would never play for his family. On that wonderful evening, as my wife and children laughed and danced, they heard my accordion. But it was my father's music.

There's a Tidal Wave Loose in Here!

*A fisherman and his son are caught
in a desperate situation.*

—

BY **LAWRENCE ELLIOTT**

Originally published in July 1960

On July 9, 1958, Howard G. "Howie" Ulrich, a 32-year-old commercial fisherman out of Pelican, Alaska, was trolling off the mouth of Lituya Bay with his seven-year-old son when he heard the 6 p.m. weather report: a possibility of high winds from the southeast.

Ordinarily Howie would have ignored such a warning, but now he stepped into the pilothouse of his 38-foot *Edrie* and radioed his partner, Julian J. "Stutz" Graham, who was running a parallel course

50 yards off his port beam. "Stutz," he said, "since the boy is aboard, I'm going into Lituya for the night."

Howie didn't much like Lituya Bay. Its mouth is constricted to a very narrow 80-foot channel by rock; violent tidal currents make navigating the channel difficult. And there were fishermen around who remembered that October morning in 1936 when several giant waves swept across the bay, leaving destruction in their wake.

Still, Lituya was the only natural harbor along 100 miles of the Gulf of Alaska coast, and Howie went in.

About ten that night, just before

Howie went below to hit the sack, a second troller put in to Lituya. In the distance it looked to Howie like Bill and Vivian Swanson's *Badger*. A few minutes later a third came in and anchored beside the second. But by that time Howie was sleeping peacefully. There was no wind. The water was glassy smooth. Small icebergs floated about, sparkling in the deepening twilight.

But one thing was ominously wrong. The gulls and terns that usually screamed above the rocky crags of Cenotaph Island in the center of the bay were silent. More than that, they were gone. Stutz Graham, who had gone on five miles north after leaving Howie, had come upon the birds at Cape Fairweather, and the sight made him uneasy. "I never saw so many of them," he said. "They must have covered 20 acres. The funny thing was, there wasn't a single one in the air. They were all squatting on the beach, like they were waiting for something."

❖ ❖ ❖

It was still light at 10:17 when an abrupt and violent shudder brought Howie Ulrich bounding out of his bunk. Not quite awake, he thought: the anchor must have pulled loose; we've run aground! The moment he came plunging out on deck, he knew the truth.

"It was an earthquake, a bad one," he said. "The water churned and the mountains shook. Those mountains—it was like they were going through some awful torture. Can you imagine what it's like to see a 10,000-foot mountain twisting and shaking?"

Clouds of snow and rock went spewing into the sky. Great chunks tore loose from the mountainsides and came avalanching into the bay. Huge pieces of ice came flying off Lituya Glacier, at the head of the bay, like a load of rocks spilling out of a dump truck.

Howie didn't know it, but in Juneau, the capital city, the earthquake jostled people in their beds. Near Cross Sound, octopus, cod and halibut in large numbers were killed by shock waves. The Alaska Communications cable between Haines and Skagway was severed in four places. In Seattle, the University of Washington's seismograph needle was knocked completely off its graph. When a final reading was taken, the quake was found to have been among the four severest in North American history, registering close to 8 on the Richter magnitude scale. (The San Francisco earthquake of 1906 had registered 8.25.)

As his boat thrashed at anchor, Howie stood transfixed by the spectacle before him. It had a hypnotic, otherworldly quality from which he had to wrench himself free.

Sonny stood beside him on the deck now, sleepily rubbing his eyes. Howie made a tentative effort to get a life jacket on the boy. He didn't feel any real sense of danger—he was fairly certain the *Edrie* could ride out the quake—but it seemed the thing to do. He didn't bother about a jacket for himself. In fact, a long time would pass before he realized that he was wearing nothing but the shorts in which he had slept. It was seconds shy of 10:20 p.m.

About 2½ minutes after he first felt the earthquake, Howie heard a rumbling, gathering roar. Soon it filled the hollow of the bay with crashing sound. Howie actually felt its vibrating impact on his bare skin. Along the top of the bay, 6½ miles away, an enormous wedge of mountain and glacier, thousands of tons of ice, rock and earth, had heaved, then plunged down into the narrow inlet, causing a cascading wave of water that now seemed to explode across the bay at an incredible height. Ponderously, inexorably, the wall of water began bearing down on the *Edrie*.

"Get below!" Howie cried to his son. Then, "Wait!" he shouted. "The life jacket!"

Terrified and trembling, Sonny stood fast as his father fumbled with the strings on the jacket. Precious seconds fled by. Fragments of panic-flecked thought jarred against Howie's brain: he had to get away from the beach; he had to haul anchor! Then he remembered that Stutz Graham and his 17-year-old son, Ken, were only a few miles away at Cape Fairweather. He ran for his radio.

❖ ❖ ❖

Stutz Graham had just turned out the forecastle light when his *Lumen* pitched forward, then rolled hard to starboard. He and his son bounded onto the deck. The sea was contorted by six-inch waterspouts; waves smashed crazily against one another and churned the water to frenzied white foam. "Start the engine!" Graham commanded. Remembering Howie, he ran to switch on the radio. A babble of excited sound came over the receiver—shouts, half sentences, cries of alarm. Then, sharper than the rest: "Mayday! Mayday! This is the *Edrie* in Lituya Bay! A tidal wave's busted loose in here! I don't think we've got a chance."

❖ ❖ ❖

Howie doesn't remember sending his "Mayday." His recollection is that as the wave tore through the bay, the first thing he did was to start his engine and throw in the full power of his anchor winch.

"I meant to head into it. I felt I had to get into deep water before the wave threw us up on the beach."

The anchor—a 64-pound Danforth—wouldn't budge. The tortured heaving of the earth had probably opened a crevice and swallowed it. Desperate, Howie let the chain pay out to its full 40-fathom length: maybe there would be enough slack to permit the *Edrie* to ride up over the wave. Then, with engine and rudder, he began maneuvering the pitching troller about so that she would be faced into the onrushing wall of water.

The wave had tapered to a height of approximately 100 feet as it cut a swath through Cenotaph Island. It now stretched from one shore to the other, 2½ miles, breaking sharply as it swept over the north side of the island. And, wherever it struck, it sheared away 100-year-old timber stands, peeled the earth to bedrock. Flung into the bay, six-foot spruce trunks were shaved as clean of bark as though they had been through a sawmill.

Howie had not quite got the *Edrie*'s bow swung into the wave when it hit. "It was like going up in an elevator," he said. "Only there seemed to be no end to it. The half-inch anchor chain snapped off at the winch like a piece of kite string, and the short end came snapping back around the pilothouse and almost took my head off."

The wave lifted the *Edrie* high up over the shore line. Swooping along above the treetops, Howie abandoned hope. "There was just nothing I could do," he said. "I could see the trees snapping off way

> ## A babble of excited sound came over the receiver—shouts, half sentences, cries of alarm.

below us. I figured we had to be dumped and smashed on the rocks."

Miraculously, the *Edrie* slid over the wave's crest and was caught by the backwash. Down and down the little troller swept. Howie threw his throttle wide and clung to the wheel in a frantic effort to keep his bow pointed at Cenotaph Island. For the first time, he began to think that he and Sonny had a chance.

❖ ❖ ❖

Neither of the other two boats anchored in Lituya Bay lasted so long. On the *Badger*, Vivian Swanson saw the great wave coming and cried out to her husband, "What can we do?" For a moment, Bill Swanson considered following the example of Orville and Mickey Wagner on the 44-foot *Sunmore*, which had anchored beside them—hauling anchor and making a run for the channel and open water. But he decided that the *Badger* could never make it in time. He moved closer to his wife and just waited.

He remembers that the wave was still sweeping them upward when he heard Mickey Wagner's last, plaintive cry on the radio, "Ma-maaaaa!" and he saw the sleek new *Summore* awash to the pilothouse and heading straight for a sheer cliff.

The Swansons' boat went up like a matchstick over the 150-yard-wide spit of rock at the mouth of the bay, up and out into the open sea. "I looked down on rocks as big as houses when we crossed the spit,"

Bill Swanson says. A quarter-mile offshore, the boat hit the bed of the sea, stern first. With the icy Gulf waters rising over them through the shattered stern, the Swansons tore frantically at the lines that secured their eight-foot skiff to the roof of the pilothouse. The water was at their knees when they shoved off from the stricken troller. Since the oars had been swept away, Bill tore loose one of the skiff's thwarts and began paddling.

By now, radios were crackling all over the area as skippers set out to account for every boat in the little fishing fleet, interdependent in crisis as never before. Racing down from Cape Fairweather at top speed, Stutz Graham kept repeating: "This is the *Lumen* calling the *Edrie*. Howie? Do you read me?"

❖　❖　❖

Howie Ulrich felt that he had been dumped, pell-mell, into another world. Inside the bay, a stench— "It smelled like an explosion in a root cellar," he said—hung in the gathering twilight. A strange fog was closing in. He could see water surging up onto the shore, forming lakes hundreds of yards inland and dumping mountains of debris on the beach. But the eeriest sight was the shore line, thick with timber only moments before, now naked, shorn to glistening rock back to a height of as much as 1,750 feet. In the bay, felled trees were pitching and tossing in unnatural currents and eddies, crisscrossed and upended like jackstraws. Great chunks of glacier ice spun round and round, grinding against one another.

Nevertheless, Howie decided to have a try at getting out of the bay. Carefully he began threading his way toward the channel.

"I could hardly see a thing by now," Howie said, "not a single landmark. I had to follow a compass course. Maybe the tide would be against me; maybe I'd take a timber through the hull on the way out. But it was still a better gamble than milling around inside until we were crushed. I tucked seat cushions around Sonny and told him to hang on for dear life."

The *Edrie* hit the channel on the full ebb tide. Howie eased his boat into the swift-running water and, in moments, the *Edrie* was being thrown toward the open sea, pitching under combers that broke solidly over the wheelhouse. Still, it held steady fore and aft, its snub nose rising stubbornly after each breaker. It seemed to Howie that he hardly breathed until, at last, the stout little troller reached the comparative calm of open water. He began to shake—a delayed reaction to the harrowing moments behind him. Then he went below and dressed.

❖ ❖ ❖

Bearing southeast at full throttle, Stutz Graham was soon forced to cut his speed, first to five knots, then to two, as the debris flung out of Lituya Bay began spreading up and down the coast line. Ken Graham lay prone across the *Lumen*'s bow, playing a flashlight on the dark and littered water, guiding his father port or starboard, and sometimes shouting, "Reverse!"

Inexplicably, Stutz Graham cut his engine as he approached Lituya. "There was no reason for me to shut down," he said. "Fact is, it was plain dangerous. I couldn't have

been in more than five fathoms of water. I might have drifted aground. It was just one of those senseless things you do sometimes. Now, I'm not a religious man, but when something like that happens—when senseless things add up to a purpose that you couldn't possibly know about—then I say that somebody or something higher up is keeping track of things."

The moment Stutz's engine faded, a new sound broke the stillness—a thin, plaintive cry.

"It could have been a bird—it sounded like a bird—but Ken and I kept running from one corner of the boat to another, trying to get a line on where it came from."

Now there was only silence, and soon Stutz turned the engine back on. In a little while he felt impelled to turn it off again. Twice more he repeated the process, and the fourth time he again heard the weak call for help. Bill Swanson's tiny skiff was almost alongside the *Lumen*'s port bow, barely four inches of freeboard remaining. Waist-deep in the 50-degree water, the Swansons were all but senseless with shock and cold. After nearly two hours of exposure, they were, in fact, only moments from an icy grave.

Stutz and Ken sent out word that the Swansons had been picked up—"Tell 'em to send a plane!"—while he got Bill and Vivian into sleeping bags and heated some coffee for them. Then he, Howie, and a third boat to arrive, Red Embree's *Theon*, began searching for some trace of the Wagners, whose boat had been anchored beside the Swansons in the bay. Soon after 1 a.m. Stutz got word that a plane had left Juneau for Dixon Harbor, about 40 miles to the southeast; he was to take the Swansons there.

Stutz suggested that Howie follow him to Dixon Harbor, but Howie declined. "There were only Red Embree and me to look for the Wagners. Suppose they were drifting around in the dark somewhere? It could have been Sonny and me, you know. I felt the least I could do was stick around."

Stutz said, "Howie's kid was just like his old man. I offered to take him in with me, but he said he guessed he'd stay with his dad."

All night long the two searchers alternately drifted and called, then cruised on to another area and called again. By now the sea was completely littered. Floating clumps of earth, roots, and trees, some still standing upright, drifted by like ghostly islands.

It was 5:30, with the morning sun already reddening the sky, when other trollers reached the scene. Howie Ulrich turned to his son. "Well, sport, what do you say to all the excitement?"

"Daddy," the boy replied, "let's go home to Pelican."

Howie hugged the slim shoulders close to him, then turned southeast and increased speed. As he cruised past Dixon Harbor, a boat hailed him. It was the *Lumen*. Stutz Graham had been standing by, waiting for his partner so they could return to Pelican together, as partner boats should. In the full light of the new day, the friends made for Cross Sound. It had been a long 24 hours.

The search for the Wagners proved futile. Except for a single brightly colored trolling pole, no trace was ever found of them.

In the spring of 1959, the Swansons bought a new boat. Part of its cost was contributed by members of the fishing fleet. As one of the contributors said, "It could have been me, couldn't it?"

And exactly one year and a day after his harrowing experience in Lituya Bay, Howie Ulrich, cruising through the Gulf of Alaska in the dead of a moonless night, ran the *Edrie* aground, tearing a hole in her starboard bow. Howie managed to beach her and, with a makeshift patch, refloat her when the tide came in. But it was a close call.

Did he think he was jinxed by the ninth and tenth days of July?

"I've got enough real things to worry about without loading myself down with superstitions," he said. Then he grinned. "But check back on July 11, 1960."

Bit by the Fitbit

*An innocent fitness fad turns into a
seductive exercise in world domination.*

——

BY **DAVID SEDARIS**
FROM THE BOOK **CALYPSO**
Originally published in June 2015

 was at an Italian restaurant, listening as a woman named Lesley talked about her housekeeper, an immigrant who earlier that day had cleaned the bathroom countertops with a bottle of very expensive acne medication. "She's afraid of the vacuum cleaner and can't read or write a word of English, but other than that, she's marvelous," she said as our antipasto plate arrived.

Lesley pushed back her sleeve and, as she reached for an olive, I noticed a rubber bracelet on her left wrist. "Is that a watch?" I asked.

"No," she told me. "It's a Fitbit. You sync it with your computer, and it tracks your physical activity."

I leaned closer, and as she tapped the thickest part of it, a number of glowing dots rose to the surface and danced back and forth. "It's like a pedometer," she continued. "But updated, and better. The goal is to take 10,000 steps per day, and once you do, it vibrates."

I forked some salami into my mouth. "Hard?"

"No," she said. "It's just a tingle."

A few weeks later, I bought a Fitbit of my own and discovered what she was talking about. Ten thousand steps, I learned, amounts to a little more than four miles for someone my size—five feet five

inches. It sounds like a lot, but you can cover that distance in the course of an average day without even trying, especially if you have stairs in your house and a steady flow of people who regularly knock, wanting you to accept a package or give them directions or just listen patiently as they talk about birds, which happens from time to time when I'm home.

I was traveling myself when I got my Fitbit. Because the tingle feels so good, not just as a sensation but also as a mark of accomplishment, I began pacing the airport rather than doing what I normally do, which is sit in the waiting area, wondering which of the many people around me will die first, and of what. I also started taking the stairs instead of the escalator and avoiding the moving sidewalk.

"Every little bit helps," my old friend Dawn, who frequently eats lunch while Hula-Hooping, said. She had a Fitbit as well and swore by it. To people like Dawn and me, people who are obsessive to begin with, the Fitbit is a digital trainer, perpetually egging us on. During the first few weeks that I had it, I'd return to my hotel at the end of the day, and when I discovered that I'd taken a total of, say, 12,000 steps, I'd go out for another 3,000.

"But why?" my partner, Hugh, asked when I told him about it. "Why isn't 12,000 enough?"

"Because," I told him, "my Fitbit thinks I can do better."

Fitbit also helps satisfy my insane need for order at the same time. I've been cleaning the roads in my area for three years now, but before the Fitbit, I did it primarily on my bike and with my bare hands. That was fairly effective, but I wound up missing a lot. On foot, nothing escapes my attention: a potato chip bag stuffed into the hollow of a tree, an elderly mitten caught in the embrace of a blackberry bush, a mud-coated matchbook at the bottom of a ditch. You can tell where my territory ends and the rest of the nation begins.

Since getting my Fitbit, I have seen all kinds of things I wouldn't normally have come across. Once, it was a toffee-colored cow with two feet sticking out of her. I was rambling that afternoon with my friend Maja, and as she ran to inform the farmer, I marched in place, envious of the extra steps she was getting in. Given all the time I've spent in the country, you'd think I might have seen a calf being born, but this was a first. The biggest surprise was how unfazed the expectant mother was. She lay flat on the grass, panting. Then she got up and began grazing, still with those feet sticking out.

"Really?" I said to her. "You can't go five minutes without eating?"

Around her were other cows, all of whom seemed blind to her condition.

"Do you think she knows there's a baby at the end of this?" I asked Maja after she'd returned. "A woman is told what's going to happen in delivery, but how does an animal interpret this pain?"

I thought of the first time I had a kidney stone. That was in New York in 1991, back when I had no money or health insurance. All I knew was that I was hurting and couldn't afford to do anything about it. The night was spent moaning. Then I peed blood, followed by what looked like a piece of gravel from an aquarium.

What might I have thought if, after seven hours of unrelenting agony, a creature the size of a full-grown cougar emerged, inch by inch, and started hassling me for food? Was that what the cow was going through? Did she think she was dying, or had instinct somehow prepared her for this?

When I returned to the field several weeks later, I saw mother and child standing side by side, not in the loving way that I had imagined but more like strangers waiting for the post office to open. Other animals I've seen on my walks are foxes and rabbits. I've stumbled upon deer, stoats, a hedgehog, and more pheasants than I could possibly count.

Back when Maja and I saw the cow, I was averaging 25,000 steps, or around 10½ miles per day. Trousers that had grown too snug were suddenly loose again, and I noticed that my face was looking a lot thinner. Then I upped it to 30,000 steps and started moving

farther afield. "We saw David in Arundel picking up a dead squirrel with his grabbers," the neighbors told Hugh. "We saw him outside Steyning rolling a tire down the side of the road." "In Pulborough dislodging a pair of Y-fronts from a tree branch." Before the Fitbit, I was in for the evening after dinner. Now, as soon as I'm finished with the dishes, I walk to the pub and back, a distance of 3,895 steps. There are no streetlights where we live, and the houses I pass at 11 p.m. are dark or dimly lit. I often hear owls and the flapping of woodcocks disturbed by the beam of my flashlight.

❖ ❖ ❖

I look back on the days I averaged only 30,000 steps and think, "how lazy can you get?" Now I'm up to 60,000, which is 25½ miles. Walking that distance at the age of 57, with completely flat feet while lugging a heavy bag of garbage, takes close to nine hours—a big block of time, but hardly wasted. I listen to audiobooks and podcasts. I talk to people. I learn things: the fact, for example, that in the days of yore, peppercorns were sold individually and, because they were so valuable, to guard against theft, people who packed them had to have their pockets sewed shut.

At the end of my first 60,000-step day, I staggered home with my flashlight, knowing that I'd advance to 65,000 and that there would be no end to it until my feet snap off at the ankles. Why is it some people can manage a thing like a Fitbit, while others go off the rails and allow it to rule, and perhaps even ruin, their lives?

While marching along the roadside, I often think of a TV show that I watched a few years back—*Obsessed*, it was called. One of the episodes was devoted to a woman who owned two treadmills and walked like a hamster on a wheel from the moment she got up until she went to bed. Her family would eat dinner, and she'd observe them from her vantage point beside the table, panting as she asked her children about their day. I knew that I was supposed to scoff at this woman, to be, at the very least,

entertainingly disgusted, the way I am with the people on *Hoarders*, but instead I saw something of myself in her. Of course, she did her walking on a treadmill, where it served no greater purpose. So it's not like we're really that much alike.

In recognition of all the rubbish I've collected since getting my Fitbit, my local council named a garbage truck after me.

Then my Fitbit died. I was devastated when I tapped it and the little dots failed to appear. Yet I felt a great sense of freedom. It seemed that my life was now my own again. But was it? Walking 25 miles, or even running up the stairs and back, suddenly seemed pointless, since, without the steps being counted and registered, what use were they? I lasted five hours before I ordered a replacement, express delivery. It arrived the following afternoon, and my hands shook as I tore open the box. Ten minutes later, my new master strapped securely around my left wrist, I was out the door, racing, practically running, to make up for lost time.

1,000 Men and a Baby

They longed for home—and opened their hearts to a special child.

———

BY **LAWRENCE ELLIOTT**

Originally published in December 1994

ne lonely Saturday night in July 1953, a medical orderly at an Army dispensary in war-devastated Korea went out to have a smoke and kicked a bundle of newspapers out of his way. A feeble little cry shivered up from the darkness.

It was a child—a gasping, emaciated infant.

Soon the orderly was racing toward the Star of the Sea Children's Home in Inchon. There he handed the bundle to a nun who unwrapped the scrawny little body. The baby was a boy, perhaps a month old. And his eyes were blue.

The war was entering its fourth year. Inchon had been overrun, liberated, shelled and starved, and the Star of the Sea orphanage had been spared little. Staffed by overworked French nuns and a dozen Korean aides, it was run by Sister Philomena, a crafty, tough-minded Irish nurse.

Her orphanage was so desperately overburdened that when the children became teenagers they had to be sent out on their own. There was never enough food or clothing. What would she do with this half-Caucasian baby?

Sister knew in her heart that there could never be a place here for a blue-eyed child. He would always be scorned as "the white one." When her back was turned, the Korean aides ignored the baby. Even if he somehow managed to grow to adulthood, she realized, he would be a pariah—despised and harassed as the abandoned offspring of an American soldier.

So when the USS *Point Cruz*—an escort carrier that had been in the thick of the action—dropped anchor in Inchon harbor early in September, Sister Philomena had an idea. She sent a message to the chaplain, Lt. Edward O. Riley.

They were old friends. At times, with the connivance of the *Point Cruz*'s captain, Father Riley brought the children things from the ship's stores: powdered milk, cough medicine, aspirin. When he arrived at the orphanage, Sister Philomena told him about the baby the orderly had brought her from ASCOM—the U.S. Army Service Command headquarters. Then she took him to the nursery.

Blue eyes stared up at them. The infant was all ribs and swollen abdomen. A rash covered his face. "I haven't proper medicine or food," Sister Philomena said. "Surely you can do something,

Father. After all, he's an American."

Father Riley brooded about it, then went to talk to his skipper.

"Does this baby have a name?" the skipper asked.

"George—after the orderly who brought him in," said the chaplain.

"What are the chances he might be adopted by a Korean family?"

"Zero."

"Then here's what I want you to do," said Capt. John T. Hayward, nicknamed Chick, who had once been expelled from a military academy, never finished high school, and thus knew something about starting out against the odds. "Find some Korean official who will issue this kid a passport. But first we're going to bring him aboard the *Point Cruz* and keep him here until he's healthy."

Father Riley was elated. But he felt obliged to ask how the Navy would take to the idea of housing an infant aboard an aircraft carrier.

"Hayward's Law," came the crisp reply, "holds that, in an emergency, regulations are to be intelligently disregarded."

"God bless you," said the

chaplain gruffly, and went off to battle the Korean bureaucracy. A week later he was back, sagging with discouragement. He had trudged all over Inchon and beseeched countless government functionaries. But no birth certificate, and no passport.

Chick Hayward didn't flinch. "I guess we have to go right to the top." Taking a bottle of whiskey out of his safe, he said, "Father, this is my last bottle. Maybe you'll find someone in the foreign ministry in Seoul who needs it more than we do. Don't come back without the passport."

❖　❖　❖

The hospital ship USS *Consolation* had been in port three weeks before Lt. Hugh Keenan, a surgeon from Spokane, Washington, set foot on land. It was a blazing hot September morning, and his two companions, old hands in Inchon, suggested a visit to the Star of the Sea orphanage. "We can get out of the sun and Sister Philomena will give us tea."

But Sister had more than tea on her agenda. She fixed a canny eye

on the newcomer and, having ascertained that he was married and had an eight-year-old daughter, led him to the nursery. When Keenan came back he was holding a rashy, blue-eyed baby. "Here," Sister Philomena said, producing a bottle, "you feed him."

Holding the child eased an ache the surgeon had carried a long time. He and his wife had lost several babies during their marriage—the last one, a boy, about a year before. As he left he promised, "I'll bring something for that rash."

He was back the next day with ointment. Then he sat down and began feeding baby George. "Tell me, doctor," Sister Philomena asked, "is it likely that you might want to adopt a little tyke like this one?"

"Yes, it's likely," Keenan said.

When he returned to his ship, he asked his captain for advice.

"Lieutenant, your job is to take care of military personnel," the captain said. Keenan told Sister Philomena that adopting George was out of the question. But he kept coming back to hold the baby.

Then came a long stretch when

he couldn't get shore leave. When he finally got back to the orphanage Sister told him George was gone. Her friend, Chaplain Edward Riley, had obtained a passport for him and taken him to the *Point Cruz*. "He's going to send George to an orphanage in America."

"The hell he is!" Keenan yelled as he ran out.

❖ ❖ ❖

When Father Riley carried "George Cruz Ascom" up the gangway of the *Point Cruz*, a thousand men lined the rail. For days, they had worked to prepare a nursery in the sick bay. Ship's carpenters had built a crib and playpen. Both were so full of homemade rattles and toys that there was barely room for George. A foot high stack of diapers had been cut from Navy sheets and painstakingly hemmed in the ship's laundry.

The baby was put in the charge of two hospital corpsmen, both seasoned fathers. The flight surgeon, a pediatrician in civilian life, had the galley make special formula. Within days the listless, spindly infant began filling out and

worming around in his crib.

So many men requested permission to visit the nursery that Captain Hayward instituted "Baby-san Call." After nap time each afternoon, the ship's public address system would blare out: "Attention all hands! Baby-san on the hangar deck from 1400 hours!" Men would run for their cameras

> *Father Riley, stricken, assumed Keenan had been sent by naval authorities.*

and file past the bomb cart that had become a baby carriage. They would coo at George and snap his picture. Some offered George a forefinger and he would curl his tiny fist around it and laugh.

"That baby had a thousand uncles," said William J. Powers, the petty officer in charge of the hangar deck. "By then, the armistice was signed and we were all waiting to go home, and along comes this little kid to hit us right in the heart. It was as though he was the peace we'd been fighting for."

❖ ❖ ❖

George had been aboard the *Point Cruz* more than a week the day Lt. Hugh Keenan came stomping up the gangway looking for Father Riley.

Father Riley, stricken, assumed Keenan had been sent by naval authorities. He admitted they had a baby on board. They were looking for an orphanage back in the States.

"What if I told you I wanted to adopt the baby?" Keenan said.

Father Riley gasped. "I'd say God bless you, my son—he's yours!"

They embraced and went looking for Hayward. The captain fired questions at Keenan, but the young surgeon's answers were sensible. The three agreed that George would stay aboard the *Point Cruz*. Since Keenan still had a year to serve, Captain Hayward would try to arrange passage for George to the States.

When the news was announced to the crew at dinner that night, a cheer ripped through the mess.

Back on the *Consolation*, Hugh Keenan was struck by the numbing realization of what he had done. He went at once to the wardroom and wrote his wife. "I am making arrangements to send you a Christmas present that I hope you will love." The days crawled by as he waited for her reply. When it came, the envelope was fat and the letter was long. The answer? Yes!

❖ ❖ ❖

Things were not going well for Father Riley. Korean nationals needed a visa to enter the United States, but when he applied for one, the U.S. consulate told him the quota was filled. Maybe next year.

As time passed, a visa for the baby seemed out of reach. Then, in mid-November, Hayward was invited to a dinner in Seoul where he was to receive a decoration. Vice President Nixon also was scheduled to attend. At the reception there was a good deal of talk about "Chick Hayward's baby"—every flag officer in Korea having heard the story by this time. An admiral friend of Hayward told Nixon about George and his desperate need for a visa. Nixon turned to Ellis O. Brigg, the American ambassador in Seoul, and spoke the magic words: "Can you help out here?"

Seven days later, the visa came. In late November, Lt. Hugh Keenan kissed his new son goodbye and handed him over to the crew of the *Point Cruz*, which was about to set sail for Japan. Several days later, "1,000 uncles" cheered while the bosun's mate piped George Cruz Ascom, IBfc— Infant Boy, first class—over the side, and the baby was turned over to Father Riley, his escort to America via military transport ship.

❖ ❖ ❖

The *Point Cruz* finally made it back to the United States in December 1953. Father Riley went on to Central America, where he served as a missionary until his death. Chick Hayward, the one time high school dropout, became a vice admiral and, with the USS *Enterprise* as his flagship, became the first admiral to command a nuclear task force.

In America, George became Daniel Edward Keenan—Daniel for Hugh's father, Edward for Father Riley. Growing up in Spokane, where his father returned to practice general surgery, Danny dreamed of becoming a sportswriter. He graduated from Washington State University in 1977 with a degree in communications. Today he's married and works as sports editor of the biweekly *Grant County Journal* in Ephrata, Washington, a town of 5,300.

One by one, the men of the *Point Cruz* had returned to peacetime pursuits, raised families, made careers. Over the years, they lost track of each other, but they never stopped wondering about "their" baby.

Bill Powers, the former hangar deck chief, had served 30 years in the Navy. He told his four children the story of the baby on the aircraft carrier, told it to his eight grand children, and he can hardly wait until his five great-grandchildren are old enough so he can tell it again.

When a reunion of the *Point Cruz* crew was organized for September 1993, Bill was

determined to have "George" there. He telephoned Daniel Keenan repeatedly, and encouraged him to attend the gathering. "Son, I knew you when you had to be burped after you ate. You have to come!"

Once the word spread that "George" would be there, a special expectancy took hold of the veterans. Our baby is coming! The former sailors crowded around to meet a handsome, well-built man, his eyes now turned to brown.

"I would go to the sick bay just to see you," said Donald J. Houlihan, recalling those magical moments in the improvised ship nursery.

"I held you in my arms," one said. "I changed your diapers," another added with a laugh.

On the last night of the reunion, Danny Keenan rose to bid the men farewell. How do I thank them for saving my life, he wondered. The faces he looked out upon from the podium where he stood were still strangers to him, but he was touched deeply. And then the words came.

"Without you good men, I wouldn't be here," Danny said quietly. "Not in this hotel, not in this country. And maybe not even on this earth."

The men of the *Point Cruz* were ordinary men. They had saved a life without asking for praise or thanks. And now, late in their lives, they could see that their long ago act of kindness had been something of great importance.

For a moment no one spoke. There was really no need. As it had once been a long time ago on the *Point Cruz*, it was again: Danny Keenan was surrounded by an ocean of fatherly love.

The Kidnapping of Christine Aragao

Beaten and trapped with her children, her only hope was the ingenuity of the FBI.

———

BY **MALCOLM MCCONNELL**

Originally published in February 2001

The Christmas party was still lively, but Christine Aragao knew it was time to leave; it had been a long day, and her two young sons were tired. Home was across a busy avenue in the Oceania Towers condominiums north of Miami. So her husband, Alceu, handed his keys to Christine, insisting that she take his car. He would walk home later with their daughter, Juliana, he said.

Christine was soon backing her husband's silver Porsche into its slot in the underground garage. Reaching over, she lifted up one-year-old Alexandre and opened her door, while Alceu Jr., nine, slipped out the passenger side. It was just after 9 p.m. on the evening of Monday, December 13, 1999.

As she exited the car, Christine sensed a blur of movement. A pair of hands grabbed her shoulders, and she heard an electric crackle. Her right shoulder and arm went limp, and Alexandre tumbled to the ground. A bald man with a bull neck savagely punched the right side of Christine's face. She screamed, and his huge fist struck again, fracturing her right cheekbone.

"Shut your mouth," the man said, as Christine's world went dark.

She awoke on the backseat floor of the family's SUV, a Lincoln Navigator. She saw another man restraining Junior and heard baby Alexandre shrieking.

"What's going on?" she shouted. "This is not because of you," the driver replied. "It's about your husband." Disoriented, in severe pain, Christine had no idea what he meant. The vehicle sped through city streets, but it wasn't very long before it stopped. Christine heard a garage door grind shut; then she was dragged out. Someone pulled a black mask over her eyes, tied her in a chair and put a rolled towel in her mouth. She felt a door slide closed near her battered face. Alexandre cried in the distance.

Sitting in the Aragaos' richly furnished duplex penthouse the next morning, FBI Special Agents Jim Lewis, Ed Knapp, and Renae McDermott listened as Alceu Aragao told them what little he knew.

He obviously seemed in anguish, and the blood and scuff marks found on the garage floor were certainly signs of a kidnapping, as was the scream of a woman heard the night before. Still, the FBI had to consider all the possibilities. Was this a domestic spat that had escalated into violence, with Christine storming off?

The Aragaos were American citizens, having built a small family business, Ipanema Enterprises, into

A bald man savagely punched the right side of her face. She screamed, and again his fist struck.

a lucrative electronics import firm operating in Miami as well as their native Brazil. Was the woman's disappearance somehow related to the company? Could there be any underworld involvement?

Lewis, a former cop in Fairfax, Virginia, asked Alceu to take a polygraph test to clear his name so that he could assist the FBI if ransom demands came in.

"I'll do anything I can to help,"

Alceu told the three FBI agents.

Meanwhile, Special Agent Knapp interviewed one of the valet-parking attendants, a Venezuelan named Jean Carlo Ferreira. "There's something wrong about this guy," Knapp told Lewis. "He changed his work shift to be on duty last night. Says he checked out the scream, but found nothing unusual."

The security camera, however, showed the Navigator leaving the parking garage at 9:13 p.m., when Ferreira should have seen it. Lewis ordered polygraph tests for all the attendants.

Hours earlier, before dawn, Christine Aragao was taken out of a bedroom closet in a rented house on Northeast 26th Avenue, some eight miles from the Oceania Towers. Removing her mask and loosening her bindings, Ewin Oscar Martinez, the man who had beaten her the night before, said her two children were being well cared for.

Then she listened, her fear and confusion mounting, as Martinez paced around the bedroom, talking rapidly in Spanish-accented English. Alceu had business rivals in Brazil,

he said, who had contracted him—through gangsters—to kill the entire family. The American police, he added, also were part of the plot. Martinez told her that he could never murder such a "beautiful" family. "So I planned to bring your whole family to this house. Then we'd fake some pictures of you dead, send them to the Brazilian

> *The plan was foolproof, Martinez boasted. Soon they'd be in Venezuela, their bank accounts bulging.*

———

mafia and collect our $700,000. But why were you driving his car?"

Finally he stopped talking, replaced her blindfold, and told her to think about what he said.

In fact, the story was fabricated. Martinez, a Venezuelan illegally in the United States, had been spying on the Aragao family for months, along with his principal ally, the parking attendant Jean Carlo Ferreira.

They'd planned to grab Alceu first, taking the rest of the family afterward. Then Alceu Aragao would be forced to reveal every bit of information—safe combinations, passwords, PINs, and account numbers—that Martinez, a self-styled computer expert, would need to ransack all of the family's personal and business accounts, savings and investments. The plan was foolproof, Martinez boasted to his confederates. Soon they'd be back in Venezuela, their own bank accounts bulging with the Aragaos' assets.

But the scheme unraveled. They thought that only Alceu Aragao drove the Porsche. When Christine climbed from it instead and began screaming, Martinez and his accomplices had no choice but to shoot her with a stun gun, grab the children, and get out of the garage.

Martinez figured that if he could persuade Christine to believe his wild tale about the Brazilian mafia, she might persuade Alceu to distrust the police and come to them.

Alceu Aragao passed his polygraph, and by Wednesday, December 15, all his phones had been connected to FBI recorders. Technicians from the federal government and a local cell phone company would try to trace any incoming calls. It was assumed that the kidnappers held Christine and the children at a fixed location, so the more frequent and longer the calls, the better the chances of finding that site.

Jean Carlo Ferreira's polygraph, on the other hand, suggested that he was involved in the kidnapping. Knapp's team put Ferreira under surveillance. Meanwhile, Assistant U.S. Attorney Stacey Levine and FBI Special Agent Brenda Moxley rushed through the subpoena process to investigate Ferreira's telephone records, hoping to identify possible co-conspirators.

Christine Aragao looked in the bathroom mirror and groaned. With the blindfold now removed, her right eye was barely visible inside a blackened socket; her face was swollen and streaked with blood. She splashed water on her cheeks with her left hand; her right arm was still useless from the stun gun.

To assure the woman that her children were healthy, Martinez brought Junior to the room where she was being held. The boy cried out, shaking, "Why did they do this to you, Mama?" Martinez took him away.

Alexandre didn't even recognize his injured mother. The infant howled as she pulled him onto her lap and tried to console him.

Christine heard several other men in the house, but never got a clear look at their faces. Meanwhile, Martinez kept insisting that her husband and daughter were being watched, and that she must get them to join him for their own safety. "This is a deadly serious game," he said. "If we win, your family will live. If we lose, we'll all die."

Dazed from lack of sleep and in constant pain, Christine found it increasingly hard to think clearly. More than once. her terrorized mind drifting, she wondered if Martinez was telling the truth.

❖   ❖   ❖

On Wednesday afternoon, Martinez handed Christine her cell phone and stood above her. "Call your husband," he said, thrusting a brief script at her. He warned that the contact must last only a few seconds.

When Alceu answered, she spoke with robotlike inflection. "I don't want to go to Brazil, OK?" she said in English, referring to an upcoming family trip.

"I can't hear you," Alceu replied, trying to stall, as Special Agent Lewis had asked.

"I don't want to go to Brazil," Christine repeated in the same lifeless voice. Then she hung up.

Martinez took the phone and grinned. "Excellent," he said. Only when all the Aragaos were together, he repeated, would he be able to fool the gangsters and save their lives.

She was still deeply frightened, having earlier seen Martinez handling two semiautomatic guns. She wondered if the so-called execution pictures he said he would stage would really be fake.

Listening to the tape of the brief

call, Special Agents Lewis and McDermott noted the tone of Christine's voice. "She sounds weird, like she's reading from a script," Lewis said.

"She's sending us a signal," McDermott added. There was no doubt now that she was under duress.

Early Thursday, Ewin Martinez

Alexandre didn't recognize his injured mother. The infant howled as she tried to console him.

---

had Christine Aragao write a letter to Alceu on a laptop computer, telling him about the Brazilian gangsters and their main hit man. "This person now turned out [to be] our friend," she typed.

She begged her husband to break off contact with the police and to arrange a secure meeting where he and their daughter, Juliana, could join their benefactor, who would protect the entire family.

On one level of her battered consciousness, she knew these words were false. But with the ordeal now in its third day, fear, pain and exhaustion were pushing Christine to the edge. Like many hostages, she was falling prey to the Stockholm syndrome—a need to believe that her captors were her protectors.

Later Christine also called Alceu on the cell phone to say that a letter had been sent to his downtown office. Because Martinez was certain he had her under control, he allowed her to speak Portuguese.

Alceu asked to speak to Junior. When he came on the line, the boy said that the kidnappers had given his mother "some kind of electricity" that paralyzed her arm. Alceu closed his eyes in distress.

Parking attendant Ferreira's telephone records revealed dozens of calls between his cell phone, another registered to Ewin Oscar Martinez, and back to Ferreira's pager. Of special interest to the FBI was a flurry of calls that had come just before and after the kidnapping.

On their own, however, these

records gave no clue about the kidnappers' location, and one of the FBI's greatest frustrations was not knowing if Christine and the two children were still in South Florida. They got a break Thursday night. Knapp's surveillance unit watched Ferreira talk for ten minutes at a public phone in Coconut Grove during a downpour.

Agents found one of the kidnappers on a couch and thrust weapons at him. "Don't move!"

"Young man's got something on his mind," said Knapp, a former Navy SEAL.

A trace revealed the call went to a Miami cell phone number. Now the odds seemed better that the kidnappers had not yet left the area.

The letter from Christine arrived at her husband's office around noon on Friday. For the next several hours, Martinez ordered Christine to make a series of brief cell phone calls, explaining how they wanted Alceu and Juliana to elude the police, hide near Orlando, and wait until they heard from her by cell phone.

Exhausted, in dread, and still terribly confused, Christine complied with Martinez's demands. She knew her life and the lives of her sons depended on it. As she was making the calls, Martinez allowed Junior into the bedroom with them.

Meanwhile, as Alceu tried desperately to prolong each brief call from Christine, technicians struggled to locate her cell phone. It was difficult, frustrating work.

❖ ❖ ❖

Then a breakthrough came during one call. Alceu asked if she was already in the Orlando area. The question jarred Christine back to reality. Suddenly she recalled the terror of the high-speed ride in the SUV, and blurted out in rapid Portuguese, "We are very close to our house, only about 15 minutes."

This crucial piece of information confirmed that the technical team was on the right track. A little more than an hour later, Special Agent Lewis's secure radio crackled. The hostage house was at 19825 Northeast 26th Avenue.

During the next six hours, Alceu took several more calls from his wife. First he suggested meeting near Miami. Next he laboriously worked out a secure rendezvous at a Palm Beach hotel for the next day. And as he delayed, the rescue forces assembled for a raid on the hostage house.

Finally, at 10:30 p.m., the acting SWAT team commander, Special Agent Alexis Vazquez, deployed his 25 men in three teams, surrounding the house. At Vazquez's order, they sprang into action. To distract the kidnappers, they exploded a flashbang grenade with a thunderous crack, smashed through glass doors at the rear and raced toward the bedrooms.

Agents found one of the kidnappers on a couch and thrust weapons at him. "Don't move!"

"What's happening?" Christine cried out from the larger bedroom. "It's the gang," Martinez said, herding them into a bathroom.

Junior cried, the baby wailed, and Christine was crushed by panic.

And then it was all over. The agents burst into the room and overpowered Martinez. Within moments Christine and her children were hustled into an ambulance.

At Aventura Hospital later, Alceu bent to kiss her battered face. They held Junior and the baby close, too overcome even to speak. During that terrible week, neither had truly expected to see the other alive again.

Christine Aragao is still recovering from reconstructive surgery on her face. Ewin Oscar Martinez, Jean Carlo Ferreira and another conspirator, Pedro Caraballo-Martinez, have each been convicted of five federal felonies and sentenced to life without parole. All are appealing. Two other suspects, not in the house at the time of the raid, have been arrested, and two more remain fugitives.

Princess Power

*At an uncertain time, these young women
offer kids a little magic—and hope.*

—

BY ASHLEY LEWIS

Originally published in February 2018

lsa, it's you!" It was the four-year-old's surprise birthday party, and her favorite Disney character, Elsa from *Froze*n, had arrived. The two jubilantly began to sing the movie's big song, "Let It Go," and were soon joined by Tinker Bell and four other fairy-tale princesses: Anna, Ariel, Jasmine, and Snow White. You would swear you were celebrating at the most magical place on earth.

But this wasn't Disney World. It was the pediatric cancer ward at a hospital on Long Island in New York, and the princesses were college students who volunteer for A Moment of Magic, a nonprofit organization whose mission is to lift the spirits of sick children.

It all began once upon a time with a family movie night featuring *Frozen.* Kylee McGrane, now 23, noticed that she and Elsa had matching blond hair and big blue eyes. McGrane and her friend Maggie McAndrew, then both sophomores on service scholarships at the College of Mount Saint Vincent in New York City, were searching for a new community project, ideally one with children. That sparked an idea—dressing up as Disney princesses and visiting

Kylee McGrane, aka Elsa, and the other princesses have visited more than 8,000 children.

pediatric cancer patients. "When kids are in a hospital for so long, they don't get all the magic that most kids do," says McGrane. "It's nice to give them time to be themselves."

In 2015, after raising $2,000 on a GoFundMe page to pay for costumes and travel expenses, McGrane and McAndrew landed their first gig, at Cohen Children's

It all began once upon a time with a family movie night featuring Frozen.

Medical Center in New Hyde Park, New York. They dressed as Elsa and her sister, Anna, to the squealing delight of the girls and blushing smiles from the boys. They spent nearly three hours singing songs, taking pictures, and traveling from one bedside to the next until they had visited and chatted with every one of the 50 children.

"To see the kids believe in me, my character … it was life

changing," says McGrane.

Of course, a princess can work only so many miracles at once, so McGrane and McAndrew recruited their peers. Today, A Moment of Magic has 400 volunteers from 11 colleges around the country.

They also have a growing kingdom of fans. Shara Moskowitz from New Jersey says that her seven-year-old daughter, Avery, still talks almost every day by phone or text to the princesses she met nearly two years ago at her birthday party. Avery was receiving treatment for a neuroblastoma.

"My daughter found something that she really needed to connect to," says Moskowitz. "These girls gave her that moment of imagination, freedom, and happiness of dreaming."

Call of the Wild

*Could a child's love for a kitten
overcome its feral nature?*

—

BY **PENNY PORTER**

Originally published in February 1997

or wild creatures that roamed our Arizona ranch, life was hard and hunger was constant. Feral dogs lusted after our newborn calves. Frantic raccoons plundered my chicken coop. Coyotes howled their endless distress. But it was the piteous cries of wild cats, solo wanderers of the desert, that tore at my heart. With no place to call home, these castaway descendants of domestic cats reverted to a primal life. And every year when hunger stalked the parched mountains and ranges, many sought refuge on our property.

One cold March morning I was milking my cow while our five domestic barn cats rubbed against my jeans, impatient to be fed. They don't know what hunger is, I thought, trying to count the skeletal wild cats cowering behind feed bins. Most were ill. Many were pregnant. Some were hideously scarred, mute evidence of desperate battles for life.

My chore was interrupted when Jaymee, the youngest of our six children, rushed into the barn cupping a snow-white newborn kitten in her hands. Behind its left ear was a copper patch of calico. "All of its brothers and sisters are dead!" Jaymee cried.

"I'll bet the great horned owl got them," I said. "You've got to find its mother—it needs to nurse."

"She's dead too!" wailed Jaymee.

"What are we going to do, Mama?"

Jaymee had watched us struggle to keep orphaned calves and foals alive. Now she'd found something just the right size for a six-year-old: a precious scrap of life she could hold, love, and take care of by herself. "Without a mama it'll die, won't it?" she asked.

"Yes," I answered. "It'll take a miracle to save it."

We brought the kitten inside, wrapped it in a wool mitten and fed it antibiotic-laced milk from an eyedropper. Then we placed it in a round incubator we used to hatch chicks of rare-breed hens.

"Can I keep the incubator in my room?" Jaymee asked.

I nodded. "But don't tell Daddy about it yet. You know how he feels about cats." Wild cats can have rabies and ringworm, and Bill worried our cattle could become infected. I knew Jaymee would get attached, and something told me this cat wouldn't be around for very long. If she took off, I was sure Jaymee's heart would break. But for now, so much hope shined in my little girl's eyes that I had to help.

Soon afterward Bill—unlit pipe clenched between his teeth—came in for breakfast. "Darn mice chewed holes in nearly every sack of grain in the barn," he said, gulping his coffee. "You'd think our cats"—meaning our pet cats—"could keep them under control. That's why we have 'em. But they have to spend all their time chasing off those wild ones. I've never seen so many wild cats. They're nesting all over the

> ## *Miracle. There could be no other name for this tiny, pink-nosed surprise.*

place. Those miserable creatures look sick." I decided that for now I'd keep quiet about Jaymee's kitten.

That night Jaymee and Becky, her nine-year-old sister, fed the tiny kitten, then returned it to the plastic-domed incubator. I heard Becky whisper to Jaymee, "I counted 22 wild cats in the barn this morning! Daddy's having a conniption."

"Does he know we really have 23?" Jaymee asked.

"Not yet."

Nine days later Jaymee showed her father the kitten still in the incubator. Bill huffed a little and left the room. The next morning the kitten's eyes opened, and Jaymee named it Miracle.

There could be no other name for this tiny, pink-nosed surprise. My hope was that we could raise Miracle as a domestic cat, a barn cat. But more and more I saw signs that she would never be tied down. Instead of sleeping in her own bed like a domestic cat, Miracle preferred hiding in closets and behind drapes. Other times we found her in Bill's boots or snoozing under beds. The household question became "Where's Miracle?"

At last the morning came when Bill caught Miracle sky-diving from the drapes. And when she spiraled up Bill's jeans with claws unsheathed, he decreed that the enclosed back porch would become her new home.

One morning Jaymee was late for breakfast. "Mirry's not on the porch," she said miserably.

"She has to be there somewhere," I said. We searched everywhere, but no kitten.

"I'm going to put food in her bowl anyway," Jaymee said, glancing at her father. "She's just playing a game, you know."

Of course, I thought. A game wild cats excel at. Hiding!

For days Miracle's bowl was empty by morning, yet we still couldn't find her. Then we noticed black paw prints from the fireplace to the food and water and back again. "Daddy!" Jaymee squealed. "Mirry's in the chimney! We've got to get her out!"

"I'm not going up there after a cat," Bill grumbled. "She'll come down."

Jaymee turned to her 19-year-old brother. "Please, Scott," she begged. Moments later his long arm reached through the partially opened damper. "Got her!" Scott shouted, pulling the coal-black ball of fluff out of the flue.

"Oh, Mirry, you bad girl!" Jaymee exclaimed, then rushed off to clean the kitten up. Unlike most cats, Miracle relished being bathed—and especially liked the blow-dryer.

We offered Miracle marbles, jacks, and fluffy ribbons that domestic cats like to play with, but she was never interested. Instead she waited impatiently for trips outdoors, where she came to life, darting into alfalfa fields or crouching outside my chicken coop, trembling with desire at the sight of 200 chicks. "Look, how cute! She wants to play with them!" Jaymee said.

Play? A twitching tail? Tiny claws extending and retracting? I wasn't so sure. I'd read that the skill to kill must be taught by a cat's mother. But I couldn't help wondering if such a trait might come more naturally to Miracle. Soon after, at the age of seven months, the nighttime yowling began. Was it her call of the wild?

"She sees things in the dark that we can't see," Jaymee said at breakfast. "Secrets and ..."

"... Tomcats!" Bill added. He was stiff-necked and grouchy from sleeping with his head under the pillow, trying to block out Miracle's nocturnal wailing. "Darn cat," he muttered.

One evening Bill came in for dinner with a handful of rattlesnake rattles. "We found a nest of more than 50 of the critters over at Cowan's ranch," he said. He selected the biggest and shook it. Instantly Miracle's nose pushed against the kitchen window. Her

Camouflaged against the weathered metal barn roof crouched a battered little cat.

back arched, her flinty eyes sparked. We gave her a rattle to play with, and suddenly it was clicking and skittering across the floor like a hockey puck, Miracle in fierce pursuit. Our little cat honed her feline skills on this new toy—and prey.

One day I discovered a round sore on Miracle's forehead. At first I suspected she'd been hurt until blisters and circles erupted on Jaymee's face and neck as well.

"Ringworm," said the vet after examining both cat and child under a diagnostic blue light. There the pair glittered like glowworms on a summer night. After administering the treatment for Jaymee and Miracle, the vet said, "And warn Bill to watch those bulls. This strain could prove contagious."

That night Bill came in for supper, beat. "Two of the show bulls have ringworm," he said.

Inwardly I cringed. I thought of the quarantine, the cost of antibiotics, and the lime/sulfur dips for animals that weigh close to 2,000 pounds. I wanted to tell Bill about Miracle, but Jaymee beat me to it. "Oh, Daddy!" she said. "Think how beautiful the bulls would look under the blue light! Mirry and I sparkled like angels!" Bill didn't get angry, as I'd expected. Even he couldn't help grinning at Jaymee's description.

One evening a few weeks later, Miracle didn't come when we called. Then the phone rang. "Does your little girl have a white cat?"

asked a hay buyer who'd picked up a ton of alfalfa just before noon. He lived 60 miles away.

"Yes," I said.

"I reckon it likes to ride in trucks," he continued. "Didn't know it was there till I got home." A muscle flicked in Bill's jaw as he reached for his hat. Moments later he and Jaymee disappeared into the darkness for the 120-mile round trip to fetch her cat.

Before long, Miracle became a seasoned wanderer. Although cars and trucks were a favorite mode of travel, she vanished more often on foot and was gone for days, and even weeks, at a time.

On Miracle's first birthday I heard Scott yell from a horse corral. "Miracle! Get outta there!" And in the next breath, "Dad! Rattler!"

Bill grabbed a shovel from the pickup truck, and I dashed for the antivenin kit. The diamondback had struck a mare between the nostrils. The horse was staggering, pawing the ground, her eyes white-rimmed with panic. In minutes her head began to swell. She couldn't breathe. Quickly Bill inserted a breathing tube and administered the antidote. We prayed the crisis would pass. Then Scott said to his father, "If it hadn't been for Miracle, that flash of white, I wouldn't have seen this happen. The cat was going bonkers, Dad, leaping around and jumping at those rattles." He looked at me. "Mom, I think the snake got Miracle too."

When we found the little cat, she lay motionless—eyes sealed, her head swollen. The bottle of antivenin serum was empty. "I'll try some cortisone," Bill said. "It's all we've got." I laid the lifeless ball of fluff gently in her box. Jaymee knelt beside her kitten, murmuring, "You'll be OK, sweetheart." After two days in a coma, Miracle started to improve. We vowed we'd never let her outside again. But as her strength returned, so did her nomadic ways.

Miracle was 2½ when she disappeared for the last time. We missed her terribly—even Bill, in his own private way.

Over the next few years Jaymee would come to love many cats, but the memory of Miracle always remained closest to her heart. Often, before bedtime, she would come with me when I checked on the chickens or a newborn foal. With her flashlight Jaymee would light up empty mangers and passageways between bales of hay. "Better be careful," I'd remind her. Jaymee's answer was always the same: "I am, Mama. But I can't stop looking for Miracle."

One evening three years later, Bill came in the back door, his eyes bright with mischief. "Jaymee!" he called. "Come outside a minute!" We all followed.

Camouflaged against the weathered metal barn crouched a battered little cat. Its dusty fur was puckered with scars, its right ear pasted to its skull. But the left ear, though torn, betrayed a trace of calico.

"Mirry!" Jaymee whispered, her face glowing with excitement.

All of us shared Jaymee's joy, but I also felt concern because I was sure this was no longer the "Mirry" she'd loved years before.

This was a battle-hardened wild cat. In her world there could be no room for memories of the little girl who had held her and bathed her and cherished her quirky little ways. Jaymee had been shattered when Miracle disappeared for those three years. Would the hurt be even worse now when Miracle failed to recognize her?

Meanwhile, spellbound, we all watched as Miracle's eyes fixed on a small bird nearby. "No, Mirry!" Jaymee screamed.

The cat hesitated. Then, shifting her gaze toward Jaymee's familiar voice, she eased down and leapt into Jaymee's outstretched arms. "I knew you'd come back!" Jaymee said. "I knew it!"

Except for occasional two-day trips, Miracle roamed no more. She ate cat food, left mice on the back doorstep, and seemed to settle into to domestic cat life—until the morning Bill found her on the seat of his tractor. Her rugged little heart had simply stopped. She was seven years old.

"At least Mirry died at home," Jaymee said quietly. "She died with her family."

Jaymee and all of us had learned a lesson that would stay with us forever: Even in the strangest of animal cultures, a child's love can overcome the ultimate call of the wild.

How We Kept Mother's Day

The author's family decides to give their mother the gift of rest and quiet.

—

BY **STEPHEN LEACOCK**
FROM THE BOOK **THE LEACOCK ROUNDABOUT**
Originally published in May 1950

ne year our family decided to have a special celebration of Mother's Day, as a token of appreciation for all the sacrifices that Mother had made for us. After breakfast we had arranged, as a surprise, to hire a car and take her for a beautiful drive in the country.

But on the very morning of the day, we changed the plan a little, because it occurred to Father that it would be even better to take Mother fishing. As the car was hired and paid for, we might just as well use it to drive up into the hills where the streams are. As Father said, if you just go out driving, you have a sense of aimlessness, but if you are going to fish, there is a definite purpose that heightens the enjoyment.

So we all felt it would be nicer for Mother to have a definite purpose. And anyway, Father had just got a new rod, which he said Mother could use if she wanted to—only Mother said she would much rather watch him fish than try to fish herself. We made a sandwich lunch in case we got hungry, though of course we were to come home to a big festive dinner.

Well, when the car came, it

turned out that there wasn't as much room as we had supposed, because we hadn't reckoned on the fishing gear and the lunch, and it was plain that we couldn't all fit in.

Father said not to mind him, that he could just as well stay home and put in the time working in the garden. He said that we were not to let the fact that he had not had a real holiday for three years stand in our way; he wanted us to go right ahead and have a big day.

But of course we all felt that it would never do to let Father stay home, especially as we knew he would make trouble if he did. Anna and Mary would have stayed and gotten dinner, only it seemed such a pity to, on a lovely day like this, having their new hats. Will and I would have dropped out, but we wouldn't have been any use in getting the dinner.

So in the end it was decided that Mother would stay home and just have a lovely restful day around the house, and get the dinner. Also it turned out to be just a bit raw out of doors, and Father said he would never forgive himself if he dragged Mother round the country and let her take a severe cold. He said it was our duty to let Mother get all the rest and quiet she could.

Well, we had the loveliest day up among the hills, and Father caught such big specimens that he felt sure that Mother couldn't have landed them anyway. Will and I fished, too, and the two girls met some young men friends along the stream, and so we all had a splendid time.

It was quite late when we got back, but Mother had kept dinner hot for us. We sat down to a big roast turkey. Mother had to get up a good bit during the meal fetching things, but Father noticed it and said she simply mustn't do it, and he got up and fetched the walnuts from the sideboard himself. When dinner was over all of us wanted to help clear the things up and wash the dishes, only Mother said that she would really much rather do it, and so we let her, because we wanted to humor her. When we kissed Mother before going to bed, she said it had been the most wonderful day in her life, and I think there were tears in her eyes.

A Life in Buttons

Bought at auction, a vintage cookie tin reveals a lifetime of memories.

—

BY **KAREN GRISSINGER**
FROM **COUNTRY WOMAN**

Originally published in July/August 2020

"**G**oing, going, gone, for $3 to bidder number 43, the lady in the last row, white hat." I had just won the bidding for a 1950s cookie tin at an estate sale outside McConnellsburg, Pennsylvania, near the farm where my husband and I live.

Delighted at my victory, I gave the box a shake. Inside were dozens—maybe even hundreds—of buttons, pins and other items, all glittering in the sunlight. It reminded me of my mom's button box. As a girl, I'd always enjoyed digging through it, just as my own daughters enjoyed looking through mine.

I listened to the auctioneer's patter as more objects were bid on and sold. Soon my eye caught the movement of a swing on the front porch of the house. A petite older woman sat and watched the happenings in her yard.

As I carried my purchases to my car, I stopped to chat with her. She told me she was selling almost all her possessions because she was moving to a nursing home in town.

Her eyes fell to the button box, and when she looked up, they were glistening with tears. I asked whether she minded if I sat with her awhile. She slid over to make room for me next to her on the swing.

I took the lid off the tin, and her gnarled hand lifted a handful of buttons and then slowly dropped them back into the container. Her fist closed around a delicate pearl button, now yellow with age. She smiled as she told me about the birth of her first child and the special pearl-buttoned christening outfit that would be worn by five more babies before time wore the garment thin.

I noticed a large, brass military button and asked her about it. "From my first husband's uniform," she said. "It's one of the few things I had to remind me of him when he didn't return home."

They had been married seven months before he left to serve his country in World War II. "I married his best friend two years later, and we had a good marriage," she told me. "That's the way it was in those days. Someone always looked out for the widows and children."

When I pulled a small key from the box, I heard the sharp intake of her breath. It was the key to a music box that played a special love song, she said. She had lost it years earlier. From my hand to hers, I passed the key to her memories.

We found a Sunday school pin holding a bar for perfect attendance for every year except one. She explained, "The year my mother was sick with cancer, I stayed home on Sundays with her so my father could get to church. He never missed a Sunday until he died, 15 years ago."

After our chat, I set the woman's box of memories down on the swing and slid my hands into hers. I knew we would talk again, when I went to visit her at her new home. And I knew that when I returned to my own home, my heart would pull me to my sewing room, where I would rediscover my own lifetime of memories in my own button box.

Deadly Cargo

They survived the crash, only to be held captive by their own ammunition.

—

BY **CHRISTOPHER DAVIS**

Originally published in July 2001

Eyes ahead, watching the earth slowly rising to meet the plane, Dave Hall guided the single-engine Piper Lance toward the landing strip at the airport in tiny Medina, Ohio. To his right, Roger Guthric fiddled with the buttons on a hand-held navigation device, looking up every so often to check on the weather. It was a blustery February morning in 1999, and a storm was moving in, bringing a swirling mix of sleet and snow.

As special agents with the Bureau of Alcohol, Tobacco and Firearms (ATF), the two men were on their way to Louisiana for a week of routine SWAT training. Their first stop was Medina to pick up agent Eric Frey, another member of Guthrie's Special Response Team.

Tall and powerfully built, Guthrie was known around the ATF office in Detroit as a man with nine lives. A decade earlier, the former Army Ranger walked into an apartment to serve a warrant. Someone thrust an assault weapon in his face and fired. The bullet glanced off Guthrie's cheekbone, taking part of his face with it. Now the scar snaking across his right cheek added a certain intensity to his green eyes.

By the time the agents met Frey at the airport and topped off the wing tanks with fuel, a heavy squall was blowing, and visibility had dropped to about a quarter-mile. The men spoke little as they fought the wind and loaded the new passenger's equipment next to the arsenal already stowed on board. The plane now carried six loaded handguns, three submachine guns and enough shells and bullets to keep the agents busy for a week. Three vests in the passenger cabin

Something big tore through the trees and slammed onto the forest floor.

each held ten shotgun shells and some 200 rounds of ammunition in clips.

While Hall and Guthrie went into the airfield office to check the weather report, Frey grabbed a broom and swept snow off the plane's wings. Hall emerged a few minutes later, explaining they'd been given a five-minute window for takeoff.

"Let's get moving," he said, feeling the chill through his blue nylon jacket. Hall eased through the aircraft's front door, which was on the passenger side, and slid over to the pilot's seat. Guthrie got in next and secured the door, while Frey climbed into the back through the rear door on the pilot's side. Soon the plane sped down the strip, lifted its nose and headed toward the shadowy line of forest at the end of the runway.

Guthrie turned back to his global positioning device and continued punching in coordinates. A moment later he glanced out the window and saw a flash of branches…

"Trees!" he yelled. That was all he had time to say.

❖ ❖ ❖

Kerry Clark pulled on a pair of sneakers and hurried through the sleet and snow out to his garage to make sure his truck would start. A burly man with a salt-and-pepper beard, he had been a trucker for 25 years. He knew that despite the weather, he'd have to crank up his rig before long and head off to work.

Satisfied that the truck was in working order, Clark stood in the doorway of his garage for a minute to let the dog run around. He hardly noticed the buzz of a small plane taking off at the airport a half-mile away. But then he was startled to hear the wild whine of an engine running wide open, followed by a loud *crack*! Something big tore through the trees and then, with a sickening thud, slammed onto the forest floor.

❖ ❖ ❖

Roger Guthrie opened his eyes. The engine was silent. The pounding was over. After crashing from tree to tree through the woods, the plane had finally come to rest. Now all was strangely quiet.

Still strapped in, Guthrie sat for a moment, dazed. Where was he? Had he been unconscious? And what about the others? Were they alive?

He looked over and saw Dave Hall slumped at the console, unconscious and struggling to breathe. "Dave! Dave!" he yelled, shaking him. No response.

Wincing at the pain in his right leg, Guthrie turned to check on Eric Frey in the back seat. He heard moaning, but could see only a crumpled mass of metal where the back of the plane had been. They were hurt, and yet somehow they'd all lived through the crash.

Out his window Guthrie saw a bright flash. Fire was spreading from the ruptured fuel tank in the plane's wing, just outside his door, blocking his escape.

❖ ❖ ❖

"A plane's gone down!" Kerry Clark yelled to his wife as he dashed into the house. "Call for help!" Then, without bothering to grab boots or a coat, he hustled across the road and through an icy field toward the smoke.

❖ ❖ ❖

Unbuckling his harness, Roger Guthrie pulled himself out of his seat and began squeezing through the opening where the windshield had been. Suddenly he heard gunfire. Shots rang out inside the plane as he dragged himself onto the muddy ground. The ammo was going off! He tried to stand, but his injured leg buckled under the weight and the pain.

Bullets were flying everywhere,

"My training had prepared me for just about anything," says Roger Guthrie. "But I wasn't ready for this."

popping holes in the fuselage. But his friends were trapped in there; he couldn't just leave them. Leaning through the window, Guthrie unbuckled Hall's harness and tried to grab him by his jacket to pull him out. The nylon garment only melted and tore away in his hands. Flames were now creeping up the wing and toward the cabin.

Guthrie reached again and, seizing the belt in Hall's trousers, managed to muscle the 190-pound pilot through the opening and out of the cockpit. Grabbing Hall under the arms, he tried to pull the unconscious man a safe distance from the burning plane. But it was hopeless; he stumbled on his one good leg and fell into the slippery mud and ice.

There was no choice but to leave

Hall where he lay, dangerously close to the burning wreckage, and try to get Frey out before the whole thing caught fire.

Staying low in the hail of bullets, Guthrie crawled around to the plane's back door and tugged at the handle. It was jammed. He looked in and saw Frey, unconscious under the collapsed roof. He knew there was ammunition back there,

> ## Guthrie tried to grab Hall by his jacket. The nylon garment melted and tore away in his hands.
> ———

and flames were only inches away.

Ten years after his own brush with death, Guthrie was standing at another door—and inside was another mindless assailant, ready to shoot. He yanked hard on the handle and managed to get the door open. After struggling to unfasten Frey's harness, he grabbed the injured agent by his belt and pulled him free, just before the cabin filled

with flames. With a new burst of explosions, more bullets screamed through the air.

Limping and sliding, Guthrie dragged Frey the few feet to the spot where he'd left Hall. Then he crouched low and turned his back to the inferno, hoping the bullets wouldn't find them.

❖ ❖ ❖

To Kerry Clark, the scene he was approaching looked like a war zone. Fire rained down from burning branches all along the 200-foot gash the plane had carved through the trees. Clark could hear explosions inside the wreckage, now burning furiously. The air reeked of gasoline.

"Anybody alive in there?" he called out, expecting the worst.

"Yes—we need help!" Guthrie shouted back. He saw Clark inching closer and warned, "Watch out. That's live ammunition going off."

Clark lowered his head and paused. *Who are these people?* he wondered. *Who's traveling with a plane full of ammunition?*

Through the smoke he could see the outlines of three men, two of them lying on the ground and the other crouched next to them. All were perilously close to the fire. Bullets sang through the air, kicking up snow and chipping bark off trees. Flames 15 feet high leapt from the wreckage. He realized he might get killed if he got any closer. But without his help, these men would die.

Who are these people? *he wondered.* Who's traveling with a plane full of ammunition?

Moving cautiously, Clark made his way to the group, ducking behind trees as he ran. Guthrie called to him over the roar of the flames. "We're ATF agents," he said. "Help me get these men out of here and behind cover!" Together they dragged Hall behind a tree to shelter him from the fire and bullets.

Clark then ran back toward the plane, using his arm to shield his face from the furnace. With Guthrie limping and helping as he could, Clark dragged Frey across the snow, sat him against a tree and wrapped his own sweater around him. Then he took off his gloves and put them on Hall's hands.

Once he knew his fellow agents were safely away from the heat and the bullets, Guthrie sank behind a tree and tried to catch his breath. Soon he heard voices in the distance—the shouts of rescue workers making their way through the muddy woods. Then he knew, at last, the nightmare was over.

Guthrie and the other agents were seriously injured in the crash, yet less than six months later they all had returned to active duty. No one at the office was surprised to see Guthrie back on the job. After all, they figured, the man with nine lives still had a few of them left.

The Funniest Football Game Ever Played

Cumberland vs. Georgia Tech—old grads (even Cumberland's) view it with pride for the number of records it set.

—

BY O. K. ARMSTRONG

Originally published in October 1955

Nothing in football history can match the game between Cumberland University and Georgia Tech at Atlanta, Georgia, on October 7, 1916. The score was Tech 222, Cumberland 0.

For many years, neither school was particularly proud of the performance. But now the game has become legendary—something to tell the kids about when fall winds blow across the gridirons. Talk to any Cumberland alumnus about that game and you'll see a glint of pride in his eye. It brought his old school a great distinction: the biggest intercollegiate defeat on record.

"We took a glorious licking!" says George E. Allen, who was the Cumberland manager and a substitute player. Allen lived down the disaster to become an adviser to several U.S. presidents, a director of the Reconstruction Finance

Corporation, and a commissioner of the District of Columbia. When he talks of that game it is with the voice of fond recollection: "It was positively the worst football game ever played!"

In his on-the-spot account of the game, the late sportswriter Grantland Rice reported, tongue in cheek, "Cumberland's greatest individual play of the game occurred when Fullback Allen circled right end for a six-yard loss."

"Not so," says George Allen. "There were several plays in which we lost only three yards!"

Cumberland University, located in the small town of Lebanon, Tennessee, was the alma mater of Cordell Hull as well as many other statesmen and legislators. Moreover, it had boasted champion football teams of the South in 1903 and 1904. By 1916, however, it was making its law school famous and paying relatively little attention to football. Meanwhile, Georgia Tech, under Coach John W. Heisman, had been building up a formidable football reputation. Heisman— known as "The Wizard"—aimed to create the greatest football team of his age.

When, in the spring of 1916, Cumberland's baseball team soundly trounced Tech, Tech's students and alumni howled for revenge on the gridiron. Heisman offered Cumberland a $500 guarantee to come to Atlanta for an October game, and Cumberland accepted.

David Harsh, head of a law firm in Memphis, Tennessee, who played on the Cumberland line, declares: "We never should have taken on Tech. They had us somewhat outclassed." (Probably the greatest understatement in the annals of college football.)

A. L. McDonald, a lawyer in Louisville, Kentucky, who survived the game as a Cumberland halfback, heartily agrees. "We had had very little practice," McDonald recalls. "But our manager, the tightwad, said we couldn't afford to lose the $500 guarantee."

Manager Allen adds: "As we went through Nashville, we tried to borrow a few Vanderbilt players, but they had a hard game coming up and couldn't spare any. Three of our boys got lost in Nashville and missed the train. That left us only 16 on the squad, including me, as we headed for the Second Battle of Atlanta."

To make matters worse for Cumberland, Lawrence W. "Chip" Robert (now head of Atlanta's largest engineering firm) was the mastermind of a scheme. Chip had been a football, track, and baseball star at Tech, and was serving as athletic director.

"Several of us alumni," says Robert, "got Old Heis to agree to use two teams, alternating by quarters. We promised a steak dinner to the team that rolled up the biggest score. That fixed it. Holler 'Steak!' at a Georgia Tech man and he'll run for a touchdown every time."

Heisman, however, showed a certain quality of mercy. He went along with the Cumberland coach's plea that the quarters be shortened from 15 minutes to 12½.

The official scorer's report of the game, preserved in the Tech archives, begins: "Preas kicked off for Tech to Carney, who was downed in his tracks. Gouger made three yards. McDonald failed to gain and punted to Preas, who ran the ball back to the Cumberland 20. Strupper went around left end for a touchdown. Preas kicked goal. Score: 7–0.”

All of which took about one minute of playing time, and was typical of the rest of the game. Cumberland would receive and kick; then Tech would go for a touchdown.

As Charles W. Warwick, the Cumberland left end who now is a West Palm Beach, Florida, attorney, explains, “They would trample us down as if we were weeds.”

The Cumberland team had a classy set of signals —they thought. Quarterback Morris Gouger, now president of the National Bank of Robstown, Texas, told me, “Each player was named for a vegetable. If I wanted to send the right halfback through left tackle, I’d call ‘Turnip over cabbage!’ Or a pass from quarterback to left end, ‘Tomato to carrot!’ The trouble was that Tech made vegetable stew out of us!”

With 30 seconds left in the first quarter, the official record reads: “Spence kicked 45 yards to Gouger, who returned ten. Ball now on Cumberland’s 20. Gouger lost five. McDonald lost five. Pass failed and

quarter ended. Score: 63–0.” Nine touchdowns, and Preas had kicked all nine extra points.

As the weary Cumberland team moved to the other end of the field, they saw with consternation a new team swarm out against them—new except for Jim Preas. Old Heis had kept him in, sensing an all-time kicking record.

“Beginning the second quarter,” declares the official written report, “McDonald kicked to Turner, who returned to Cumberland’s 20. Senter went for a touchdown. Preas kicked goal. Score: 70–0.”

E. W. McCall, now an insurance executive in Houston, Texas, went along as a substitute player on the Cumberland team. He says that he had some vague promise from Allen that he might not have to play at all. But when casualties reduced the ranks of his teammates, he was ordered in, with an admonition from the cheerful Allen to “turn the tide.”

“On every play I got flattened,” he said. “Not only Bill Fincher, their All-American tackle, but every Tech man seemed to be about six inches taller and six inches wider than I was."

The score for the second quarter exactly matched the score of the first: 63 – 0. Preas had kicked 18 consecutive points after touchdown. And the two Tech teams were tied for the steak dinner.

Old Heis always made an impressive speech to his squad between halves, and he ran true to form on this historic day. He strode in, waved for silence. "You're doing all right, team," he declaimed. "We're ahead. But you just can't tell what those Cumberland players have up their sleeves. They may spring a surprise. Be alert, men! Hit 'em clean, but hit 'em hard!"

In the Cumberland locker room, the coach and manager worked feverishly to revive the players. Also, the coach told Heisman that Cumberland might run out of substitutes, and managed to get the quarters shortened to ten minutes.

The most experienced player for Cumberland was R. E. "Pete" Gray, who had played football for several seasons at the Oklahoma University. Gray, who remembers that he was one of six Cumberland players to struggle through the whole game without relief, told me:

"I started at right half. Every time Tech ran a play toward my side a big, tough redhead named Shaver would take me out with a block that jarred every bone in my body. The game was a case of running all afternoon on a fast track."

When the teams came out for the third quarter, Pete Gray asked a Tech player if they had any Sigma Nus on the team. "Sure, Red Shaver over there is one," was the response. Pete rushed up to the man who had blocked him so unmercifully in the first half and gave him the fraternity grip. "After that," Pete declares, "more of the plays went around the other end."

Even with the shortened quarters, Tech ran up 54 points in the third and 42 in the fourth.

It was in the middle of the third quarter that George Allen came in for his moment of glory. His teammates say the game might have ended from their sheer exhaustion had it not been for George's encouraging words: "Hang on, boys. Remember that $500 guarantee!"

"One of Allen's more brilliant plays," recalls his teammate B. F. "Bird" Paty, now also an attorney in West Palm Beach, "was when he attempted a punt. It was a good, hard kick, but the ball hit our own center squarely in the back of the neck and bowled him over."

Tech's great lineman, Canty Alexander, drew the loudest cheers of the game. When most of the Georgia Tech players had scored touchdowns, Canty protested that he ought to be given a chance at one. Captain Tally Johnston agreed. Quietly he passed the word among his teammates. Canty was shifted to halfback and the ball was snapped to him. But to the surprise of the Cumberland team, every man in the Tech line stumbled and fell. The Cumberland players then swarmed over Canty for a five-yard Tech loss.

This was Cumberland's one spectacular achievement. On the next play, however, the Tech line pushed the whole Cumberland team back of the goal and Canty followed to score his touchdown.

Captain McDonald contends that football's huddle system began with this game—accidentally. "Our boys were so groggy that they never knew what to do. So I called them together now and then to figure out how best we might live through the game. Our huddle idea spread."

In the fourth quarter, when every Cumberland man was praying for the end, one of the backs fumbled and the ball rolled toward "Bird" Paty. "Pick it up!" the fumbler shouted. Glancing toward the horde of Tech men thundering down on him, Paty yelled back, "Pick it up yourself—you dropped it!"

George Griffin, now Dean of Students at Tech, was a quarterback that day. In the last quarter he saw one of the Cumberland players wrapped in a blanket sitting at the end of the Tech bench. "Hey you," he called, "you're on the wrong bench!"

"No, I'm not," answered the battered warrior from Lebanon.

"I'm not going to be sent back into this game again!"

Pete Gray says that toward the end of the game he looked around to see if all the Cumberland players were on their feet. "I saw one of my teammates leaning against the goal post. 'Come on, get in the game—only three minutes more!' I yelled. He barely looked up. 'Heck,' he mumbled, 'what's the use? Too late to beat 'em now.'"

These records, established that day at Atlanta, have stood through the years: highest score, greatest number of touchdowns and points after touchdown; highest score for one quarter; most points kicked after touchdown by one player; greatest number of players making touchdowns (13); greatest number of yards gained in one game (978).

"To which must be added another record," says Albert Hill, a business executive in Louisville, Kentucky, and one of Tech's quarterbacks. "Neither team made a first down. Cumberland couldn't, and Tech made touchdowns instead."

At his home in Johnson City, Tennessee, big Jim Preas admits his pride in his record of 18 consecutive points after touchdown, but says, "Don't forget the most unusual play of the game. I got off a high punt which sailed over the goal line, struck a Cumberland player and bounced into my own hands for a touchdown."

Tech's right guard, George West Jr., now chairman of the board of a Chattanooga, Tennessee, firm, recalls: "As we trotted off heading for the gym, Old Heis blew his whistle, sent us back on the field and put us through a half hour's good, hard scrimmage!" But since both Tech teams had played what Heisman said was a "fairly good game," all hands were given that steak dinner.

"As for us," says George Allen, "we collected our $500 guarantee, and I showed the team the sights of Atlanta."

"Which," laments Pete Gray, "we saw through swollen eyes."

Killer Connection

The bestselling crime writer explains why she is not afraid of murderers.

—

BY **ANN RULE**

Originally published in October 2004

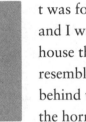

t was four in the morning, and I was locked in a house that all-too-closely resembled the mansion behind the Bates Motel in the horror classic *Psycho*. I was alone except for my dog, Toby, and a coworker, who was on the phone in an adjoining office. Wind and rain whipped the fir boughs until they screeched against the window in front of me, the ragged limbs blotting out the faint yellow of flickering streetlights three stories below. And then a hand touched my shoulder as a shadow lowered over my desk. Toby growled deep in her throat. When I put my hand on her collar to quiet her, I felt the hackles rising on the back of her neck.

Why was she acting in such a bizarre way? I whirled in my chair and smiled as I apologized for my crazy dog. My partner was holding a manila folder out to me.

He half-shook his handsome head. "No hard feelings," he said. "Dogs and I just don't appreciate each other, I guess."

Now I know why. Standing in front of me was a serial killer, a sadist whose days and nights were consumed with murderous obsession. He had killed before and would kill again, many times. I had no idea that a monster hid

The true-crime author, posing near her home on Puget Sound, carries a pen instead of a badge.

behind his perfect mask, but my dog—who loved just about everyone—sensed the danger. For once, it was fortunate that I wasn't a man's "type"; I didn't fit the profile of his victims—young, slender, beautiful, and a stranger to him. Three decades later, I shudder at the circumstances that threw us together, and how he was only the first of many serial killers who found his way into my life.

Headlong into a Life of Crime

After reading Truman Capote's *In Cold Blood* at 27, I had one big wish: to one day get inside a psychopathic killer's head and write a book about what I learned. Coming from a family of law enforcement officers, attorneys, and social workers, I always wondered why criminals did the things they did. I still wonder today.

The first murderer I met was a woman named Viola who spent months in the jail in Mountcalm County, Michigan. My grandfather was the sheriff; Viola was awaiting trial for fatally shooting her

husband. She taught me how to crochet and also explained what she called "justifiable homicide." She had bought her husband a new Ford pickup and then surprised him—and herself—when she caught him in it with another woman. Her swift retribution made more sense to me than some of the other homicides I have researched since.

Ten years later, I signed up for every criminology course offered at the University of Washington. When I was only 20, I became a Seattle police officer. Though my degree was in creative writing, my heart was in being a cop. I was eager to listen to both victims and suspects, to discern for myself what was fact and what was fiction. I couldn't imagine a better job, but after 18 months on the force, I had the biggest disappointment of my life when I failed the civil service medical exam because of nearsightedness. At 22, I thought nothing interesting would ever happen to me again.

By default, I became a writer. The first lesson in Creative Writing 101 is to write about what you know, and I knew about crime and cops and killers. In the next 14 years I churned out more than a thousand articles about real cases for *True Detective* magazine and its sister publications. Few people were very impressed with my writing credits, but, by then divorced, I was happy to make enough to support my five children on my own.

At my editor's request I used a male pen name, Andy Stack. "Who would ever believe a woman knows anything about detective work?" he asked. I set out to prove him wrong, attending scores of trials and working toward an associate degree in criminal justice.

In the early years, I didn't meet the accused, which was fine with me. But sometimes investigators introduced me to victims' families, saying it would help to have their stories told. I found remarkably brave people who had lived through the deepest tragedies and I joined their group: Families and Friends of Victims of Violent Crime.

I soon realized that if I was serious about presenting the psychopathology of murderers, I would have to spend time in prison

From jail, Ted Bundy wrote several friendly but cagey letters to Ann Rule about his case.

myself—if only for visiting hours.

In the spring of 1975, after years of rejection slips, I finally landed a contract to write a book about an unidentified serial killer who was thought to have abducted and murdered at least eight young women in Washington and Oregon. However, my contract stipulated that someone had to be arrested and convicted of the crimes; only then could my book be published.

Ted Bundy (top left), a former law student, conferred with his lawyers during his 1979 trial for the murder of two Florida college students. A Seattle homicide unit displayed photos of his first six known victims (1974).

I knew that on a summer day in 1974, the prime suspect in the case had attempted to lure several girls away from Lake Sammamish State Park east of Seattle by asking them to help him unload a boat. Tanned and good-looking, he had said his name was Ted, and he wore a full cast on his arm. The girls who refused to go with him lived, but Janice Ott, 23, and Denise Naslund, 19, walked away with "Ted" and never returned.

How would I find out who "Ted" really was? Knowing how self-absorbed serial killers are, and that they often love to read about crime themselves, I thought about putting an ad in the personals column, something provocative enough to convince him to call me. I put hints in my *True Detective* articles that I was willing to serve as an intermediary with the police.

I need not have bothered. I soon came to realize that I already knew Ted. As unbelievable as it sounds, it was Ted Bundy, the same man my dog didn't trust, who was my partner at the Seattle Crisis Clinic two nights a week for a year. Every Sunday and Tuesday during the all-night shift, we were the only people fielding phone calls from strangers in emotional distress. But despite spending 12 to 16 hours a week alone with Ted Bundy, I found out I hadn't really known him at all. It would be three years before I had the first hint about his secret life.

On September 30, 1975, Bundy called me from Salt Lake City, saying he had been arrested and was going to be in a lineup, viewed by a kidnapping victim. "Ann, I'm in a little trouble. You're one of the few people I really trust in Seattle…"

Actually, he was in a great deal of trouble. By the time Ted called me, there were not only eight missing women in Washington and Oregon, but also at least four in Utah, five in Colorado, and two in Idaho. They had disappeared during a span of 18 months. The actual toll is probably much higher than 19. After he escaped from jail twice and made his way from Glenwood Springs, Colorado, to Pensacola, Florida, the FBI estimated that Ted Bundy had killed at least 36 women.

When presented with that number, he smiled slightly and told Florida detectives, "Add one digit to that, and you'll have it."

Did he mean 37? Or 136? Or 360? Ted Bundy's name never crossed my mind when I got my book contract, and yet six months later I had to face the possibility that I might be writing about someone I knew. Fortunately, it was a nonfiction book, because the situation was too implausible to sell as a mystery novel: Crime writer discovers her friend is a wanted killer. It sounded much too contrived. But that was the way it happened. *The Stranger Beside Me,* about Bundy as I knew him, was published in 1980, and is now in its 50th printing.

Between his final arrest in 1978 and his execution on January 24, 1989, in Starke, Florida, Ted wrote me dozens of letters. He never came right out and admitted his crimes, although he once said, "Ann, I planned my escape for 2½ years. I had my freedom and lost it through a combination of compulsion and stupidity." Compulsion was the operative word. I don't think he could grasp that as long as he was free to walk the streets, he could not stop killing.

A Menace I Could Not Put into Words

I continued to write *True Detective* cases to pay my mortgage. I was probably the only true-crime writer who had known a serial killer during and after his crimes. I had written a successful book. My wish had come true. But as a result I would never again unquestioningly trust the people I met.

I had dinner twice with a very attractive detective who was popular with his fellow investigators and seemed polite and considerate. But there was something menacing about him that I couldn't put into words. Three years later, he was convicted in the shooting death of an ex-convict believed to have been involved with him in a burglary ring.

One of my first editors shook his head when I suggested a book on serial killers. "They're a fad, Ann," he said. "Like Hula-Hoops. Next year, nobody will be interested in them." Right. My next three books were about serial murderers. My crossover book—a term used to signify the difference between small sales and outright success —was *Small Sacrifices*, published in 1987.

An old friend, the late Pierce Brooks, called me in the spring of 1984 from his home in Oregon. "Ann," he said, "I can't tell you much, but I'm a consultant on an amazing case here in Eugene. You'd better get down here for the trial before some real writer hears about it. It's your kind of case."

Stung, I protested. "I'm a real writer—"

"You know what I mean," he said. "One of those bestselling writers from New York or Los Angeles may beat you to it. Come. I promise you won't be sorry."

So I spent that spring at the bizarre trial of Diane Downs. She was a flamboyant defendant, accused of shooting her three children in the mistaken belief that, if they were out of the picture, her married lover would return to her. Two of her children miraculously survived and were placed in the foster system.

While caring for children was onerous for her, Diane enjoyed being pregnant. She had even been a surrogate mother, bearing a child

For veteran Seattle detectives who thought they had "seen everything," this was something new in homicide...

THE MAN WHO KILLED HIS IMAGE

by ANDY STACK

One of the author's stories for *True Detective* magazine, written under her pen name, Andy Stack, in 1976.

for a relative stranger. "You have someone inside, a friend you can talk to," she explained. After the shootings, she deliberately conceived another child to replace the seven-year-old daughter she had killed. Hugely pregnant during her trial, she clearly loved being the focus of attention. It didn't seem to matter to her whether that attention was positive or negative.

A few weeks after her conviction, I visited Diane in the Lane County Jail. We spoke by intercom through a glass barricade, and she was animated and upbeat, becoming more so when a fellow prisoner asked for her autograph. The next morning, Diane gave birth to a baby girl. She graciously let Doug Welch, the detective who had helped convict her of murder, hold her baby. Then the child was placed for adoption.

Over time, we exchanged letters. Diane wrote mostly about how much motherhood meant to her, but avoided answering any of my harder questions. She escaped once and was recaptured, and two decades later, she is still incarcerated, in the Valley State Prison for Women in Chowchilla, California. She is up for parole in 2021. Her surviving children, who were adopted by the prosecuting attorney and his wife, are adults now—and doing well.

A Long Search for Justice

After *Small Sacrifices* came out, I got hundreds of suggestions from readers for book subjects. Obviously I couldn't look into them all, but there were times when I felt an almost physical tug urging me to

Sheila Bellush and husband Jamie with their quadruplets. Right: Sheila's first husband, Allen Blackthorne, was convicted of her murder in 2000.

help unveil the truth. I remember reading a 1997 story about Sheila Blackthorne Bellush, the young mother of quadruplets who was savagely murdered in her home in Sarasota, Florida. I was horrified and wondered who could possibly have hated her enough to shoot and stab her in front of her toddlers. But I was writing another book at the time, so I didn't pursue the case.

Then, in January 2000, I got an e-mail from Kerry Bladorn, Bellush's sister. Unbeknownst to either of us, Kerry lived two miles from my parents' ranch in Oregon. When I called her, she said, "I've been looking for you for so long. From the moment my sister divorced her first husband ten years ago, she

believed he would find a way to kill her. Sheila said Allen Blackthorne never let any woman leave him. She knew his other ex-wives were in hiding."

Sheila had warned Kerry that if she died suddenly it wouldn't be the way it looked. Allen was furious because Sheila had taken him to court repeatedly to gain full custody of their two daughters, and also for her share of their financial assets. Tearfully, Kerry had promised her sister that if anything happened, she would see that it was investigated. "And then she told me to find Ann Rule," Kerry continued, "and ask you to write a book about her."

I couldn't say no. To research *Every Breath You Take*, I went to

San Antonio for multimillionaire Allen Blackthorne's murder trial, and then to Sarasota to talk to sheriff's detectives there.

Blackthorne, the co-owner of a company that sold muscle stimulating devices, was supremely confident throughout his trial. He turned often to mouth "I love you" to his current wife, Maureen, who was sitting beside me. However, Blackthorne lost his sangfroid when the jury came back and he was sentenced to life in a federal prison.

I always spend time where the crimes occurred. In Sarasota, I stood in front of a white house trimmed in yellow, sheltered by lush tropical plantings. I looked at the garage window where Sheila's killer had entered, and silently promised Sheila I would tell the story she no longer could.

That was not the only time I felt I had received a plea from beyond the grave. In 1985 a woman named Linda Bailey Brown was shot to death in her home, a small rambler in Garden Grove, California. That apparently was not the end of Linda, though. A few weeks afterward, her husband, David, told a friend he couldn't sleep in his bedroom any longer. Something kept awakening him and his mistress, who was the 16-year-old sister of his deceased wife. "There's a ghost there," he insisted. There may have been.

I am barely adequate as a photographer, but I took a picture of the front of that house for the book I wrote about Linda Brown's case. When I picked up the prints, I was startled to see a blond woman staring from the front window. That wouldn't be unusual, except that the family who then occupied the property were Asian, with jet-black hair. And there was only an inch or two of space between the windows and the venetian blinds that covered them. No flesh-and-blood person could stand between the two. Later, when the sun was at the same height and the shadows were identical, I tried to duplicate the photos. I never could.

I visited David Brown in the Orange County Jail after he was convicted of arranging his wife's murder. Despite the overwhelming circumstantial evidence presented at his trial and the testimony of his own daughter, Cinnamon, he was glib as he urged me to reinvestigate the charges against him. "Ask my family," he said. "They'll tell you I'm a nice guy."

But David lost me when he boasted that he'd bought his late wife a funeral plot where "she has a nice view of the fountains." That expense had taken only a small portion of the nearly half-million dollars he collected on Linda's life insurance policy. David Brown paid $330,000 cash for a house for himself in the Anaheim Hills with a much better "view."

A "Plastic Surgeon" with Murder in Mind

As strange as it might seem, I once heard from a killer-in-waiting before he set out to poison his wife. Anthony Pignataro, MD, of Buffalo, New York, e-mailed me in 1998 asking if he might call me about an important matter. I provided my office phone number, and he did call—asking me to write a book about the outrageous injustices he said he had suffered at the hands of the New York State Department of Health, which had taken away his medical license. Pignataro said he was a plastic surgeon. He had never been board-certified in that specialty and his credentials were suspect, although I didn't know it then. At least one young patient had died in his office during surgery, and others came close to death.

Pignataro was a persuasively smooth man with a deep voice, and he even put his wife on the phone with me. I explained that I didn't write medically oriented books; I wrote true crime. Undeterred, Pignataro sent me a rough manuscript he said his wife had written. I glanced through it, and promptly forgot about the Pignataros. I had no way of knowing that the woman who spoke to me on the phone wasn't his wife at all, but his mistress.

More than a year later, a reader in Buffalo sent me a newspaper clipping about a woman named Debbie Pignataro who lay near death in a local hospital from some unknown poison. "Pignataro … Pignataro … ?" Then I remembered the angry doctor. Because I knew he had read my books—and two of them were about killers who used poison—I sent copies to Frank Sedita, the Erie County prosecutor handling the case. As it turned out, Debbie had been poisoned with arsenic from ant traps.

Most of us have arsenic in our blood—usually from five to ten micrograms per liter, or a little more if we eat shellfish. It's not enough to hurt us. When she was admitted to the hospital, Debbie's blood tests showed she had 29,580 micrograms per liter.

I'm happy to say that she fought her way through crushing pain and paralysis, determined to live for her children. She made it. And I wrote a book about Anthony Pignataro, who remained in prison until 2013. Needless to say, it was not the ending he had envisioned.

Waiting for the Green River Killer

After 23 books, I've become fairly selective about the cases I decide to write about. Some are too old, going back 50 years or more. Killings like those of JonBenet Ramsey and Nicole Simpson have already had what I call "saturation coverage," meaning anyone who watches television already knows all the details. And many cases simply lack suspense: He did it, he got caught, he confessed, case closed.

Truly engrossing homicides are those where the solution seems tantalizingly close, and yet detectives are stymied for months—or even years. Along with three separate sheriff's task forces, I had to wait more than two decades for the denouement of the longest-running serial murder mystery in the Northwest: the Green River Killer homicides, with at least 48 young female victims. From July 1982 to December 2001, my linen closet held no sheets or towels because it was packed with newspaper clippings, maps, audio and videotapes, and my notes about locations and suspects in this baffling series of disappearances, followed by the discovery of their decomposing remains.

Most of the victims, runaways and teenagers who had turned to life on the street for survival,

The first victims of Seattle's Green River Killer were found in the early 1980s, along the riverbanks. Many of the women (ten are shown above) were not even 18 years old at the time they disappeared.

vanished within a few miles of where I lived at the time, in South King County, Washington, practically in the flight path of the Seattle-Tacoma Airport. Sometimes I stopped to warn girls who stood in the rainy nights along Pacific Highway about the danger there, but they usually assured me they would be fine.

Sadly, many of them were not, and the toll continued to rise. I never felt "hinky"—a cops' term for intuition that something is wrong—about Ted Bundy, but given my proximity to the Green River Killer's stalking ground, I developed a feeling early on that I had probably seen him. I came to believe that at some point I had stood behind him in a supermarket, or sat next to him at a restaurant.

In the first three years of the probe, I fielded several calls a day from people convinced they knew his identity. Most were from women turning in their ex-husbands or ex-boyfriends, and many of them were chillingly convincing. Rumor had it that the killer was a cop, and I was tipped to the names of many

detectives I knew, which gave me pause.

My daughter Leslie Rule also is a writer, and we often hold book-signing events together. On several occasions she mentioned a man she spotted at our signings. "He never buys a book, Mom," she said. "He just leans against the wall and stares at you."

In 1987, a woman who sold her house to a divorced man in his late 30s called me. The man, who remained a neighbor, had later asked this woman for help removing a bedroom carpet, ruined with spilled "red paint." He matched the composite drawings resulting from Green River witnesses' observations. She and her friend suspected that he might be the killer. I met with them and agreed their suspicions were important enough for me to take them to the task force. Before I did, I drove by his house—which was less than two miles from my own. It was an ordinary little house, two blocks off the Pacific Highway.

I had no idea, of course, that the Green River Task Force was already looking closely at him. But when a

Carol Estes (with surviving daughter Virginia Graham) holds a portrait of her daughter Debra, one of at least 48 victims of killer Gary Ridgway (opposite).

search warrant was executed on his property and a meticulous combing of the house netted no physical evidence linking him to the victims, they couldn't proceed.

It would be 15 more years before Gary Ridgway was arrested and charged—initially, with four homicides of young women. Forensic science had progressed to the point where Ridgway's DNA profile could be matched absolutely to body fluids found on some of the victims. In December 2001, his picture flashed across television screens and newspaper front pages up and down the West Coast.

I didn't recognize him, but my daughter did. Leslie called me and said, "That's him, Mom."

"That's who?"

"The man I told you about—the one who watches you. It was Gary Ridgway!"

I knew she was right 2½ years later as I viewed 105 hours of taped interrogations between Ridgway and the task force detectives. I froze every time I heard Ridgway say my name. Sometimes he spoke about

Ridgway has begun serving 48 consecutive life sentences, isolated in a small concrete cell in Walla Walla, Washington. It's unlikely he will be allowed to read my book, and that's just as well. He wouldn't like it. There is no way for a sociopathic serial killer to make a good impression on anyone. While I do explore his twisted world in my book, my concern is with the lives of the young women he killed—lives cut short by a man who is addicted to committing murder.

reading my books. He also admitted why he had lied to the police at first, downplaying his cruelty, and the fantasies of torture he had toward all those lost girls.

"I heard a popular Northwest true-crime author was going to write a book about me," Ridgway said. "I wanted to make the best impression possible."

As I wrote *Green River, Running Red*, I shivered to think that I held any place at all in Gary Ridgway's thought processes. I didn't want to be inside his head or to think of him watching me when I didn't even know he was there.

Am I afraid? No. When I began writing in the true-crime genre, I made up my mind not to let it frighten me or blunt my life. I don't have nightmares because the sadness and terror goes from my fingertips into my computer.

Still, I know that in the future there undoubtedly will be other strange connections to the people I write about. And that's just part of my job, because I truly believe I'm doing what I was meant to do: speaking for victims who can no longer speak for themselves.

"You Two Must Meet!"

If you want mutual friends to get on well together, says this popular humorist, a calculated lack of enthusiasm may be just the thing.

BY **CORNELIA OTIS SKINNER**

Originally published in August 1961

When I was a small girl, my mother labored under the delusion that because she happened to be fond of a particular friend, I would automatically be fond of that friend's daughter—and vice versa. Time and again, her voice lilting with delight, she would announce that her dear friend Mrs. X was coming to tea and wasn't it lovely she was going to bring her little daughter Mary and wouldn't she and I have fun playing together! I always knew that we wouldn't—

and so always did little Mary.

As Mrs. X's car pulled up at our front door, I would watch from a second-story window in baleful mood for a first appraisal of little Mary—who was obviously in a similar mood of bale. Our meeting invariably was like that of two fledgling fighting chickens who aren't interested enough even to fight. Each of us would croak "Hello," back up against her mother, and stand motionless, wishing it were all over.

Mother would suggest brightly that we go right in to tea. Mary and I would be served first, and once our fingers were licked clean of cake icing, we'd amble away in obedience to our mothers' cheery injunction to "go play." Playing consisted of my asking Mary if she'd like to see my new bicycle and Mary's answering, "Not much." Then how about Parcheesi, I would suggest, and Mary would say Parcheesi was silly; anyway, didn't I have a dollhouse?

I did, but it was rather a shambles, with no staircases and no doors and none of the furniture made to scale. The current Mary always had—or said she had—a dollhouse completely equipped with miniature furniture, tiny chandeliers that lit up, and a working toilet in the bathroom. One contemptuous glance at my dollhouse would be enough. Mary would return to Mrs. X and cling poutingly to the arm of her chair while I hovered morosely in the background, fine-combing my dog for fleas.

Such deliberate attempts to establish affinity by outside influence are doomed from the start. I still squirm with embarrassment over the memory of a painful matchmaking experience I endured at the age

of 19. The well-intentioned but misguided matchmaker was a college classmate, and the other victim of her innocent plot was a youth from her hometown. He was tall, dark, and handsome, she told me, keen on tennis and seriously interested in the theater. Pleased at being paired in her imagination with such a Prince Charming, I agreed to attend a weekend house party to which he had been invited. Unfortunately, she had also told the young man that he and I were made for each other. And that's not the thing to tell any potential pairers-off, even a couple of poodles about to be bred.

The result was inevitable. Our initial meeting was strained to the point of nervous giggling on my part, met by manly but rather stony silence on his. Ensuing conversation didn't help. His interest in the theater was limited to his having played a minor role in a local drama group production of *Charlie's Aunt*, and when he learned that my enthusiasm for tennis stemmed from having once talked for ten minutes with Bill Tilden, any incipient ardor died a-borning.

When my conniving classmate saw to it that we were placed side by side at meals, we each talked animatedly with the person on the other side; if seated together in the back of a car, we huddled apart, silently intent on the view out our respective windows. By Sunday we were avoiding each other like enemy diplomats. The matchmaker was sadly disappointed, but only temporarily so. Within the year she married my intended, and, as far as I know, they are still living happily ever after.

A good and dear friend of mine, whom I shall call Dolly, talked to me for years about a good and dear friend of hers. "I can't wait to bring you two girls together," Dolly used to say. "You'll just love her, I know! You'll get along like a house afire" —which always struck me as a dubious way of getting along. When we eventually did meet, what we got along like was more in the nature of a well-modulated Frigidaire.

We were introduced at a party. Upon seeing the other "girl" (she is fully my age—and just let anyone try to find out what that is!), Dolly let out a series of embarrassing squeals and, clutching us each by an arm, led us into a quiet corner. Her friend and I shook hands, she told me that Dolly had always talked so much about me, and I told her that Dolly had always talked so much about her—an opener that is about as good a conversation stopper as any I can think of. "And to think you two are meeting at last!" Dolly burbled. We two pondered the enormity of that thought, and in Greek-chorus fashion echoed that, yes indeed, we were meeting at last.

Actually the woman gave every indication of being great fun and, given a chance, we might have got along splendidly. But Dolly's duenna-like presence, like Mother's of old, had a cramping effect on us both. After some further meaningless exchanges, we said how lovely it was to meet at last and that we must get together soon, beat hasty and separate retreats, and have not set eyes on each other since.

The reasons people have for bringing together spirits whom they imagine to be kindred are varied and curious. Maybe they both come from Kansas, or they both like to water-ski or they may each have read *War and Peace* from cover to cover three times. None of these coincidences, unfortunately, is enough.

Actors have special problems of this nature. One of them is the well-meaning person who decides that you must meet the So-and-So's "because they saw you act in Hartford, Connecticut." Accordingly you do meet the So-and-So's, who say that, yes indeed, they did see you act in Hartford way back in—quoting a date that sounds prehistoric—none of which gets things off on too happy a footing, especially as there is often no follow-up. They don't say, "We loved the play," or even, "We thought it stank." They merely state that they saw you and you are left high and dry to flounder into some banality like: "I'm glad they sold at least two tickets that evening."

If one wants mutual friends to get along well together, perhaps the best plan is for them to meet casually, without buildup. Indeed, a calculated lack of enthusiasm may be just the thing to bring about a true marriage of minds. Once when my husband and I were vacationing in Bermuda, there turned up at our hotel a man I had known years before. For some reason I thought he and my husband wouldn't hit it off. Only a chance encounter obliged me to introduce them.

They took to each other like long-lost brothers. In no time they were swapping the sort of stories they said I mustn't listen to, and every evening found them side by side closing the bar, while I lay upstairs in bed morosely reading a magazine. If only I had told them in advance how well they would get on, I brooded, they might have ignored each other and paid some attention to me.

The Will to Live

Badly burned in the World Trade Center,
Lauren Manning was determined to survive.

———

BY GAIL CAMERON WESCOTT

Originally published in March 2004

On a hazy late afternoon in New York City, Lauren Manning breezes through the door with an upbeat smile, her husband, Greg, at her side. A gauzy medical sleeve covers her left hand following a recent surgery, but her outstretched right hand is elegantly manicured. "Oh, this was a big deal," she says with enthusiasm. "I don't have that many nails left—I lost parts of a few fingers on my left hand—and one of my nails grows oddly. So this manicure was huge. A milestone."

Every day since September 11, 2001, has been a milestone for Lauren Manning. Burned over 82 percent of her body in the World Trade Center attack, she was given just a 15 percent chance of surviving. Now, a little more than two years later, she is planning a third birthday party for her son, Tyler. "I just visited the Children's Zoo in Central Park where we're going to have it," she says. "I didn't grow up with parties like this, but he's our only child and it brings us great pleasure."

"What's great," says Greg, "is that Lauren will be there. There was a time when we couldn't be sure..."

Lauren still remembers lying in

"Where I am today is a result of real team effort," says Lauren, with her husband, Greg.

the brilliant sunshine on the grass median outside the World Trade Center in unspeakable pain—yet "seeing every blade of grass with razor precision," she says. Walking into the north tower, unaware that a plane had struck, she had been engulfed by a fireball as jet fuel poured down an elevator shaft and exploded. On her back in the midst of the horror, with debris raining down around her, Lauren made the decision to live—for Greg and for Tyler, then 10 months old. She had kissed them both goodbye just minutes earlier in their Greenwich Village apartment, a mile away. A senior vice president and partner at Cantor Fitzgerald who was normally at her desk on the 104th floor by 8 a.m., Lauren was running late that day.

Greg had watched the towers burning from the balcony of their apartment and was certain his wife was dead. When he found her later that morning at St. Vincent's Hospital, he told her she would be fine and prayed that she would. During the next few months he wrote a collection of heartbreaking e-mails to family and friends that documented her day-to-day battle. They were compiled in a bestselling book, *Love, Greg & Lauren.*

It took Lauren, now age 43, as long as six months to return to the apartment she had left on September 11. "Talk about coming home late from work," she says, laughing. But then her voice cracks. "To be home

> ## "I wanted my life back," says Lauren. "I wanted to be able to pick up and hold my son."

with Greg, to hug Tyler and just be around him ... the sweetness of that is not easy to describe."

It had been impossible even to envision that when she first awoke in the Burn Center of New York-Presbyterian Hospital after weeks in a drug-induced coma. Her hands, horribly seared when she pushed open hot metal doors to escape the Trade Center, were immobilized in casts. Unable to talk because of a breathing tube, barely able to move, she felt trapped, helpless, a prisoner in her own body.

As she told a convention of occupational therapists in Pennsylvania several months ago, "As injured as I was, it was almost impossible to imagine I would ever regain meaningful function." But for Lauren, it was never going to be enough simply to survive. "I wanted my life back. I wanted to dial the phone, drive the car, swing a golf club, all the things I'd previously taken for granted. Most of all, I wanted to be able to pick up and hold my son."

Roger Yurt, the physician who is director of the New York-Presbyterian Burn Center, was optimistic. "Lauren is unusual," he says. "She puts out 300 percent."

The milestones—sitting up, standing, taking a step—kept coming. Three months after the attack, on December 11, Lauren walked on her own out of the Burn Center to continue her treatment at Burke Rehabilitation Center in suburban White Plains, where she would live for three months. At

Burke, Lauren began a rigorous regimen of both physical and occupational therapy. The biggest obstacles of all were her hands.

"There would be good days and bad days, breakthroughs and days when I'd feel like I couldn't do anything," Lauren says, looking back. "I still remember the first stretching of my fingers when almost every movement brought intense pain." As she moved through the exercise and therapy sessions, her eyes would well with tears. But she flatly refused to stop. "I'm fine," she would tell the therapists. "Just keep going."

Lauren has now had more than 20 surgeries, seven in 2003 alone—complex skin grafts, scar revisions—with more still to come. To get through each day, she has needed 24-hour assistance from two women who work in 12-hour shifts. Just getting dressed is daunting for her. For the first 22 months, Lauren had to wear cumbersome, pressurized Jobst garments and gloves for 23 hours a day to prevent scars from thickening and hindering her movements. "It's like wearing this really tight body stocking—the tighter the better," she says. "It's incredibly claustrophobic and hot. And impossible to get in and out of without help."

In August 2003, to her relief, the required time was cut in half; now she wears the garments for 12 hours at night. "Oh, freedom!" she exclaims. "If Greg or Tyler and I are going someplace, I can now just run out the door without all that paraphernalia. I used to need help just getting a jacket on. Now I can put it on myself."

Certain losses are permanent.

Because of her fragile skin, Lauren cannot go outside without special sun-blocking protective clothing. "I used to love lying out in the sun for hours," she says wistfully. "Remember baby oil and all that?"

Between surgeries, a daily routine has evolved in the Manning house. Greg takes morning duty with Tyler, who is now an energetic toddler enrolled in preschool, getting his milk and starting his breakfast. Lauren once loved to cook, but she spends little time in the kitchen now.

"My skin is still so sensitive," she says. "If I get a cut, it takes twice as long to heal. So I have to be very careful."

Tyler, enchanted with his first backpack, loves to yell, "Bye, Mom, I'm going to school!" while Lauren revels in the ordinary everyday-ness of it all. Greg, a senior vice president at Eurobrokers before 9/11, departs next. Since November 2002, he has been a member of the management team at Cantor Fitzgerald, Lauren's company, which lost 658 people in the attack. "It's more than just rebuilding a business," Greg says. "It's working on behalf of families of people who were Lauren's colleagues."

While Lauren hasn't been back to the office to visit—"It's not the time yet," she says—she did speak at the firm's Central Park memorial on the anniversary of 9/11. She asked families and friends to clap instead of standing for a moment of prayer. "I want to clap until my arms ache," she told them, "to make so much noise that God can hear us … that we celebrate the time we had with them." The applause was

On February 9, 2002, Senator Hillary Clinton went to Burke to meet Lauren and other 9/11 victims.

thunderous. She also quoted from a favorite Wordsworth poem that comforts her: "We will grieve not, rather find strength in what remains…"

Those words have become a sort of mantra. "I'm angry, absolutely," she says, "but I don't live with it. I don't want to give the terrorists any more time than they have already taken from me. I'm grateful to be alive."

Lauren is usually out of the house by 9:30 a.m. Most weekdays she does some kind of physical or occupational therapy. Several days a week, she spends hours with therapists at New York-Presbyterian Hospital working on exercise equipment and computer-controlled resistance machines. Other times, she works out at home or at a neighborhood gym—aerobics, treadmill, free weights.

"Sometimes," she says, "I just grab onto a bar and try to hang from it with as much body weight as I can. Some ranges of motion I'll never regain." The skin on Lauren's back is tight because of skin grafting. "But I have to maintain what I have," she says. "It's a constant fight."

Ordinary tasks have gradually become easier. "I can do some buttons, others not. It obviously takes a lot longer to put on a button-down Oxford than a sweater." She can't put on a necklace without help, and she cannot thread a needle. Putting on an earring can take forever. "But remember," she cracks, "I only have to put on one, since I lost part of my left ear."

Greg remains awed by Lauren's diligence. "She does absolutely everything she has to do. And now we're seeing results." She, in turn, is awed by her husband's support. "He is an incredibly hands-on, powerful human being. He may forget the garbage and his office is more than a mess—but where it counts, he delivers."

Their progression to what Greg calls "the normal stuff of life" is steady. They go out to favorite restaurants, spend evenings with friends. Lauren can now drive a car again for short periods of time. She waters her vines on the balcony and wonders if it's too late to plant mums. At night, she reads stories to Tyler. There are, increasingly, the blissful moments when they forget what they've been through.

Last winter, they watched as two feet of snow fell at their weekend house in Dutchess County, north of the city. "Lauren and Tyler and I were out there," remembers Greg, "not worried about anything, just having fun, running around in the snow, having this wonderful time."

Lauren's eyes briefly mist. "It was just such normal joy," she says.

Last summer, both Lauren and Tyler visited a riding stable and trotted around on horses. Then, one afternoon, watching Greg and Tyler out in the yard with a Wiffle ball and bat, Lauren was astounded to see her son pop one high in the air. "I got right out there and batted with him," she says. "That was really great. That's the stuff that matters." She roughhouses with her son regularly. Greg used to worry that she might hurt herself; now he says he feels more like a referee.

"Lauren and Tyler have a fabulous relationship," he says. "People have asked us, 'What will you tell him about 9/11?' We'll tell him what he needs to know. What he knows right now is that his mom is here. That's enough."

Well, This Is Awkward

A cartoonist and author catalogues some of life's less-than-fine moments.

———

BY **JESSICA HAGY**

Originally published in March 2014

Accidentally running over the foot of a lawyer's child with your shopping cart. Being unsure whether you are or are not on a date. That word you're unable to put your finger on. Swimsuit season. Being bitten by a toddler. Asking "When are you due?" and being told "It's benign, actually." Prominent dog testicles. Looking like a tourist. Forgetting the names of people who think they're important. Wearing socks with holes to the airport. When the circus lion angrily decides he's had just about enough of this nonsense, thanks. Sweaty handshakes. American flags made in China.

Being stopped because they've heard that one before.

When it's your fault we need a cleanup in aisle seven. All the things you should have said but didn't. All the things lost in translation. Cold sores. When no one has anything nice to say at the funeral. Inadvertent triple entendre. Cries for attention that involve visible thongs. Breaking up with your boss.

Opening awful gifts in front of the person who gave them to you. Small talk at the urinal. Faded bumper stickers for candidates who lost. Forgetting the baggies before walking the dog.

Karaoke.

Magic tricks that don't quite work. Not being asked to perform an encore. Mispronouncing a common word in the presence of linguists. Rich people who have no idea what things cost. Any conversation that begins with "Let me tell you about my placenta." Being served a fine cut of an endangered species in a delicate balsamic reduction on a bed of arugula. Your Internet browsing history. First and last dates. Parrots that swear at guests.

Teenage poetry.

The casual racism of elderly relatives. Saying "I love you," and hearing "Oh, OK." The honesty of the extremely inebriated. The honesty of curious children. When someone angrily asks, "Are you flirting with me?" Rattraps in restaurant bathrooms. The honor of being a bridesmaid.

Calling your neighbor's dog by his wife's name.

Telemarketers who are just trying to save some lives. Damp seat cushions on public transit. Lazy eyes. Struggling to compliment creepy-looking babies. Being the flabbiest person at the gym. Beardless Santas. Long, thick hairs in soups, on soaps, and in nostrils. Apologizing for being successful.

First dates and last dates. Parrots that swear at guests. Teenage poetry.

When Dad won't give you his ideal kidney. Speaking now instead of forever holding your peace.

Lice.

The red sock in the load of white towels. Adult tantrums. Not being allowed into the club. Sharing toothbrushes. Comparing scores on standardized tests. Sanctimonious parenting advice. Medical exams that require the donning of a gown.

Comparing salaries. Forgetting where you parked Grandma. Telling a funny story you didn't know was a secret. Reheating tuna fish in the office microwave. Every baby shower that has ever been thrown.

Accidentally flashing a gang sign.

Loud snorting. Becoming your mother despite decades of effort to the contrary. Adoring things that are not at all popular. Not getting the joke.

Being the joke.

Not knowing when to quit. Quitting while you mistakenly think you're still ahead. And so on.

I Hunted Down the Woman Who Stole My Life

With the police unable to act, Karen Lodrick took matters into her own hands.

BY **ANITA BARTHOLOMEW**

Originally published in January 2008

aren Lodrick ordered a latte at Starbucks while waiting nervously for the bank on San Francisco's Market Street to open. She had been anxious and distracted of late, but couldn't help noticing the scruffy-looking pair standing next to her: a tall man wearing a navy baseball jacket and a large woman in jeans and Gucci glasses, carrying a brown suede coat and a Prada purse. The woman looked vaguely familiar.

The distinctive faux-fur trim along its edges looked as unkempt as the woman who held it. And then—bingo—she knew. Karen's ID had been stolen five months before. Her bank account had been emptied, and her life sent reeling out of control. The coat she was looking at was the same one she'd seen in the bank surveillance tape, worn by the woman who'd stolen Karen's identity.

Karen followed the pair onto the patio and watched as they settled at a round table under a burgundy window awning. She called 911, asked that a police officer meet her, then settled at the next table.

Just the day before, Karen's bank had called after closing hours to tell her that she'd left her driver's license at a branch on Market and Church streets. But Karen had never been to that branch. And her real driver's license was still in her wallet.

The con artist must have come back to retrieve the phony license.

A cell call from her friend Ed Fuentes interrupted her thoughts. She walked toward the hedges that bordered the Starbucks patio, out of earshot of the pair, and told him her suspicions.

The large woman and her companion stole glances at Karen, looking increasingly nervous. Then they got up from the table and separated. The man turned south; the woman headed north.

"Ed, I've got to go," she told her friend. "I've got to follow her."

"Don't do anything crazy, Karen," said Fuentes. "She could have a gun."

"I've got to do it." She feared that if she didn't act, the identity thief would disappear, along with any hope of ending her bad dream. The chase was on.

For five months, the thief had dipped into Karen's accounts as if they were her own private piggy bank. She scammed thousands of dollars more, using credit cards she opened in Karen's name. The banks were unable to stop her. The police could do nothing. Creditors demanded payment for the thief's transactions. Karen closed her accounts, only to have the criminal crack open the new ones she'd opened and drain those too.

The woman turned a corner. Karen's phone rang. The caller ID said "unknown caller." Karen looked up the street and saw that the woman had her cell phone out. Could she be checking to see if the real Karen Lodrick was on her tail? And where were the police?

As Karen approached a recycling center at the corner of Buchanan Street, a man looked at her, then at the woman she was following.

"Do you know her?" she asked.

"No. Do you?"

Karen told him she thought the

woman had stolen her identity. "You're not the first person to say that about her," he said, arousing her suspicion about him as well. Was he an accomplice? Karen again called 911 as the woman took off up the hill, looking over her shoulder at Karen every few seconds.

"I need somebody to come to Buchanan and Market," Karen told the 911 operator who answered. "She is running. I need the police."

"What's the problem, ma'am?"

"This woman has been taking my identity. For the last five months. It has been a living hell."

❖ ❖ ❖

There had been an odd voicemail from Karen's bank waiting when she returned home to San Francisco in November 2006 from a family reunion in Michigan. Karen called back, and the service rep asked if she'd made any large withdrawals, mentioning one in the amount of $600. Karen assumed it was a bank error and asked the rep to verify the debit card number.

"That's not my card," she said.

The bank representative

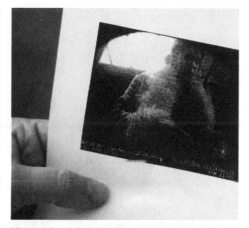

Karen Lodrick holds the printout of the alleged suspect, shown here using an ATM to withdraw funds from Karen's account.

insisted—mistakenly, as Karen later learned—that someone had called from Karen's phone to order the new debit card. After much back-and-forth, Karen convinced the rep that it wasn't hers, and he canceled it. What he failed to mention was that a second new debit card had been issued on her account. And it was still open.

Concerned after the bank rep told her the order came from her home phone, Karen asked her neighbors if they'd heard about any break-ins. They hadn't. But several people in her building mentioned that they'd seen mailboxes hanging

Maria Nelson had six prior criminal convictions.

open. A thief had apparently broken into the mail and stolen at least four envelopes: two with debit cards and two that provided the debit card PINs.

As far as Karen knew, the thief had stolen $600. Bad enough, but not life-altering. It wasn't until she got to the bank, and a representative turned the computer screen around for her to see, that she understood what had occurred. The screen showed dozens of withdrawals, just over the past few days. About $10,000 was gone. Karen's balance was zero. Her overdraft protection plan had automatically deducted

another $1,200 from savings to cover the shortfall after the thief had cleaned out the checking account.

Karen filed a police report, closed her now-empty account and submitted a claim. With no money to cover checks, she couldn't pay her bills, her rent. She couldn't even buy groceries. Late fees were compounded by black marks on her credit report. And that was just the beginning.

At five foot two and 110 pounds, Karen Lodrick was tiny compared with the nearly six-foot-tall woman carrying the brown suede coat. Block after block in downtown San Francisco, Karen chased the woman, keeping the 911 operator on the phone to let her know exactly where they were.

She lost sight of the woman after she turned a corner. But as Karen looked through the French doors of a stately old apartment building, there she was again. One glance at Karen and the woman took off down the hill toward Market Street, a main thoroughfare with multiple lanes in either direction.

Traffic whizzed by. Locals

strolled the tree-lined sidewalks and walked in and out of funky coffeehouses. Some, toting bags of bottles and aluminum cans, meandered toward the recycling center. People of every description moved along Market Street.

But Karen didn't see any police officers.

As the identity thief passed an abandoned shopping cart, Karen saw her arm swing out. She tossed something inside. Karen raced to the cart. "I got what she dropped," she told the 911 operator. "It's a wallet. A Prada wallet." Karen wanted to look inside, but she had no time.

The thief then ran into a busy intersection against the light and flagged down a taxi. Karen panicked. "She is not going to get away," she cried to the operator. "I am not going to let her escape." She caught the taxi before the driver pulled out.

"Don't let her go!" she implored. "She's an identity thief." The driver lifted his hands off the wheel and held them up. Her escape thwarted, the woman got out and confronted Karen.

"Why are you chasing me?"

For an instant, Karen felt doubt. What if this wasn't the thief? She tried to convince the woman to wait for the police. But she took off down Market Street again, toward Octavia, where the freeway spilled out its traffic. Karen kept after her.

A vintage orange streetcar pulled up to the bus stop, and the woman jumped aboard, Karen right behind. Adrenaline pumping, she was totally focused on the thief.

"Please don't drive away," Karen told the driver. The thief quickly ducked off again. "Why don't you just wait and you can talk to the police?" Karen called.

To Karen's surprise, the woman answered, saying she was on probation and would be arrested. Karen now had no doubt she'd found the right person.

It drove Karen crazy that it took about two weeks for the bank's credit card division to process the problem and recredit money to her account. She felt hopeful when the bank called to tell her it had a surveillance video of the thief. On it Karen saw a big, dark-haired woman in a suede coat and designer sunglasses at an ATM. Karen signed an affidavit that she didn't know the woman and got a printout of her image, and that was it.

Meanwhile, the thief reached deeper into Karen's life. She used her Social Security number and other information to obtain a counterfeit driver's license, showing Karen's license number but the thief's picture. With the license and the Social Security number, she reopened accounts that Karen had closed years before.

One day, the Dell computer company called Karen to confirm that it was all right to send "her" $7,000 order to an address different from the one on her account.

"Close that account and don't deliver those computers," she told Dell's rep, explaining that someone had stolen her identity. She asked for the address the thief had wanted the equipment sent to. Dell refused to give her the address, saying she'd have to put the request in writing.

Karen placed fraud alerts with the credit reporting agencies. But that didn't stop the thief from opening more accounts in Karen's name. Again and again, she asked the bank to put an alert on her account, but when she checked, it wasn't

Spotted at Starbucks

Thief tosses wallet

Cops make arrest

MARKET ST.

DUBOCE AVE.

GUERRERO ST.

OCTAVIA BLVD.

GOUGH ST.

Karen stops taxi

Thief attempts escape at bus stop

there. The thief got into her new bank account, and the cycle began again. She was at her wit's end.

To add to her frustration, the bank claimed Karen had failed to come in to view the surveillance video. It didn't matter that she'd signed an affidavit. The bank couldn't find it and cut off access to her funds. She viewed the video again and signed another affidavit. The bank lost that one too. She signed another.

Now, with a phony driver's license, the thief was stalking her third checking account.

For half an hour, up and down the streets, around corners and into alleyways, Karen Lodrick, frightened but determined, pursued the woman with the suede coat. Karen lost her twice when she slipped into buildings to hide. And then she lost her a third time at an indoor parking lot. "It's over," she told the 911 operator. Exasperated and exhausted, Karen zipped open the Prada wallet.

Two of her bank statements were tucked into one side of the large wallet. On the other were the two debit cards used to clean out her account in November. She also found one of her own paychecks. But what chilled her most were tiny "cue cards" with her name, Social Security number, driver's license number and address.

The 911 operator assured her that an officer would be there soon. When the cop arrived a few minutes later, Karen told him what had occurred, feeling little hope that he'd find the woman now.

But only moments later, the officer found her—crouched between a car and the building, smoking a cigarette.

"Idiot! You should have kept running," Karen told her.

The arresting officer said the identity thief, Maria Nelson, had at least 60 prior arrests, was indeed on probation, and was wanted in another jurisdiction for similar crimes. When Nelson came before a judge 44 days later, however, thanks to a plea deal with the prosecutor, she was sentenced to only time served plus probation.

Meanwhile, Karen keeps getting billed for phone service and items at a department store that she didn't buy.

My Mother Barked like a Seal

The quintessentially embarrassing mom got better with age—the daughter's age, that is.

———

BY **JEANMARIE COOGAN**
FROM **LADIES' HOME JOURNAL**

Originally published in May 1994

My mother was a great handicap to me when I was little. She was different. I learned this very early, when I first began going to other children's houses. There, when the mother opened the door, she said something sensible, like "Wipe your feet" or "You're not bringing that junk in here."

At our house, however, when you rang the bell, the letter slot would open, and a little high voice would pipe out, "I'm the chief troll here. Is that you, Billy Goat Gruff?"

Or a syrupy falsetto would sing the first few lines of "Barnacle Bill the Sailor": "Who's that knocking at my door?"

Other times the door would open just a slit and my mother, crouched down to our eye level, would say, "I'm the new little girl here. Wait a minute, I'll call my mother." Then the door would close for a second and reopen, and there would be my mother—regular size. "Oh, hello, girls," she'd say. "I didn't know you were there."

In that awful first moment when my new friend would turn to me with a "what kind of place is this" look, I knew how it felt to open a closet and have the family skeleton sprawl all over you. "Mo-*ther*," I would bawl, but my mother would never admit to being the little girl who had opened the door. "You girls are kidding me," she'd say. We'd wind up protesting that a little girl had opened the door, when what we really meant was that no little girl had opened the door.

It was all very confusing. And different. That was the hard part. She was so different from other mothers.

Like the seal in the basement. When we were outside while my mother was washing or ironing in the basement, we would often hear a cheerful barking coming from down there. Mother's explanation was that it was our seal. Every Friday, she made a great show of unwrapping the fish (which eventually wound up on the dinner table) for the seal. Though kids made countless dashes to the basement to catch the creature, he had always "just gone for a ride in the bakery truck" or "was taking his swimming lesson at the Y."

This seal was smart and would answer questions by barking once for "yes" and twice for "no." His reputation soon spread. Children came from blocks around to ask questions of the seal at our basement window, and the seal was always good for a few barks.

I was mortified to be pointed out as the girl with the seal, but my mother was equal to the occasion. Often when a crowd of little boys huddled at our window, waiting for a bark, my mother would open the door and call out gaily, "Hello, little girls."

My mother was no different with grownups. She often greeted an acquaintance by poking a finger in his back and growling, "Stick 'em up." The fact that adults liked my mother was no comfort to me. It was easy for them. She wasn't their mother.

Furthermore, they didn't have to put up with the "Interested Observer." My mother often carried on conversations about us with this invisible person.

"Would you look at the kitchen floor," my mother would say.

"Mud all over it and you just finished scrubbing it," the Interested Observer would say with sympathy. "Didn't you tell them to use the basement door?"

"Twice!"

"Don't they care how hard you work?" the I. O. wanted to know.

"I guess they're just forgetful."

"Well, if they'll get the clean rags under the sink and wipe it up, it'll help them to remember in the future," the I. O. would advise.

Immediately, we'd get the rags and go to work.

Luckily my mother improved with age. Not hers—mine. I was about ten the first time I ever realized that having a "different" mother could be a good thing.

The playground at the end of our street had a cluster of formidably high trees. To be caught climbing them brought out every mother for blocks, shrieking "Come down! You'll break your neck!"

One day, when a bunch of us were dizzily swaying in the top branches, my mother passed and caught sight of us silhouetted against the sky. We froze, but her face as she looked up was dazzling. "I didn't know you could climb so high," she shouted. "That's terrific! Don't fall!" And off she went. We watched in silence until she was out of sight. Then one boy spoke for us all. "Wow," he said softly. "Wow."

From that day on, I began to notice how my classmates stopped at our house before going home; how club meetings were always held in our kitchen; how friends, silent in their own homes, laughed and joked with my mother.

Later, my friends and I came to rely on my mother's lighthearted good humor as a support against adolescent crises. And when I began dating, it was wonderful to have a mother whom boys immediately adopted and a home where teenagers' craziness was not just tolerated, but enjoyed.

Everyone who knew my mother liked her. Many people loved her. All have said kind things about her. But I think the one who best described my mother was that boy, high in the tree, long ago.

"Wow," he said softly.

And I echo, "Wow."

50 Seconds from Death

Unconscious and plummeting to earth,
the novice skydiver appeared to be doomed.

—

BY **ROBERT KIENER**

Originally published in June 2017

hristopher Jones is packed tightly into a Cessna 182 with a dozen or so other trainee skydivers as they fly over the Australian countryside just south of his hometown of Perth. It's shortly after 4 p.m., and this will be Jones's fifth jump in his accelerated free-fall training program and his first time jumping solo, without being tethered to an instructor.

As the plane climbs through the clear, crisp November sky, Jones, 22, goes over today's procedure in his mind. His heart is racing, but he's confident that he's ready for his first solo jump. Stay calm, he tells himself as he sits in the back of the plane, mentally ticking off the maneuvers he has to make.

Just after the plane reaches 12,000 feet, a green light begins flashing on the wall in front of him, a signal that the pilot has given his OK for the jump to proceed. Though Jones will be managing his parachute by himself, he will not be alone. Veteran parachutist Sheldon McFarlane, who has 25 years and some 10,000 jumps under his belt, will be right behind. McFarlane slides open the plane's side door and motions for Jones to take up the ready position near the door.

Although he is protected by a helmet, goggles, his jumpsuit, and two parachutes (a main and a reserve), Jones winces as he feels the cold air rush into the plane. The whipping wind is so noisy that he can hear nothing but his own heartbeat. He is nervous but focused on McFarlane, who will guide him through a prescribed set of maneuvers using hand signals and radio commands via headsets they both wear. McFarlane will also film the jump so that Jones can watch it later.

As Jones clambers into position, holding on tightly to a rail above the open door to brace himself, he begins the pre-jump cadence he has learned: "Check in," he says, with a thumbs-up to McFarlane, indicating that he's ready to jump.

"OK," answers McFarlane, with a return thumbs-up.

Fighting the strong winds, Jones looks down at the green-and-brown checkerboard pattern of the countryside. In the distance, he sees the bright blue of the Indian Ocean.

"Sky!" he shouts, indicating that

he knows in which direction to jump and has gotten his balance. McFarlane gives him another thumbs-up.

Today's solo skydiving jump is the culmination of a lifelong dream. Jones fell in love with flying after going out in his uncle's small plane. He loved it so much, he'd planned to become a pilot when he grew up. But his hopes were dashed when he was diagnosed with epilepsy at age 12. Doctors told him that his condition would prevent him from ever getting a pilot's license.

Years later, after skydiving in tandem with an instructor in Europe, he fell in love with the sport. Free-falling through the sky was exhilarating, almost like flying. He was hooked. He told his parents, "If I can't fly a plane, I'll jump out of one instead."

As a rule, people with epilepsy aren't allowed to skydive alone. But Jones hadn't had a seizure in more than six years, so his doctor gave him a letter stating that he was fit to sign up for lessons. The recent university graduate sailed through the classes at the WA Skydiving

Academy in Jandakot, a suburb of Perth.

"A star pupil," one of the instructors, Donna Cook, called Jones. Other staffers agreed. Jones's tandem jumps, for which he was tethered to an instructor, had gone off without a hitch. He was ready to solo.

So today, at last, he's about to step out of an airplane by himself. All told, the jump should take about two minutes, from leaving the shelter of the plane to landing on the ground some 12,000 feet, or two miles, below. This is how it went:

12,000 FEET. As Jones prepares to jump, he missteps and nearly slips out of the Cessna. That's a bit messy, thinks McFarlane, though this kind of stumble is not unusual for first timers. But Jones catches his balance and turns his back to the bright sky, grabs onto the hanging bars on either side of the door, and arches his back into the jump position. He shouts to McFarlane, "Up! Down! Hard arch!"— skydiving lingo for "Ready, set, go!"—and leaps out of the plane.

Jumping just seconds behind Jones, McFarlane reaches him, relieved to see that Jones has recovered from his clumsy exit and is free-falling in the perfect "box man" position: belly to the ground, his body arched upward with arms and legs spread for stability and control. Both skydivers

Jones is unconscious, unable to open his parachute, and falling fast.

are free-falling and will continue to plunge without opening their chutes until they reach 5,000 feet, in less than a minute. (It typically takes ten seconds to free-fall the first 1,000 feet, then 5½ seconds per 1,000 feet after that; skydivers plunge at a speed of approximately 120 miles per hour.)

McFarlane points to the altimeter on his wrist. Jones follows his cue to check his own. So far, so good,

thinks McFarlane. He flashes a thumbs-up.

9,000 FEET. As both jumpers free-fall, McFarlane signals Jones to begin an aerial left-hand turn. The jumper starts to make the turn, but suddenly stops and is buffeted to the right. Not good, McFarlane thinks. Jones continues to drift right as McFarlane wonders, What the heck are you doing?

8,000 FEET. Jones fails to recover from his missed left turn and also is not following McFarlane's other commands. The veteran instructor quickly realizes something is wrong.

Suddenly Jones's knees come up into his chest, and he flips over like a turtle onto his back. His arms flail as he falls through the sky. He's losing it, thinks McFarlane.

Come on, Christopher, he says to himself. Right yourself!

7,000 FEET. Jones continues to fall, spinning helplessly on his back. McFarlane has seen other first timers suffer from sensory overload and become incapacitated. He thinks this may be what Jones is experiencing. However, that usually occurs on one of a student's first tandem jumps, and Jones completed his without a problem. But this is a solo jump, and, of course, the stakes are higher: Jones's life is on the line.

"Come on, Christopher!" McFarlane shouts out loud this time. Unaware that his student has epilepsy, he doesn't know that Jones is suffering a seizure and has blacked out. He is unconscious, unable to open his parachute, and falling as fast as a speeding race car to the ground below.

6,000 FEET. Jones continues to plummet, spinning and spiraling out of control, now with his head pointed downward. McFarlane knows he has to act fast. Although Jones, like every WA Skydiving student, is fitted with an Automatic Activation Device (AAD) that will automatically open his main parachute at 2,000 feet above the drop zone, McFarlane realizes that would give the jumper little time to regain control. He could easily fly into a tree, river, or power line or, worse, break his neck in an uncontrolled landing. He also knows AADs can fail.

5,000 FEET. Beep, beep, beep.

McFarlane's preset audible altimeter begins beeping in his ear, signaling that it's time to deploy his main chute for a safe landing. He ignores the sound as he makes the decision to free-fall down to Jones, grab him, and open his parachute for him. McFarlane lifts his chin and swoops his arms back, speeding toward his student like a hawk pursuing its prey. It's a risky maneuver. He has to avoid becoming entangled if Jones's chute opens in the wrong direction. In that worst-case scenario, both men could fall to their deaths.

McFarlane soon realizes that he's coming in too fast. Afraid that he will crash into Jones or that Jones might suddenly pull the rip cord and entangle both of them, he aborts the effort. Jones is still on his back, unconscious, and falling uncontrollably.

4,500 FEET. BEEP, BEEP, BEEP. McFarlane's altimeter alarm is beeping even louder as he pulls on both toggles to slow his chute, a step known as flaring, to buy him a few more seconds as he descends. But he's running out of time to

12,000 feet: The skydivers exit the plane.

8,000 feet: Jones is out of position. No one realizes that he is having a seizure.

deploy his own parachute. Even highly skilled skydivers don't open their chutes any lower than 2,000 feet, and McFarlane will reach that height in just 14 seconds.

Still, he decides to dive again to try to reach Jones. This time he swoops like Superman and manages to grab Jones's harness and roll his body sideways. It's crucial to get him in the proper position before pulling the rip cord, or his chute could entangle them both. Holding tightly to the harness with his right hand, McFarlane uses his left to grab Jones's chute handle and then pulls it hard. The main parachute billows out and up, swinging Jones around so that he is sitting upright in the harness.

Thank God! thinks McFarlane as

the force of air filling the chute sends Jones upward into the sky. But Jones is still unconscious, still unaware that he is falling to the earth, though more slowly now, beneath his billowing yellow canopy. A crash landing could easily kill him.

4,000 FEET. McFarlane opens his own chute, then executes a series of midair turns to speed up his descent.

During any jump, an instructor is stationed on the ground to watch the action and radio commands to the jumpers.

Today's drop zone safety officer, Donna Cook, has been radioing Jones but getting no response. When his chute opens, she is relieved. "Way to go!" she tells him.

But Cook's relief quickly turns

8,000 to 4,500 feet: Jones free-falls uncontrollably.

4,500 feet: McFarlane reaches Jones and pulls his parachute's release cord.

to concern as she again gets no response and sees Jones drifting far off course. She radios him again: "Keep yourself upwind of the target. Turn right." As Jones continues to move away from the drop zone, Cook realizes something is seriously wrong.

3,500 FEET. Cook watches Jones fly farther off course. Maybe he has blacked out or become incoherent. Or perhaps his radio has failed. Whatever the problem is, Jones isn't following any of her commands. But she continues to guide him on the radio, praying that he can somehow hear her: "Turn right, Chris! Turn right!"

3,000 FEET. Slumped over in his parachute, Jones finally regains consciousness. He feels as though

he is waking from a deep sleep. But as he comes to, he sees the ground beneath him coming closer and closer. He lifts his head and is amazed to discover that he is drifting down to earth under an opened parachute canopy.

How the ... ? he wonders. He realizes he has blacked out, and his skydiving training instantly kicks in. He checks his altimeter, which reads 3,000 feet. The last time he remembers checking it was at 9,000 feet, following McFarlane's instructions. He doesn't know how long he has been out, but he knows he has to act fast.

Check the canopy, he tells himself. He looks up to see that it is open and none of his lines are twisted.

Back on the ground, instructor Sheldon McFarlane (left) and his grateful student Christopher Jones.

Orient yourself, he tells himself next, and he looks for the drop zone, a white fabric arrow far off to the west. Before he can run through the other landing procedures, he hears the crackle of the one-way radio in his helmet.

"Chris! Chris!" he hears Cook say. "Fly toward the ocean. To your right!" He sees that he is far off course and tugs hard on his steering handle.

2,000 FEET. As the wind helps carry him, Jones pulls on the parachute toggle to direct him closer to the drop zone, which he can now see beneath him. Now he's back on course. Seeing Jones finally

He doesn't know how long he has been out, but he knows he has to act fast.

responding to her commands, Cook is ecstatic. "Great!" she radios him. "You're doing great!

"Turn your back to the ocean," she says. Jones follows her directives.

"That's it! You're doing it!" Cook tells him. Afraid of losing contact with him again, she keeps radioing commands.

1,000 FEET. McFarlane, who has already landed, shouts to Cook, "This was one of the worst stage-five jumps I've ever seen!" He still has no idea that Jones had a seizure. (Although Jones and his doctor can't say for sure why he had a seizure that day, a lack of oxygen at high altitudes and stress can bring one on.)

300 FEET. Jones prepares to land close to the drop zone. As he nears the ground, he mentally runs through the steps he has learned to touch down safely. Like a veteran skydiver, he flares his chute moments before his feet hit the ground running. Perfect!

Cook keeps up her chatter. After Jones executes a faultless two-point landing and begins gathering up his chute, she is close to tears.

"You did great!" she radios to Jones.

The first thing Jones does upon landing is to go to McFarlane and hug him tightly.

"Thank you very much," he says, explaining that he suffered an epileptic seizure. "You just saved my life."

For his quick thinking and courageous actions, McFarlane was awarded the Gold Cross from the Royal Life Saving Society, Western Australia. Although Jones hasn't had a seizure since that day, he says his skydiving days are over.

To watch the video of the jump and rescue (shot from McFarlane's helmet camera), go to rd.com/skydiver.

America's 10 Funniest Jokes

In a noisy, cramped back room at Factor's Deli in Los Angeles, eight comedy legends put down their pastrami sandwiches long enough to help choose the nation's top gags.

———

BY **ANDY SIMMONS**

Originally published in June 2009

t's mayhem. Amid the clamor of pickle trays and pastrami-bearing waiters, eight old friends have gathered for their biweekly lunch. They're all talking over one another, and no one's listening. But somehow they can hear Arthur Hiller regaling Sid Caesar with a story about Billy Wilder. Gary Owens, Rocky Kalish, and Matty Simmons croon ear-wrenching, plate-shattering harmony on the old Benny Goodman standard

"Undecided." Hal Kanter and Monty Hall trade stories about working with Jimmy Stewart, both favorable and not ("Jimmy was a brigadier general during World War II, and he never let you forget it," says Kanter). Any silence is filled by a Gatling gun salvo of one-liners from John Rappaport: "Hear the one about the Israeli newspaper reporter who yelled to his editor, 'Hold the back page!'?"

These eight comedy legends, who range in age from their 60s to their 90s—and with about 422 years of

A PRIEST, A MINISTER, AND A RABBI WANT TO SEE WHO'S BEST AT HIS JOB...
8
HEINZ
TOMATO KETCHUP

comedy under their collective belt—meet every other week to kibitz, eat, and reminisce. But mostly, they're there to exercise their comedy chops by cracking wise at every opportunity.

It's this group whom *Reader's Digest* has asked to choose America's all-time best jokes. The magazine's editors have winnowed down the thousands of submissions our readers sent in. Our judges' job is to pick ten from that collection. That is, if I can get them to concentrate on the jokes.

"Excuse me, excuse me!" I yell over the din. I begin handing out sheets of paper containing the gags. "Can we start with the jokes?"

Rappaport begins: "A guy goes to his doctor's office and says, 'Give it to me straight. I know I'm sick. How long do I have?' The doctor says, 'Ten…' 'Ten what?' asks the patient. 'Years? Months?' 'Nine… Eight…'"

"That's a good joke. I vote for that one," says Hiller.

"It is a good joke, but it's not on our list," I say.

Rappaport peruses the list and offers to read the monk joke, which pits him against Hall, who also wants to read the monk joke. Instead of either reading the monk joke, they start telling their own favorite monk jokes. "Maybe we can read a joke from the list?" I suggest over the laughter.

Kalish taps a spoon against a glass of Dr. Brown's diet cream soda. "Point of order!" he shouts. That's what the guys yell when they want everyone's attention. It doesn't always work, but that's what they yell. "I'm going to read one," he says. "And remember, gentlemen, *Reader's Digest* is picking up the tab today, so you know what that means: Eat as much as you want."

Joke #1

A man, shocked by how his buddy is dressed, asks him, "How long have you been wearing that bra?" The friend replies, "Ever since my wife found it in the glove compartment."

– *Submitted by Braeden Silvermist*

They all laugh, except Kanter, who sneers, "It's so old."

"It doesn't matter if it's old or not," I say. "The point is, is it funny?"

No one's listening, because the joke genie has been let out of the bottle, and the gags (none from our list) start flying.

Simmons begins: "A grandmother is watching her grandchild playing on the beach when a huge wave comes and takes him out to sea." Caesar leans in to hear. He knows what's coming. They all do—it's their favorite joke from their stockpile of gags. "She pleads, 'Please, God, save my only grandson. I beg of you, bring him back.' With that, a big wave washes the boy back onto the beach, good as new. The grandmother looks up to heaven and says, 'He had a hat!'"

"Very funny, but I want to give you a line read," says Rappaport. "It should be 'He had a *hat*.'"

"No no no," says Kanter. "It's 'He had a hat.'"

"'He had a *hat*,'" insists Rappaport.

"Then she's too angry," Kanter counters. "She's not angry—she just wants the damn hat back."

"Who'd like to read the next joke?"

"'He had a *hat*?'" Simmons tries.

Owens finally launches into the next gag on the list, drawing it out for all its comic worth.

Joke #2

A ventriloquist is performing with his dummy on his lap. He's telling a dumb blonde joke when a young platinum-haired beauty jumps to her feet.

"What gives you the right to stereotype blondes that way?" she demands. "What does hair color have to do with my worth as a human being?"

Flustered, the ventriloquist begins to stammer out an apology.

"You keep out of this!" she yells. "I'm talking to that little jerk on your knee!"

– *Submitted by Nancy Gomes*

"Great," I say. "Who'd like to tell—"

"You know, that reminds me of a true story," says Owens. "It was in the '50s. The ventriloquist Rickie Layne and his dummy, Velvel, were onstage at the Copacabana. In the front row were some gangsters. Velvel starts insulting them. 'Hey, it looks like you slept in your clothes,' he says. 'Don't you make any money? Is that the best suit you can buy?' With each put-down, the mobsters are getting angrier and angrier. Suddenly, the owner of the nightclub, Jules Podell, a real tough guy, jumps onstage. He grabs the dummy and punches him so hard, his head rolls off. Podell then points at Velvel's head lying on the stage and says, 'One more joke like that and I'll kill you!'"

"True story," says Kalish, corroborating it between guffaws.

"Can we read another joke?" I ask.

"Anybody hear of a guy named Evil Eye Finkel?" says Kalish. In the '30s, Evil Eye's job was to go to boxing matches and fix some boxer with the evil eye in hopes of jinxing him.

The contest has now been hijacked by tales of all the Evil Eyes the guys have known. That's when I remind everyone that *Reader's Digest* will pick up the lunch tab only if they actually judge the gags.

The men swallow their pickles, pick up their pens, and get serious, often bickering over votes cast.

"You actually like that one?" Kanter asks Simmons after the latter voices approval of the bra joke. Simmons, in turn, points out that Kanter had little company when he voted for an ill-fated gassy-granny joke.

Here, now, the rest of the ten best jokes in America (in no particular order), as decided by our judges:

Joke #3

In surgery for a heart attack, a middle-aged woman has a vision of God by her bedside. "Will I die?" she asks.

God says, "No. You have 30 more years to live."

With 30 years to look forward to, she decides to make the best of it. So since she's already in the hospital, she gets breast implants, liposuction, a tummy tuck, hair transplants, and collagen injections in her lips. She looks great!

The day she's discharged, she exits the hospital with a swagger, crosses the street, and is immediately hit by an ambulance and killed.

Up in heaven, she sees God. "You said I had 30 more years to live," she complains.

"That's true," says God.

"So what happened?"

God shrugs. "I didn't recognize you."

– *Submitted by Hank Chawansky*

Joke #4

Every ten years, the monks in the monastery are allowed to break their vow of silence to speak two words. Ten years go by and it's one monk's first chance. He thinks for a second before saying, "Food bad."

Ten years later, he says, "Bed hard."

It's the big day, a decade later. He gives the head monk a long stare and says, "I quit."

"I'm not surprised," the head monk says. "You've been complaining ever since you got here."

– *Submitted by Alan Lynch*

Joke #5

A guy spots a sign outside a house that reads "Talking Dog for Sale."

Intrigued, he walks in.

"So what have you done with your life?" he asks the dog.

"I've led a very full life," says the dog. "I lived in the Alps and rescued avalanche victims. Then I served my country in Iraq. And now I spend my days reading to the residents of a retirement home."

The guy is flabbergasted. He asks the dog's owner, "Why on earth would you want to get rid of an incredible dog like that?"

The owner says, "Because he's a liar! He never did any of that!"

– *Submitted by Harry Nelson*

Joke #6

Two hunters are out in the woods when one of them collapses. He's not breathing and his eyes are glazed. The other guy whips out his cell phone and calls 911.

"I think my friend is dead!" he yells. "What can I do?"

The operator says, "Calm down. First, let's make sure he's dead."

There's a silence, then a shot. Back on the phone, the guy says, "OK, now what?"

– *Submitted by Gerald Doka*

Joke #7

A turtle is crossing the road when he's mugged by two snails. When the police show up, they ask him what happened. The shaken turtle replies, "I don't know. It all happened so fast."

– Submitted by Debby Carter

Joke #8

A man is walking in a graveyard when he hears the Third Symphony played backward. When it's over, the Second Symphony starts playing, also backward, and then the First. "What's going on?" he asks a cemetery worker.

"It's Beethoven," says the worker. "He's decomposing."

– Submitted by Jeremy Hone

Joke #9

A priest, a minister, and a rabbi want to see who's best at his job. So they each go into the woods, find a bear, and attempt to convert it. Later they get together. The priest begins: "When I found the bear, I read to him from the Catechism and sprinkled him with holy water. Next week is his First Communion."

"I found a bear by the stream," says the minister, "and preached God's holy word. The bear was so mesmerized that he let me baptize him."

They both look down at the rabbi, who is lying on a gurney in a body cast. "Looking back," he says, "maybe I shouldn't have started with the circumcision."

– Submitted by Mitchell Hauser

Joke #10

A poodle and a collie are walking together when the poodle suddenly unloads on his friend. "My life is a mess," he says. "My owner is mean, my girlfriend ran away with a schnauzer, and I'm as jittery as a cat."

"Why don't you go see a psychiatrist?" suggests the collie.

"I can't," says the poodle. "I'm not allowed on the couch."

– Submitted by L. B. Weinstein

A Dog like No Other

Santos led a charmed life, until one unlucky day in Africa.

—

BY PETER MUILENBURG

Originally published in June 1998

A waning moon had turned the muddy waters of Oyster Creek to quicksilver. Not so much as a zephyr stirred the inlet where our 42-foot ketch *Breath* lay in the delta of western Africa's mighty Gambia River near Banjul, the capital of Gambia. Days before, we'd sailed in off a thousand miles of ocean. Snug in this anchorage, we could still hear the surf thundering just beyond the low span of the Denton Bridge.

The chance to see Africa had brought our family back together for a couple of months. Our older son, Rafael, 20, had taken leave from college to join the rest of us: Diego, 13, my wife, Dorothy, and our little black dog, Santos.

Breath had been our only home since I had built the vessel on St. John in the Virgin Islands in the early 1980s. Life afloat had knit close bonds. Everyone had responsibilities—the boys were standing watch when they were six. And for the past eight years, Santos, our loving, feisty, 11-pound schipperke, was at our side.

When we went to bed that night, Santos lay on the cabin top, which he vacated only in the worst weather. He touched his nose to Dorothy's face as she bent low to nuzzle him goodnight. His ardent eyes flared briefly—he worshipped her—then he returned to his duty.

We slept easier with him aboard. It was his self-appointed mission to ensure that no one, friend or foe, approached within 100 yards of *Breath* without a warning. He'd sailed with us through the Caribbean, the Atlantic, and the Mediterranean, keeping sharp watch and good company, and bringing us luck. In eight years we'd never suffered a mishap.

But during the night of January 2, 1991, that would change.

❖ ❖ ❖

We were asleep when, just past midnight, our dock lines began to creak. At first I thought a passing boat might have sent a wake, but Santos would have barked. The creaking grew louder. The ropes groaned against the cleats that tethered our boat to another vessel.

On such a calm night there could be only one cause—current. My boat was tied stern to stream, and a glance over the side at water speeding past the hull alarmed me. The ebb had tripled its usual spring-tide rate. The cleats on the other boat looked ready to snap. If

anything gave, both vessels could spin off bound together, helpless to avoid destruction. I had to cast off.

We were in a difficult spot. Just a few boat lengths downstream, two high-tension power lines hung across the creek. About 100 feet behind them loomed Denton Bridge. If we couldn't turn in time, our

> ### Santos stood his ground. He was growling for all he was worth when sparks landed in his fur.

metal mainmast might hit the wires. If the boat hit the bridge, both masts would be pinned by the roadway while the hull was sucked under.

I called everyone up on deck. We cast off the lines and hung briefly to a stern anchor, but we had to let go as *Breath* was swung violently back and forth by the current's force. I gunned the engine and had almost turned the boat around when I realized that, dragged toward the bridge by the current, we were going to hit the power line. Dorothy clutched a quivering Santos, and we all held our breath.

We just tipped the wire. There was a meteor shower of sparks and we were through, but the second wire was coming up fast. I flung the wheel over hard, but we struck the wire anyway—a long, scraping skid, the top six inches of our mast pinned against the power line.

Electricity exploded down the rigging, and incandescence lit the sky. Flames leaped up inside the cabin; fuses shot from their sockets; smoke billowed out the hatches.

Then the fireworks stopped. The cable had rolled over the mast, but we were trapped between the second wire and the bridge. There was nowhere to go but back out—through the wire. Santos wriggled out of Dorothy's arms and dashed up to the foredeck to be in on the action.

The wheel hard over, we braced for impact. The mast top hit the cable, sending down a torrent of red sparks. Santos, eyes fixed ahead, stood his ground. He was growling for all he was worth when sparks landed in his fur. Uttering a high-pitched scream, he sprinted down the side deck, cinders glowing in his coat, and plunged into the water. When he surfaced, Santos was swimming for the boat, his eyes fastened on Dorothy. But the current swept him under Denton Bridge and out of sight.

An instant later a blast like a small thunderbolt hit the mainstay. My son Raffy was flipped backward off the foredeck and into the water.

Then we were through. Diego seized a fire extinguisher and attacked the flames as I steered toward a trawler tied to a concrete slab on the muddy bank. Raffy, a college swimmer, got to the bank.

Against all odds we were safe—except for Santos. Raffy called along both shores, but there was no sign of him. We spent the rest of the night tied to the trawler. As I tried to sleep, I kept thinking of Santos. I felt a helpless sorrow over his fate.

❖ ❖ ❖

The next day Dorothy walked for miles down the beach, talking to beach attendants, tourists, vendors at every hotel. Nobody had seen our little black dog.

·She offered a reward over the ship's radio, notified the police, and posted signs. It was touching, but it seemed futile. Just beyond the bridge were broad flats of sand pounded by row after row of massive breakers. The thought of Santos funneled helplessly into the surf made me wince.

Days later we'd repaired *Breath*, but Santos hadn't turned up. "Honey," I told Dorothy, "we've got to get on with our life—do the river, cross the Atlantic, get back to work."

"But what if he survived?" she asked. "What if he finds his way back, and we're gone?"

"It's hard to believe he survived that surf," I said flatly, "and then swam till dawn."

She searched my face, looking for a reprieve from reality. Then her eyes flooded and her voice broke. "I just didn't want to abandon him."

With heavy hearts the next morning, we hauled the anchor for our trip upriver.

❖ ❖ ❖

Our loss really hit home 50 miles upstream where we anchored. A strange face suddenly peered in the porthole and inquired if we wanted to buy a fish. The fisherman had paddled up silently alongside us. When Santos was alive, that could never have happened. Now we sorely missed the zealous barking we'd so often tried to hush.

Not a day went by without one of us bringing up another Santos story. He might have been small, but he was absolutely fearless. Santos had a classic Napoleon complex. He had to have respect, and he got it by making bigger animals run from him. He was all bluff. But with a histrionically vicious growl and a headlong charge, he had put to flight Rottweilers, herds of goats, troops of wild donkeys, and even a meter reader.

Once, on the island of St. Lucia, an elephant brought over by a rich estate owner emerged from the woods into a clearing where Santos was merrily scattering a flock of chickens. Our dog reacted in character: He charged. The elephant panicked, flaring its ears, splitting the air with its trumpet call, and smacking the ground with its trunk as Santos dodged and darted underfoot.

We'd never see another like him, I thought as I steered upriver.

Soon after, I woke one night to an empty bed. I found Dorothy sitting in the moonlight. From the

Santos had put to flight Rottweilers, herds of goats, troops of wild donkeys, and even a meter reader.

way her eyes glistened, I could tell she'd been thinking of Santos. I sat down and put an arm around her. After a while she spoke. "You know what I miss most? His shaggy mane filling the porthole. He liked to watch me cook. Now every time a shadow falls over that port, it reminds me of the love in those bright black eyes."

We watched the moon slip below the treetops; then, our hearts filled with grief, we went back to bed.

Two weeks passed as we made our way 150 miles up the Gambia River. One afternoon Dorothy and I were reinforcing the deck awning when I saw a catamaran with a man on board inspecting us with binoculars.

"Are you the Americans who lost the dog?" he called.

"Yes," I said cautiously.

"I don't know if it is yours, but the police at Denton Bridge have a small black dog that was found on the beach."

Everyone tumbled up on deck shouting, "Oh, my God! Yes! Yes!" But I cautioned, "Someone might have found a stray mutt and just brought it in, hoping for the reward. Don't get your hopes too high."

❖ ❖ ❖

Dorothy and I took a series of bush taxis and old buses back to Banjul the next morning. With hope and trepidation we caught a taxi to Denton Bridge to see if Santos had truly survived.

"You've come for your dog!"

the police officer on duty greeted us. He turned and called to a boy, "Go bring the dog." Dorothy and I waited on tenterhooks.

There, led on a ratty piece of string, was Santos. He walked with a limp, his head down. But when Dorothy called "Santos," his head shot up, his ears snapped forward, his whole body trembled as that

"Are you the Americans who lost the dog?" he called. "The police have a small black dog that was found on the beach."

—

beloved voice registered. He leapt into her arms and covered her face with licks. Dorothy hugged him, her eyes filled with tears.

The police officer told us that the morning after we'd hit the power lines, a Swedish tourist was walking the beach and found Santos—about six miles from Oyster Creek. The

Swede smuggled the wet, hungry animal into his hotel room and fed him. When the Swede had to fly home, he gave Santos to the police.

We noticed Santos's muzzle seemed whiter, and when we patted him on his right flank, he sometimes yelped in pain. We wondered what he'd experienced as he was swept into the surf and carried along the coast. We marveled at his fortitude and his luck. But most of all, we were grateful to have him back.

Next morning we made our way back upriver. We arrived just after sundown and shouted for the boys.

"Do you have him?" they called. Dorothy urged the dog to bark. His unmistakable voice rang across the river, to be answered by a cheer of wild exuberance.

Later that night we toasted Santos with lemonade. No need for champagne when euphoria spiced the air we breathed. Santos was back. Our family was intact.

The Book That Changed My Life

Celebrated writer Rick Bragg reflects on the enduring message of courage and kindness in the classic novel To Kill a Mockingbird.

BY **RICK BRAGG**

Originally published in May 2010

y first copy was dog-eared and sunbaked, the pages brittle and brown, as if the paperback had rested in the back window of an old Pontiac instead of on a library shelf. Some kind of pestilence— water bugs, I believe—had gotten to it before I did, and it was hard to tell, as I turned to that first page, which of us would get more from it. I was an ignorant teenage schoolboy and read it because a teacher told me to, prodded as if by pitchfork

down the hot, dull streets of a town called Maycomb in the desolate 1930s, and pressed into the company of a boy named Jem, a mouthy girl named Scout, and an odd little chucklehead named Dill whom, I am fairly sure, I would have beaten up and relieved of his milk money. I would have preferred the Hardy Boys, preferred to gallop alongside the Riders of the Purple Sage, but I was afraid of teachers then, and so I read. "Maycomb was an old town, but it was a tired old town… Somehow, it was hotter then… There was no hurry, for there was nowhere to go…" I missed a few words, bug-eaten or besmirched, but I read on, to a shot-down rabid dog, and a neighbor, Boo Radley, in hiding, and a young black man named Tom Robinson who is wrongly accused of raping a young white woman. And, of course, there is Atticus Finch, the lawyer who offers reason, and kindness, and some thin hope. He tries to save Robinson, but, as the pages turned, I saw that it would take more than one good Alabama man to make this sorry world all right.

To Kill a Mockingbird was published in 1960, but it was the middle 1970s before it reached Roy Webb Road in Calhoun County, Alabama, and me. I began reading Harper Lee's novel in the skimpy shade of a pine outside my grandmother's house, fat beagles pressing against me, begging for attention, ignored. At dark, I kept reading, first on the couch, a bologna sandwich in one hand, then in my bed, by the light of a 60-watt bulb hanging from the ceiling on an orange drop cord.

When my mother came in from her job as a maid and unplugged my chandelier, I replayed the story in my head until it was crowded out by dreams. I woke the next morning smelling biscuits, and reached for the book again.

I remember this, some 35 years later, the same way I remember where I was when Elvis died or the first time I saw Paul "Bear" Bryant walk a sideline on a Saturday in fall. Some things are just important. And as the pages fluttered by, the ragged 50-cent paperback shook my conscience, broke my heart, and took me into its landscape forever. I believed, at the time, I was the only person in the whole world who felt like that.

It was my first grown-up book, a story not pat or perfect, about children coming of age in a time when reality falls wretchedly short of ideals. Even as a lynch mob threatens Tom Robinson, Atticus Finch refuses to condemn the cruel conventions of his community and is willing to absorb the mob's hatred himself, stoic, till a villain named Robert E. Lee Ewell strikes at his own children. Atticus is not the book's only hero. Another steps from the closet, the shadows.

Many people see *To Kill a Mockingbird* as a civil rights novel, but it transcends that issue. It is a novel about right and wrong, about kindness and meanness. As a child

> **As so much poison spewed from so many courthouses, political platforms, and Klan picnics, it was a kind of poultice that should have drawn out that meanness.**

in rural Alabama in the 1960s, I had seen such stories burn past me, somehow unreal and distant, as buses were overturned, as civil rights workers were beaten or shot from speeding cars. I did not truly feel those hatreds, or understand them, until I read that book.

Now that I know this novel's place in history, I wonder: How many readers have gone with me into those pages and returned in some way different, in some way changed?

I am not talking about book sales, although Lee's Pulitzer Prize–winning novel is one of the most popular books of all time. It has sold an estimated 40 million copies, is a staple of school curricula, and has been translated into some 40 languages. It also made a glorious transition to screen in 1962 in the Academy Award–winning adaptation written by the great Horton Foote and starring Gregory Peck. Lee has been covered up to her chin in awards and citations and presented with every trophy short of a gold monkey.

But her novel's finest, most profound legacy is quieter, almost private—something between Lee and one reader at a time.

❖　❖　❖

You get to know readers, a little bit, if you write books for a living. You get to see the depth to which they love a book. *To Kill a Mockingbird* is not just the kind of book people hold in their hearts; it's the kind people hold to their hearts, wrapping their arms around it and pressing it against their breasts as if they could feel a heartbeat in its paper. I have seen people do that to copies signed and unsigned.

We writers should all be so lucky, to write a book people actually hug.

Don Brown, a retired newspaper editor who works across the hall from me at the University of Alabama, told me he has picked up countless books in his life, but this one he never really put down.

"I don't think you do," said Brown, now 73, who has a signed copy. "And I am so proud of it."

It is not a complicated book, to him.

"It is a sermon," he said, "on courage as much as anything else."

In the collected essays *Critical Insights: To Kill a Mockingbird*, author and English professor Edythe M. McGovern notes that a 1991 survey by the Book-of-the-Month Club and the Library of Congress Center for the Book found the novel was "most often cited as making a difference in people's lives, second only to the Bible."

For Southerners, especially those who were alive in the segregated South, it was a reminder of our finer nature. As so much poison spewed from so many courthouses,

> *I did not need Harper Lee to tell me it was wrong to treat people badly because of color. What Lee did was make me think about it.*

statehouses, political platforms, and Klan picnics, it was a kind of poultice, a story set in the 1930s that should have drawn out that meanness and shamed the wrongdoers of the 1960s into doing the right thing.

It did not. But it was, I guess, the closest thing to an antidote we would have for a long, long time.

❖ ❖ ❖

We were not political, my family and me. My people swung hammers, poured steel, heaved sticks of pulpwood onto ragged trucks, and made a little liquor deep in the pine forests along the Alabama-Georgia line. The women worked hunched over the spinning frames in the mill, breathing air that was thick with cotton. Men broke down truck tires in dirt-floor garages, their sledges ringing through the trees, and broke each other's bones, now and then, over a woman, or an insult, or an open jug. They sinned and got saved, backslid, then did it all over again, jerking in the grip of the Holy Ghost as if they had grabbed hold of a naked wire. They did a little time, some of them, till their mamas bailed them out, but most of them just punched a time clock, fed their babies, and watched wrestling live from Birmingham on their black-and-white TVs. In late summer and early fall, they picked cotton in the fields beside black men and women, and if there was ever a conflict there, I was too dumb to see it. My mother worked on her knees cleaning the homes of the better-off white ladies in town and took in laundry. If anyone needed a prophet to tell us we were better than someone, better than anyone, I guess it was us.

He came to us from Barbour County, a pugnacious little man named George Wallace, who promised to protect us from the outside agitators who were coming down here to destroy our way of life.

It made no sense to me as I started school in Calhoun County in 1965. Were they going to take away our sledges? Were they going to unplug my mother's iron? Were they going to stop us from digging a ditch?

But still, we went to see him, to see the show. I remember a rally in Anniston, the county seat, remember a band playing "Dixie," and an undulating canopy of Confederate battle flags, a whole auditorium of Stars and Bars and fluttering red. The little man got everyone all worked up. The guv'ment in Washington would not force us to go to school or otherwise have unwanted close association with colored people, he promised. I did not really understand it much. It was, though, quite a show.

Not long after that, our daddy got fairly well drunk and ran off. Things got bad for a while, till the black family that lived down the road brought my mother some

"I keep coming back to it. It lives," said Jones.

———

food, including some good corn. I liked corn, so I liked them. I was six, I believe.

I did not need Harper Lee to tell me it was wrong to treat people badly because of color. I was raised right that way by my gentle mother. What Lee did was make me think about it, longer, deeper, as a man. I would not stand in the company of men who spouted meanness, or be a go-along, come-along racist for the sake of so-called good manners or peace in the family.

It is not much, maybe, to say, to claim. But there was more to me after reading that book than before.

I hear it from people my age over and over again.

Many scholars have said that *To Kill a Mockingbird* was never intended as a civil rights book and, powerful as its message was, did not register among the demagogues and night riders who tried, with terror and violence and the law itself, to hold back time. It was not widely banned by people in power, merely ignored. The violence of the 1960s, the murders of civil rights workers in Mississippi, the bombing of the 16th Street Baptist Church in Birmingham, and more, unfolded even as the book was still being lauded in literary circles.

But as those crimes smoked and then grew cold, the message in *To Kill a Mockingbird* lived on.

Doug Jones was a college student at the University of Alabama in the middle 1970s, then a law student at the Cumberland School of Law at Samford University. He remembers that he watched the movie first, then read the book.

Gregory Peck and Harper Lee on the set of *To Kill a Mockingbird*, 1962.

"It was a dose of conscience," he said, "of right versus wrong."

Some three decades later, he was the U.S. attorney and then special prosecutor who convicted the two surviving Klansmen who bombed the 16th Street Baptist Church, killing four little girls, in 1963.

They had bragged of their crime, those men, certain no one would reach so far back in time to punish them. But Atticus, even in black and white, had endured in the mind of Jones and others who worked to make their case.

"The duty of a lawyer is to seek justice," Jones said. "You do it in a professional way, even if it is not popular. I have read that book a dozen times, sometimes read just bits and pieces, but I keep coming back to it. It lives."

'Twas the Night After Christmas...

And all through the house was something of a mess.

———

BY **COREY FORD**

Originally published in January 1960

anta Claus has a lot of stockings to fill in a hurry on Christmas Eve, but on the morning of the 25th he can hang up his white beard and relax for the rest of the year. His bag is empty, and I'm left holding it.

There's that mountainous pile of gift wrappings in the center of the floor, for instance. You can't just throw them away. Oh, no. Any piece of holly paper more than three inches square must be smoothed out and folded once lengthwise and once across, and saved to use again next Christmas. Gummed stickers have to be pried off tissue paper, penciled messages erased from gift tags, red satin bows carefully untied, and the ribbon wound into loops with one end tucked inside. Little boxes are placed inside bigger boxes and carried upstairs to the attic.

Everything else is shoved into the fireplace, including one fleece-lined glove, the envelope of nuts and bolts for Junior's unassembled bicycle, and a $25 gift certificate from Uncle Herbert; and a match is touched to the excelsior, producing a blast of flame. If you hear the sudden patter of feet on the roof, it isn't Santa

Claus. It's the local fire department, arriving to combat a chimney blaze.

Christmas night is generally devoted to trying to remember which relative gave what to whom. Personally, I think there should be a law requiring each donor to state clearly on his gift (1) what it's for, (2) how much it cost, and (3) where it came from so we can take it back. Last Christmas we wound up with seven tags left over, and we're still trying to account for the following:

- A set of highball glasses with Spanish dancing girls painted on them. Aunt Agatha's card was with them, but when you hold the glasses up to the light the girls don't have any clothes on, and that doesn't sound like Aunt Agatha.
- A piece of hand-painted pottery that looks like a syrup jug, except that there's a place to screw it on the wall. It might be a soap dish, but that doesn't explain why it lights up when I plug it in.
- A little Christmas whatsit that Cousin Ellie knitted herself. We're not sure whether it goes on top of something, like a tea

caddy, or whether something goes inside it, like a hot water bottle. But I never heard of a hot water bottle with sleeves.

My solution is what I call Ford's All-Purpose Thank You Letter, which runs more or less like this: "Just a line to say how much we appreciate your nice Xmas remembrance, you couldn't have surprised us more, we haven't got one like it, it will certainly come in handy, and how did you ever guess it was something we always wanted?" To be on the safe side, I send the letter unsigned.

Then, of course, there's the Christmas night phone call. This always turns out to be from my wife's brother in California, and doesn't come in until two the next morning because all the circuits are loaded. Judging by his voice, so is my wife's brother. The mouthpiece is handed rapidly from one member of the family to another while I sit sleepily on the edge of the bed in my pajamas and try to guess who's talking. The conversation lasts for 20 minutes:

Wife's brother: Hi, there, Merry

Christmas! And now hold on. Edie wants to say Merry Christmas to you.

Edie: Merry Christmas.

Me *(trying to recall which one Edie is)*: Merry Christmas.

Wife's brother *(who seems to be master of ceremonies)*: Here's somebody else who wants to say Merry Christmas.

Somebody else: Merry Christmas.

Wife's brother: And now here's little Buddy; say Merry Christmas to Uncle Corey, Buddy. *(Thirty seconds of total silence, followed by a slap and a loud wail.)* And now, before you hang up, will you put Sis back on for a minute because some other folks just dropped in to say Merry Christmas? ...

The ensuing week is given over to the annual post Yule visits. These are made by groups of gimlet-eyed relatives, who drop in ostensibly to look at the tree but actually to see whether their own greeting card occupies a prominent place on the mantel. They always arrive unannounced, and you have to be ready at any moment, day or night, to slip on those knitted ski socks or struggle into that plaid smoking jacket when you hear the first crunch of gravel in the driveway. I've found the best plan is to wear everything to bed until the holidays are over.

Which brings up the problem of just when the holidays are over. Some people say the Christmas tree should be taken down on New Year's Day. Others claim it should remain until Twelfth Night. Still others leave it up until the following year and save themselves a lot of trouble.

My own household is divided. My wife's position is that it seems too bad to take it down after all that work. My own position, on the other hand, is bent slightly forward with my head craned to one side, owing to the fact that my easy chair has been moved to the other side of the room and the cord of the reading lamp doesn't quite reach. I can't even look at television because the colored bulbs reflect in the screen. To make matters worse, the tree lights keep burning out, and I have to get down on my hands and knees and crawl under the low

branches in order to replace them.

At last I put my foot down, squashing a couple of holly berries into the rug. "That tree is coming down tomorrow," I announce, "if I have to do all the work myself." Which is exactly what happens.

The ceremony is in sharp contrast to the happy scene of two weeks ago. Gone are the excitement and shouts of "Let us help you Daddy!" The tree decorations are removed one by one, in heavy silence broken only by a few muffled sobs. Balancing on a stepladder, I lift the gilt angel off the top spindle. Amid the accusing glances of the entire family, I shoulder the denuded evergreen, leaving a trail of tinsel and fallen needles as I carry it through the house and stick it in a snowdrift in the front yard. There it leans all winter at a dejected angle, a sad reminder that Christmas is over.

Or is it? Promptly on January 2 the bills will start arriving in the mail, and by the time I get them all paid, it will be Christmas again.

"I Never Forgot You"

After more than six decades, a doomed teenage romance gets a second chance.

BY **MARINA LOPES**

FROM **THE WASHINGTON POST MAGAZINE**

Originally published in 2020 in Reader's Digest International Edition

n a sunny Saturday in April 2017, the phone rang in my grandmother's house in São Carlos, Brazil. "I've been looking for you for decades," the man on the line whispered in Italian. "You were my first love."

It had been more than six decades since my grandmother had heard the voice of Aldo Sportelli, now 83.

She pictured his youthful face and wondered what he looked like now. Aldo's voice trembled as he recalled the last time he saw her in southern Italy. He had spent years tracking her down.

For 10 minutes they caught each other up on how their lives had unfolded—both married for half a century, my grandmother widowed, Aldo's wife now in the last stages of Alzheimer's, kids, grandkids, careers.

"You just don't think this type of thing will ever happen to you," my grandmother told me.

❖ ❖ ❖

In 1951, when my grandmother, Marilena, was 14, she set off on a yearlong trip to Italy with her grandparents. Her grandfather, Antonio Lerario, was the son of an illiterate fisherman who, in 1885 at the age of 14, had left Italy for Brazil as a stowaway. He joined thousands of Italian immigrants in São Paulo, where he sold bags of rice on the street. He eventually saved enough money to open his own warehouse and went on to create a multimillion-dollar cereal empire.

After World War II, he decided to return to Italy and invited Marilena, his eldest granddaughter, to come along. In April 1951, the SS *Conte Biancamano*, an Italian ocean liner, departed the Brazilian port of Santos. My grandmother was the youngest passenger in first class, which included counts, members of the Brazilian aristocracy, and the archbishop of Rio de Janeiro.

After the ship docked in Genoa, Marilena and her grandparents took a train to Puglia, the heel of the boot. The war had been over for six years, but destruction lingered. The rubble, though, could not dampen the bleached beauty of Polignano a Mare, her grandfather's hometown. The village is perched on limestone cliffs on the edge of the sea. As a returning rice tycoon, Antonio would stay with his family in the Hotel Sportelli.

The hotel was three stories, with a terrace facing the sea. Underneath, scooped into a cliff, was a vast cave that held the Grotta Palazzese luxury restaurant. Visitors from around the world came to dine.

Marilena, who spent her days people-watching from the hotel terrace, was never allowed into the cave. After catching businessmen ogling her from the restaurant, her grandmother started shooing her to the kitchen as soon as the lunch rush began. Svelte, with a tiny waist, she exuded the kind of aloof, effortless glamour of a Hollywood movie star. Dark curls framed her face. She had heart-shaped lips, a dainty nose, and a curious smile.

While making herself useful in the kitchen, Marilena picked up Italian and got to know the Sportelli family. Aldo Sportelli, one year her senior, was smitten. Lanky, with a shy smile, he would hang around the kitchen when he came home from school. "It was my first infatuation," Aldo would tell me. They spoke about their plans for the future. He wanted to be an engineer. She had no idea what awaited her when she returned to Brazil.

After school, Aldo served the glamorous patrons in the restaurant; my grandmother spent her nights listening to the music coming from the cave below. Every now and then, Aldo joined her on the terrace, always under the watchful eye of a family member.

One day, as Marilena was going

> **Marilena, who spent her days people-watching from the hotel terrace, was never allowed into the cave.**

down the stairs to the kitchen, Aldo went in for a hug. Unsure of what to do, she rushed away.

My grandmother's family was not happy with the budding romance. The son of a hotel owner was not what they had in mind for the family heiress. Aldo's mother told him the social distance between him and Marilena was too large to bridge. "At that time, I thought they were right," Aldo recalls.

The two continued an awkward but friendly relationship over her last few weeks at the hotel. Before she left, she asked him to sign her memory book. "Marilena, if you allow it, a friendship can be an enduring bond," he wrote.

When she left, he went to the station and watched as the train pulled away. It was one of the saddest moments of his life, Aldo says.

❖   ❖   ❖

My grandmother went on to meet my grandfather in college, and by 1969, she was married with four children. Her marriage was happy, but my grandfather's jealousy limited her curiosity about the world. When they ate at restaurants, she faced the back to avoid other patrons' wandering eyes.

Shortly after the wedding, they moved three hours away from São Paulo to a town in southern Brazil. My grandfather enjoyed small-town life, but my grandmother struggled to adjust. After he died, she started spending half the year with my mother in Miami.

Meanwhile, Aldo went on to

Marilena Lerario and Aldo Sportelli met in Polignano a Mare, her grandfather's hometown, when she spent a year in Italy in 1951.

study engineering. For most of his career, he worked in urban planning for local communities. In 1959 he met Beatrice at a party. They married and had two children.

Beatrice suffered from depression, and the marriage was hard on Aldo. Their circle of friends was small, and they rarely traveled. After his mother died in 1995, he came across a wedding photo of his beloved Marilena among her letters. Her grandmother must have sent it.

"I thought, 'Where is she? How is her life?'" he recalls. "The thought that I would never again hear from the girl who captured my boyhood heart tormented me." And so began his search.

Aldo tried to reach the wedding photographer, but he was long dead. He e-mailed the mayor's office of

São Paulo, asking for information on a Marilena Lerario. "We're a city of 12 million people," Aldo was told. "We can't help you."

In 2012, Beatrice was diagnosed with Alzheimer's and Parkinson's. She eventually stopped speaking and barely recognized her children. She refused at-home care from nurses and relied on Aldo for her every need.

Finally, two decades after he started his search, Aldo contacted the daughter of a family friend who worked at the Brazilian tax authority. She found Marilena and passed him her phone number.

When Aldo phoned that afternoon, he told Marilena, "I never forgot you." My grandmother was speechless.

❖　❖　❖

The next day, Aldo called again. What did her children do? he asked. What were her days like?

"I don't even know what he looks like, and we talk every day," my grandmother said to me.

"Let's look to see if he's on Facebook," I suggested.

I pulled up Aldo's photo. He had white hair, but the same sad eyes and shy smile he had at 17. "He's handsome," my grandmother said.

I suggested they communicate by video chat. The next weekend I went to her house for a family get-together and messaged Aldo to arrange the call. My family was eager to see the man my grandmother wouldn't stop talking about.

There was Aldo on the computer screen, beaming. "You didn't use to be blond!" he said. My grandmother burst into giggles.

Week after week, Aldo kept calling. "It is nice to have someone care about me again," my grandmother told me.

The messages soon grew rosier: heart emojis and photos of flowers. "For when you wake up: Good morning," he messaged once, when it was daytime in Italy but still dark in Brazil.

My grandmother, who had shut herself off from the world, came back to life. She began dressing up for their virtual dates, putting on lipstick and fixing her hair.

"We have to take you back to Polignano!" my mother said one day. My grandmother rejected the idea, saying, "He has a wife!"

My mother was persistent, and soon Marilena called Aldo with the news. "We'll be there for two weeks in September," she said. He agreed that she should come.

Accompanied by my mother, my

"There we were, you and I, as if we had been good friends for 68 years," he wrote.

dad, my aunt, two cousins and me, my grandmother landed in Bari, nervous but smiling. When we arrived at the hotel in Polignano, a bouquet of pink roses was waiting for her. "Welcome to your hometown," Aldo had written on the card. "I hope you don't wait another 68 years to return."

The next morning we drove past miles of twisted olive groves. My grandmother sighed and said, "It's

interesting, isn't it? An old lady, seeing an old man."

Aldo had asked us to meet him at the church of San Vito, where Mass would soon be starting. When we pulled up to the entrance, he was waiting. With sky-blue eyes hiding behind silver Ray-Ban sunglasses, slicked-back hair, and a tan jacket, he was as cool an octogenarian as I've seen.

My grandmother leaped out of the car and walked toward him, her arms open.

"So beautiful," he said, trembling as he hugged her. She blushed and introduced him to the family. "It's a historic moment, a miracle," he announced.

Later, my grandmother handed Aldo two gifts. One was a new iPhone—his was old and was always cutting out when they conversed. "And this is for Beatrice," she said, pointing to the second gift. He opened it to find a gray shawl. Aldo stared at my grandmother, tearing up and mouthing, "Thank you."

We asked him out for lunch, but he said he had to go home

Marilena and Aldo in Polignano a Mare. "I thank God for allowing me the chance to be with you," he wrote to her.

and relieve the housekeeper who was watching his wife.

Aldo sent my grandmother a message late that night. "There we were, you and I, as if we had been good friends for 68 years, helping each other in sorrow and rejoicing together in joy," he wrote. "I thank God for allowing me the chance to be with you."

❖   ❖   ❖

They met for coffee daily, during the few hours he could get out of the house. My grandmother refused to be alone with him. "What would people think if they saw us alone together?" she said. "It looks bad."

At first I laughed this off as an antiquated sense of modesty. But everywhere we went Aldo seemed to run into an acquaintance. "Aldo Sportelli!" a friend would shout

223

from across the street, making my grandmother cringe.

On one date he brought his daughter and grandson. I was worried about what they would think of my grandmother, but all anxiety disappeared when we met them. Sabrina, Aldo's daughter, pulled my grandmother into a tight hug. My grandmother had brought her a necklace, which she put on right away. "Give Grandma Marilena a hug," Sabrina told Giorgio, her 12-year-old son.

"It's been a gift for Dad," Sabrina said later that day when I asked how she felt about their relationship. "He's a victim of Mother's condition."

When we weren't with Aldo and his family, my grandmother wanted to explore Polignano. It was still a charming hamlet with narrow limestone streets leading to scenic outposts overlooking the sea. But much had changed since her last visit. Red Bull had chosen Polignano as the site for its annual cliff-diving competition, and the town was now overrun with tourists.

The restaurant in the cave was still operating, and my grandmother, who was allowed to watch guests dine there only from a distance at 15, wanted to see it up close. On one of our last nights in Polignano, we descended the 60 steps into the cave for dinner.

When we emerged onto the wooden deck, the view took my breath away. We were suspended some 30 feet above the sea. The emerald water's reflection danced against the cave's limestone dome.

Aldo had refused to come because the memories of losing the nearby Hotel Sportelli in a financial dispute 20 years ago were too painful. My grandmother respected his decision.

"Isn't it amazing?" she said, gazing out at the sea. "Only nature knows how many millions of years this has been here."

The next day, at another coffee shop, Aldo pulled out a family photo dating from 1934, and my grandmother studied it. "I met every one of them," she said. "We've had this shared life together. Isn't that crazy?" Aldo updated her on what had happened

When we emerged onto the wooden deck, the view took my breath away. We were suspended some 30 feet above the sea.

to each person in the photo.

"When do you leave?" he asked.

"Tomorrow," she said.

They still had 40 minutes before Aldo had to head home. After chaperoning every moment the two of them had spent together, I left my grandmother alone to enjoy the last moments of her last date.

❖　❖　❖

The next morning, Aldo, Sabrina, and Giorgio met us at the hotel. We thanked them for their hospitality and for making my grandmother so happy. "Our family will be an extension of yours," my dad said.

I was surprised to see tears running down Sabrina's face. "Take care of him," my grandmother said, hugging her. She nodded, sobbing.

Aldo took my grandmother's hand in his. "Now, I will do the hardest thing: turn around and walk away," he said.

My grandmother didn't allow herself to indulge in the finality of the moment. She gave Aldo one last hug, and, as we walked away, she held up her phone and said: "I'll see you tomorrow."

Aldo and Marilena continue to speak daily. Marilena says she may visit Italy later this year if she is in good health. Aldo's wife is still alive but her health continues to decline. Aldo has told Marilena that he believed her to be the love of his life when they first met and that their reuniting was "a blessing from God."

The Almost-Perfect Kidnapping

The capture of ten-year-old Kenneth Young loomed for years as one of the few unsolved major abduction cases in the FBI's history.

BY **JOSEPH P. BLANK**

Originally published in June 1971

is ransom for $250,000 made it then the second-largest payoff in the annals of FBI cases. Yet more than 30 months had passed without a clue being found to the identity of the criminal. And time was on his side: California's three-year statute of limitations on the kidnapping felony was running out...

Around midnight on Sunday, April 2, 1967, Arline and Herbert Young returned to their Beverly Hills, California, home after visiting friends. Mr. and Mrs. Young looked in on their four children. All were sleeping soundly, and the Youngs went to bed.

An hour later a car turned quietly into the drive, and a man softly climbed the Youngs' outside steps to the second-floor deck. The sliding glass door to Kenny's room, where he slept alone, was unlocked. The man entered, stepped to the bed, and gently but persistently shook Kenny's shoulder. When the startled boy uttered the first squeak of a yell, the intruder hit him with four blows on the head and said, "Shut up or

226

I'll kill you." Quickly, he wrapped adhesive tape across Kenny's mouth and eyes, dropped an envelope on the bed, and guided Kenny, dressed only in undershorts and socks, down the steps and into the car.

"All clear?" he whispered into a walkie-talkie.

An accomplice on the corner three houses away replied, "All clear."

About 20 minutes later, the kidnapper parked and led Kenny up a flight of steps and to a bed with a bare mattress. He placed the boy face down, tied his hands and feet to the bed with wire, and plugged his ears with wax.

Monday morning at the Young house was routine except that Kenny did not come down for breakfast. At eight, Mrs. Young went upstairs to awaken him. There was the envelope on the empty bed; inside, a typed carbon-copy message read in part, "Do not call the police or your missing merchandise will be vindictively destroyed. Give a reasonable explanation to all interested parties concerning the absence of this merchandise. We

need $250,000—in hundreds only—be at the pay phones at the Standard station, northeast corner of Westwood and Ohio, at 6 p.m. on Wednesday."

Kenny's up to another one of his practical jokes, Mrs. Young thought as she showed the note to her husband. Young went to his son's room and took in the scene: bedding strewn on the floor, and the glass door open. As the truth hit him, he felt a surge of anger, then terrible fear. He turned to his wife and said, "I don't think it's a joke." They looked at each other, embraced, and cried for a while. Then, ignoring the warning, Young said, "I'll call the police."

Minutes later, Beverly Hills police arrived, followed shortly by FBI agents. A fastidious check of Kenny's room, the outside staircase, and driveway produced no clues, no fingerprints. And the letter was too fuzzy to trace the typewriter used to write it. The Youngs were counseled by the FBI agents to follow the kidnapper's instructions to the letter. They would take no direct action until Kenny was safely home.

Although the agents had assured the Youngs that the kidnapper was interested only in the money, not in harming Kenny, time passed excruciatingly slowly for the next two days. The parents avoided speculative talk about Kenny, but each ring of the telephone sent their nerves twanging. "Why Kenny?" they kept asking themselves. "My God, what's happening to him?"

On Wednesday afternoon Young, the chairman and president of the Gibraltar Savings & Loan Association, put up stocks from his own and his father-in-law's resources as collateral and borrowed 2,500 hundred-dollar bills. FBI agents briefed him: "We'll have our men spotted throughout the Los Angeles area. Make the conversation as long as possible so we can try to trace the call. Try to remember every detail. Under no conditions will we do anything to jeopardize the safety of your son. Our work begins after his return."

Young reached the Standard station at 5:35 and waited, tensely. At six o'clock the phone rang and a voice ordered: "Go to the corner of Sepulveda and Moraga. There's another Standard station there, with a telephone booth. Goodbye."

At the second station, Young waited an interminable 45 minutes before a white 1965 Chevrolet with license plate NBD770 drove up and its driver motioned Young to follow.

The white Chevrolet stopped in a barren area near the San Diego

> *There was the envelope on the bed; inside, a typed carbon-copy message.*

freeway. Staring at the rearview mirror in the near-darkness, the apprehensive father saw a slim man with wraparound sunglasses step out of the car. Young was struck by the man's walk—"deliberate, easy, self-assured"—and his thick black hair with so perfect a hairline that Young thought it might be a wig.

The kidnapper stopped at the doorpost behind Young's left shoulder. "Hand me the bag," he ordered.

"When will I get my son back?" Young asked.

"Tonight. Go home and wait for a call."

Young handed the money over and said, "God help you if anything happens to my son."

While the frantic father waited for the promised telephone call, Kenny slept in the rear seat of a car in the basement garage of an apartment house. He had been given four sleeping pills before being placed there by the kidnapper sometime after the payoff. At 3 a.m. he awoke groggily, rang the bell of an apartment, and told the sleepy occupant, "I've been kidnapped and I'd like to call home."

On April 10, Los Angeles police found the Chevrolet abandoned in a shopping center parking lot. It proved to be a stolen car, which the thief had modified with switches that deactivated the brake lights and overhead interior light. Analysis of dirt vacuumed from the floor revealed earth that contained both freshwater and saltwater diatoms —minute shell-like particles that are virtually indestructible. In only one place in Southern California, scientists told the agents, did the diatoms occur together: the abandoned Grefco Mine laboratory, where earth with freshwater diatoms had been trucked in from out of state. But agents could not attach any significance to this conclusion at the time.

Though the ensuing routine of detective work turned up no definite clue as to the kidnapper's identity, the FBI realized that it was dealing with a criminal who had a law enforcement background. The canyon where the money changed hands was a dead zone for radio transmission, a fact generally known only to law officers. The kidnapper had approached the Young car like a policeman, standing by the doorpost to avoid being struck if the driver suddenly flung open the door. The use of overhead and brake-light turnoff switches was little known outside of law enforcement agencies (which use them to assure blackout of their cars during nighttime surveillance activities). And not a single ransom bill had surfaced.

In questioning and eliminating hundreds of suspects, agents checked out former law officers and private investigators involved in shady or illegal activities, but their efforts were fruitless.

As the months passed, the investigation became a plodding but never-waning game to keep talking with suspects, alert for the slightest wisp of a clue; to watch for the ransom bills and assume that the kidnapper would remain in crime because he couldn't spend the money for a long time; and to hope that he would make a mistake.

The Youngs moved to another house to help Kenny forget his frightful experience and acquired two large watchdogs. After two years the family retained little hope that either the kidnapper or the money would be found.

On September 29, 1969, Eugene Patterson, an ex-convict, was arrested for the armed robbery of a supermarket in Alhambra and was also identified as one of the two men who had held up a theater the previous September. Patterson readily admitted his guilt

and named Ronald Lee Miller, a 38-year-old special agent in the Intelligence Division of the Internal Revenue Service, as the planner of the robberies.

When police arrested Miller, a search of his apartment produced more than 14 guns and an extensive array of disguises. Although he calmly and confidently denied all charges, and nothing specifically linked him to the Young case, his alleged criminal involvement and his experience as a law officer fit the skills of the kidnapper. FBI agents wanted to know more about him.

They began asking Patterson about his relationship with Miller, urging him to try to reconstruct his activities during late March and early April two years before. He disclaimed any knowledge of the kidnapping. It could have ended there, but agents intuitively believed he was withholding information. Patiently, almost amiably, they continued talking to him. Finally, on February 12, 1970, Patterson started to tell what he knew about the crime.

He had met Miller in 1962, he said, and subsequently teamed up with him in a number of robberies. Then, early in 1967, Miller talked with him about a kidnapping. His job as an IRS agent gave him access to confidential information about wealthy people, and he displayed a list of names, including Young's. Miller drove Patterson in a

As the months passed, the investigation became a never-waning game.

government car to the old Grefco Mine and told him it would be the ideal place to hold the kidnap victim. On the night of April 2, Miller and Patterson drove in two cars to Beverly Hills. Miller handed him a walkie-talkie, stationed him on a corner, and told him to call a warning if anybody appeared. The following day Miller gave him $1,000 in twenties without any explanation.

When Patterson told Miller some weeks later about being questioned by the FBI, Miller replied, "If you involve me, you will be taken care of."

Was Patterson telling the truth? He represented the primary and damning witness against Miller. If evidence supported Patterson, the case could go to a grand jury. With the statute of limitations having less than two months to run, the FBI intensified its investigation.

Miller, who scoffed at the accusations and denied everything, was an unusual personality. An employee of the Internal Revenue Service since 1964, he was considered knowledgeable in surveillance techniques, typewriter evidence, and the operations of Swiss banks where money could be deposited in numbered, secret accounts. In discussing hypothetical crimes with one colleague, he stated that "hot" cash could be kept away from the law by having it picked up by a courier from a Swiss bank.

Bureau artists altered several photographs, including Miller's, by adding the wraparound sunglasses and straight hairline described by Young. When agents then asked Young if he recognized the kidnapper, he promptly picked Miller's picture. Soon afterward, Patterson's common-law wife revealed that she had picked up an extension phone prior to the kidnapping and briefly heard her husband and Miller discussing the question of "hiding the kid."

Miller denied that he had driven Patterson to the Grefco Mine in a government car. IRS records, however, showed that Miller had use of car 90110, a 1963 Plymouth, between April 3 and 7. The FBI located this car, and lab analysis of scrapings from its wheel wells and the undersides of its fenders proved that the car had indeed been at the Grefco Mine. At 6:55 on the Wednesday evening when the ransom money changed hands, Miller claimed that he was interviewing an automobile dealer on a government matter 30 miles from the barren freeway site. The daily office diary that Miller kept scrupulously verified this, and the dealer confirmed Miller's visit. But in reconstructing the details of that day, the dealer remembered that Miller had actually talked with him in the early or mid-afternoon, not in the evening.

The Los Angeles grand jury heard the evidence against Miller and returned an indictment on March 31, 1970, just four days before the statute of limitations expired. In August, Miller was convicted of the two robberies, and in September he was found guilty of the kidnapping and sentenced to life in prison.

For the FBI, the case remains open until the $250,000 ransom money is returned to its owner. If and when Miller is paroled, agents will be watching for those $100 bills.

Ronald Lee Miller almost pulled off the perfect kidnapping. And if any one word is likely to rasp across his nerves for the rest of his life, it is "almost."

Bad Puns Are How Eye Roll

Inside the hypercompetitive, sometimes groan-inducing world of pun competitions.

———

BY **PETER RUBIN**
FROM **WIRED**

Originally published in November 2017

n the surface, the guy wasn't particularly fearsome—pudgy, late 30s, polo shirt, plaid shorts, baseball cap. He looked completely at ease, one hand in his pocket, the other holding the microphone loosely, like a torch singer doing crowd work. And when he finally began talking, it was with an assurance that belied the fact that he was basically spewing nonsense.

"I hate all people named John," he said with bravado. "Yeah, that's right, that was a John diss!" The crowd roared. John diss. Jaundice. A glorious, groan-inducing precision strike of a pun.

If you're an NBA rookie, you really don't want to go up against LeBron James. Anyone's trivia night would be ruined by seeing Ken Jennings on another team. And if you find yourself at the world's biggest pun competition, the last person you want to face is four-time defending champion Ben Ziek. Yet that's exactly where I was, on an outdoor stage in Austin, Texas, committing unspeakable atrocities upon the English language in front of a few hundred onlookers.

The rules of the 39th annual O. Henry Pun-Off World Championships "Punslingers" competition are simple: Two people take turns punning on a theme in head-to-head rounds. Failure to make a pun in five seconds gets you eliminated; make a nonpun or reuse a word three times, and you've reached the banishing point. Round by round and pair by pair, a field of 32 dwindles, until the last of the halved-nots finally gets to claim the mantle of best punster in the world.

My first-round opponent froze when his turn came to pun on waterborne vehicles. Seriously, yacht a word came out. Canoe believe it?

Eventually, there we stood, two among the final eight: me, a first timer, squaring off against the Floyd Mayweather of the pun world. I'd been a little jittery in my first couple of rounds, sure, but now I was punning above my weight, and I knew it. Once the judges announced that we'd be punning on diseases, we began.

"Mumps the word!" I said, hoping my voice wasn't shaking.

Ziek fired back: "That was a measle-y pun." Not only was he confident, with a voice that was equal parts game show host and morning radio DJ, he was nimble enough to turn your own pun against you.

"Well, I had a croup-on for it," I said. Whoa. Where'd that come from?

> *If you find yourself at the world's biggest pun competition, the last person you want to face is Ben Ziek.*

"There was a guy out here earlier painted light red," Ziek said. "Did you see the pink guy?"

"I didn't," I responded. "Cold you see him?"

Again and again we pun-upped each other. From AIDS to Zika we ranged. Almost five minutes later, we'd gone through 32 puns between us, and I was running dry.

Ziek, though, had a seemingly endless stockpile and tossed off a quick alopecia pun; I could have bald right then and there. As far as my brain was concerned, there wasn't a medical textbook in existence that contained something we hadn't used. As I stood there, silently sweating, the judge counted down, and I slunk offstage to watch the rest of the competition—which Ziek won, for the fifth time.

235

The author, standing at top left, among his fellow Bay Area punslingers.

Knowing I'd lost to the best cushioned the blow, but some mild semantic depression lingered.

When I was growing up in the 1980s, my father's favorite (printable) joke was "Where do cantaloupes go in the summertime? Johnny Cougar's Melon Camp." This is proof that—well, that I grew up in Indiana. But it's also proof that I was raised to speak two languages, both of them English. See, there's the actual words-working-together-and-making-sense part, and then there's the fun part. The pliant, recombinant part. The part that lets you harness linguistic irregularities, judo-style, to make words into other words. It's not conscious, exactly, and whether this is nature or nurture, the result is that I play with language all the time.

"I can't listen passively to someone speaking without the possibility of puns echoing around in my head," says Gary Hallock, who has been producing and hosting the O. Henry Pun-Off for 26 years. He has seen the annual competition grow from an Austin oddity to a national event.

It's almost surprising that it took so long. Verbal puns may date back to at least 1635 B.C., when a Babylonian clay tablet included a play on the word for wheat. Humor theorists generally agree that comedy hinges on incongruity: When a sentence or situation subverts expectations, that's funny (Also, yes, humor theorists are a thing.) And of the many kinds of wordplay—hyperbole, metaphor, even letter-level foolery such as

After a muggleful of Harry Potter puns, I find myself in the semifinals.

anagrams—nothing takes advantage of incongruity quite like puns.

They come in four varieties. In order of increasing complexity, you've got homonyms, identical words that sound alike but differ in meaning ("Led Zeppelin's guitarist was interrogated, but detectives weren't able to turn the Page"); homophones, which are spelled differently but sound the same ("I hate raisins! Apologies if you're not

into curranty vents"); homographs, which sound different but look similar ("If you're asking me to believe that a Loire Cabernet is that different from a Napa Cabernet, then the terroirists have won"— terroir being the French word for the environment in which wine grapes are grown); and paronyms, which are words from different languages that sound similar and often come from the same Latin root ("I ate so much cucumber chutney at the Indian restaurant that I have raita's block").

Simply put, a good pun is a joke that hinges on wordplay. A truly formidable punner knows that and frames a sentence to make the pun the punch line. But was I a truly formidable punner? I'd thought so—my lifelong dream is seeing Flavor Flav and Ellen Burstyn cohosting a talk show so it can be called Burstyn with Flavor. But after Austin, I had my doubts. I'd cracked under pressure; until I tried again, I'd never know fissure.

❖ ❖ ❖

The Bay Area Pun-Off is just one of a handful of competitive punning events popping up across the country, such as Punderdome 3000 in New York City, Pundamonium in Seattle, and the Great Durham Pun Championship in Durham, North Carolina. (No experience is necessary—you just sign up and hope your number gets picked.) On this Saturday night, a week after O. Henry, I am in a high-ceilinged performance space in San Francisco's Mission District, looking for redemption. We commence with a marathon on tree puns designed to winnow the field from 12 to 8.

"I'm just hoping to win the poplar vote," one woman says.

"Sounds like a birch of contract to me," says someone else.

A lanky British guy I'll call Chet rambles through a shaggy-dog story involving a French woman and three Jamaican guys to finally arrive at a tortured "le mon t'ree" punchline. The crowd eats it up.

After someone delivers a good line, I admit that I end up being pretty frond of it. Things go oak-ay, and I'm on to the next round.

After a muggleful of Harry Potter puns, I find myself in the semifinals against an engineer named Asa. The host scribbles the mystery topic on a chalkboard hidden from sight, then turns it around. It says … diseases. The same category that knocked me out in Austin? The category I dwelled on for the entire flight home, thinking of all the one-liners that had eluded me?

This time, there's no running dry.

> ## As long as I've got the words to try, I'll keep using them to create incongruity. Or maybe I'll just plead raita's block.

Not only do I remember all the puns I used against Ben Ziek, I also remember all the puns he made against me. So when Asa says "I'm really taking my mumps," I shoot back with, "That's kinda measle-y, if you ask me." I reprise puns I'd made in Austin ("Did you see that Italian opera singer run through the door? In flew Enzo!"); I use puns that I'd thought of since ("My mom makes the best onion dip. It's HIV little concoction you'd love").

Asa fights gamely, but I have innumerable disease puns at my fingertips, and it's not much longer before the round is over.

And then there are two: me and Chet. I'm locked in. No nerves, no self-consciousness, just getting out of my brain's way and letting the connections happen. When the host announces the theme—living world leaders—I don't even try to stockpile puns. I just wait, and they come.

Chet opens the round: "Ohhh, BAMA. I don't know anything about world leaders."

Hearing Obama conjures up a mental image of Justin Trudeau. Before the laughter even dies down, I nod my head encouragingly. "True, though—that was a decent pun!"

It's Austin all over again, just in reverse. Now I'm the quick one, and Chet's the one who has to scramble. My turn? No problem: "I am Bushed."

Chet has used a total of three U.S. presidents and two British prime ministers; meanwhile, I've been from South Korea to Germany, by way of Canada.

Even better, I've got another continent in my pocket. "Have you guys been to Chet's farm?" I ask the audience. "He has this group of cows that won't stop talking." I wait a beat before taking the audience to Africa with a nod to Zimbabwe's president. "They are seriously moo-gabby."

What happens next is a blur. I can't even tell you what comes out of Chet's mouth, but it's either nothing or it's the name of someone dead. Either way, the Bay Area Pun-Off is over.

This may be my only taste of victory in the world of competitive paronomasiacs (a fancy word for pun addicts), and I may never know the secret to the perfect pun. But as long as I've got the words to try, one thing's for sure: I'll keep using them to create incongruity.

Or maybe I'll just plead raita's block.

My Journey to Moscow

The noted TV personality gives a heartwarming report about the love and hope that remains in Russia, despite the arrogance and power of the Communist elite.

—

BY **ED SULLIVAN**

Originally published in March 1960

When the State Department invited me to take a variety show to the Soviet Union as part of the new cultural exchange program, I was both delighted and honored.

My nominal employer was to be the Soviet Ministry of Culture, the bureau that has complete control of all the arts. Since a deputy minister was in New York with the visiting Bolshoi Ballet, I made an appointment with him to arrange details of my tour. When I arrived, I found the deputy flanked by three other men, and I learned my first lesson about Soviet bureaucracy—no one man seems to have authority to decide anything; everything is done by committee.

I came directly to the point. I was

Ed Sullivan, circa 1948, when he began hosting his long-running variety show.

ready and eager to build a variety show of top American stars that would play two weeks in Moscow and two weeks in Leningrad. But first I needed permission to tape a television show in Russia for subsequent showing here in the United States. I wanted to film our stars against backdrops of Red Square, Gorki Park, the subway, and the Moscow River, and also scenes of the famous Russian circus and the puppet theater.

The deputy minister heard me out, then said, "We will discuss this point later on the agenda."

"No, Mr. Minister, this is the first point to discuss," I said. "I am building a show headed by top stars. These people make for a single performance more than you are offering them for an entire month. The only way I can afford the tour is by producing a television show about it."

The deputy minister nodded and said, "We will discuss this point later on the agenda."

"There are no other points unless we agree on this," I insisted.

The deputy conferred with his colleagues. Finally he said, "You have permission."

My wife and I flew into Moscow on a gray August afternoon and were soon installed in a suite in the Hotel Ukraine. I turned at once to the problems of staging our show. Our director, Bob Precht, was having difficulties. "The stagehands don't know how to do anything,"

When I arrived, I learned my first lesson in Soviet bureaucracy.

he moaned. "They've never seen a show like ours, they have no conception of the fast changes necessary, they don't know how to handle scenery. In fact, there's nothing to hang the scenery on."

"I never heard of a theater that couldn't hang scenery," I said.

"Theater! We're assigned to the amphitheater in Gorki Park. Seats 14,000 people—under the stars!"

I had battled out this question with the Russians in New York, explaining that ours was a small, intimate show, and they had agreed to put us in a regular theater.

"I'll see the Ministry of Culture boys tomorrow and straighten everything out," I said.

Next day I discovered that we had a new team of culture ministers to deal with. The four new men, like the old, were formally polite but without warmth. I presented my problem, explaining that it had already been agreed I was to have a theater. They were sorry, Gorki Park it was.

I went on to the next problem. I had hired videotape trucks and crews to film my Moscow TV show, but the trucks were still in Paris, awaiting Soviet visas and gas coupons. This was something to consider in due time, the deputy minister said. I said I was paying these trucks and crews $7,000 a day while the deputy minister considered something that had already been decided. We would meet again tomorrow on this problem, the deputy minister announced.

The ministers and I met the rest of that week with no break in the deadlock.

Finally the night arrived for the opening of our show in Gorki Park. We'd had no dress rehearsal, and all was chaos backstage. At eight o'clock the audience began to flood into the arena. Their appearance seemed to confirm all my preconceived ideas about the Russian people—stolid, humorless, suspicious. What an audience to play to! I began to sweat.

Nine o'clock came. Saying a small prayer, I gave the signal to strike up the overture, a medley of old American tunes: "Yankee Doodle," "Sidewalks of New York," "Turkey in the Straw," "Home on the Range," "California, Here I Come!" and "America the Beautiful." As the songs boomed out into the chill Russian night, I suddenly got a lump in my throat. I felt like saying to those 14,000 Russians: This is us, our land, our hopes, our fun. We want you to like us, but if you don't—well, we don't intend to change to suit you.

The orchestra went from the overture into the first number:

"Autumn Leaves," sung by the Barry Sisters. It was a quiet, nostalgic song sung with finesse by two fine artists. The last note died with infinite sweetness, and there was a moment of silence. Then it came—waves of thunderous applause. I had never heard anything like it. The thousands of faces that a moment ago had seemed so stolid were now illumined with pleasure and gratitude.

From that point on, our show was a sensation, with every act receiving an ovation. As I watched our performers become one with that Russian audience, I realized how superficial are the barriers that divide people. The 43 Russian musicians in the orchestra assigned to us played "Turkey in the Straw" with a joyous lilt because notes on a staff are the same in all languages. The audience responded to our songs, laughed at our light comedy because their ears and their eyes and their hearts were the same as ours.

I had learned some Russian phrases and just before the finale I made a little speech of thanks. After that I said, "I'm certain there is not a mother in this great audience who wants another war in which her son might be killed. Believe me when I tell you that there is not a mother in America who wants war. That's why we've come here, not only to entertain you, but to tell you that."

At the conclusion of the show the audience rose from their seats and headed not for the exits but for the stage. Thousands converged on us and I felt some alarm; but they stopped at the orchestra pit—and threw flowers. At least half that audience had brought bouquets with them, expecting to like us, and soon we were knee-deep in blossoms.

When we were finally able to leave we had to push through hundreds of people lingering around our cars. Hands reached out to touch us, voices were raised in greeting, and even if we could not understand the language, we understood the tone. Typical was a little woman who grabbed my hand and said in broken English, "True, true—tell America no mother wants war. God bless you."

As I was driven off, I thought

to myself: The men in the Kremlin have failed! For 40 years they've preached hatred of America, but the people do not hate us.

Every night of every show we saw this truth demonstrated. One evening Little Buck, a tap dancer, did a sliding split, caught his heel, and twisted his ankle cruelly. Immediately three Russian doctors

> *The thousands of faces that a moment ago had seemed so stolid were now illumined with pleasure and gratitude.*

came up from the audience, cradled him in their arms, and carried him off to be X-rayed. He had only a sprain, but they treated him as if he were the most important case in all the land.

It was not just onstage that we received plaudits. Our musical director's chambermaid would not let his laundry go to the hotel; she took it home and did it by hand. Taxi drivers would not accept tips, saying that the American guests must take home good memories of Russian hospitality. And all of us had the experience, at one time or another, of a Russian approaching us on the street to shake hands, then leaving in our palm a small, hard candy. We were extraordinarily touched by this small gesture of friendship.

There was only one thing that was marring our stay. Day after day the Ministry of Culture and I conferred, while the video trucks remained in Paris and I was fast losing my temper. At last I goaded them into a decision. It was—*nyet*! I could not film Red Square, or the Moscow River, or the subway, or the circus, or the puppet theater.

I stormed out of the ministry and back to the hotel. My wife had to listen to my raging as I paced back and forth. Almost unnoticed was a hotel official who had come to check on some housekeeping detail. He said in English, "Why don't you write Khrushchev?"

I turned on him in amazement and demanded, "What did you say?"

"This would not happen if Khrushchev knew about it," he said. "If you send him a telegram in care of the Central Committee of the Communist Party it will be in front of him within an hour, no matter where he may be."

"What have I got to lose?" I said, and sat down to write the telegram. I gave it to him straight. I said that the Ministry of Culture had gone back on its word, that it was jeopardizing the whole cultural exchange program between our countries and was, in effect, sabotaging the world's efforts toward understanding and peace. I signed the telegram with an angry flourish, sent it off, and went to bed.

I came awake the next morning to the sound of the telephone. It was the Ministry of Culture, requesting most urgently and respectfully a conference with me at once.

When I arrived at the meeting I found that my four zombies had suddenly acquired smiles. Did I have any problems they could help me with, they asked.

That nearly threw me, but I played along. As if it were the first time I'd made the request, I said that I wanted to film Red Square.

"*Pozhalesta*!" they said. It was a simple word that meant "But of course! What man of intelligence could think otherwise?"

"And the Moscow River?"

"Pozhalesta!"

"And the circus? And the puppet

> ## "This would not happen if Khrushchev knew about it," the official said.

theater?"

"Pozhalesta ... pozhalesta ..."

"And what about my video trucks stranded in Paris?"

"They'll be sent visas at once. No trouble at all."

When I returned to my hotel, I sought out the man who had told me to write Khrushchev. I said, "That was a great thing you did for me."

He said quietly, "I didn't do it for you, Mr. Sullivan. I did it for my country."

Our month ended, the television show was at last on tape, and it was time to go home. Our plane was scheduled to leave at an early hour, and when we arose it was still dark. The hotel was ghostly; the dining room would not open for another two hours. We dressed quickly and carried our bags down to the lobby to meet the rest of our party. The moment we came onto the main floor, the doors to the dining room burst open to reveal all our tables set and our regular waitresses smiling and ready to serve us an enormous meal.

"Why did you do this?" I asked one of them.

She said, "You are our guests. And we want you to have a good hot breakfast before your long journey." Then she said with a shy smile, "We want you to remember us."

A sullen dawn was breaking as we got to the airport. When our flight was announced, the four men from the Ministry of Culture suddenly appeared, to give us a properly austere farewell.

As I took my seat and glanced out the window, I saw them standing stiffly in the posture of authority. I thought how different these men were from the other Russians I had met—the musicians, the taxi drivers, the open-hearted waitresses, the thousands who had been our audiences and responded so warmly to our efforts. It was as if these men were not Russians at all, but an alien elite who had failed completely to impose their image on the country.

For all their arrogance and power, there remained in this ancient land more love than hate, more hope than despair.

Almost Ready to Do My Taxes!

There's always something better to do than taxes.

—

BY **EMMA RATHBONE**
FROM **THE NEW YORK TIMES**
Originally published in April 2017

**W**hoop! First gotta warm my tea.

OK, OK, OK, done. Let's do this. Except I think I left the back door open. Just gotta check.

Yup. Closed. Phew. Now I can finally settle in and get started.

Wait. Is that caterpillar trying to cross the windowsill? I have to see this. I definitely need to check out this scene, and it's definitely going to take me 45 minutes of just staring at this caterpillar and watching it rear up and wave its little arms around like a tiny emperor. Maybe I should put it on my finger. Maybe I should just pop it into my mouth. Ha!

I'm back. Time to really get my hands dirty here. OK, let's see, gathering my forms. The gathering storm! A perfect storm! Shoot. Thing is, I'm pretty sure I need to call Aunt Diane. I never call her, and it's not even her birthday or anything, but I'm pretty sure I've got to call and twist a lock of hair around my finger and wander around the house while she's talking and pick a sticky thing off the fridge, then study my fingernails, then hold up a wooden spoon and just kind of slash it through the air in an inconclusive way, not even imitating anything.

OK. I really need to do this. Now. Like, now. Checkmate, taxes! You're about to get done. Except, speaking of chess … You know, I haven't played any games lately. Had some fun. You know? Who says a 36-year-old woman can't have some fun? I need to have some fun before I do this, clean out the cobwebs. I mean, we're all gonna die one day! Maybe I'll paint my bedroom floor as a checkerboard and then … kinda hop around on it. Sounds like fun. Sounds outrageous and fun, and I am on it.

OK, I actually just did that. I just painted my bedroom floor with black-and-white squares, and it took six straight hours, and I hate it. Now I really, really, really need to get started on these taxes.

And I will. I really will. But here's the thing: I just found a promotional bouncy ball in this drawer, from a veterinarian or something, and it's neon green, and I didn't even know I had it. But, I'm sorry, I have to spend some time with this bouncy ball. I've gotta bounce this ball! Like, when else am I going to do this? There's. No. Time. Like. The. Present. When. It. Comes. To. Randomly. Bouncing. Some. Ball.

So that's what I'm going to do. I am living my best life, I am living my best me, and that involves taking the opportunity of a lifetime during the lifetime of the opportunity and going outside and standing in the driveway with this neon ball like it's the '90s and … Oh no. Now it's in a gutter. Well, that's what happens when you dream.

I'm not afraid to dream. And I'm not going to apologize for not having started my taxes even though I really need to do them, and if I could just start this list of business expenses in an Excel sheet, then I'd be "all set," as people from many walks of life say.

It's just, I haven't practiced my signature in a while.

The Case of the Blasted Bank

The bank employees had no idea what was going on beneath the surface.

———

BY **EVAN MCLEOD WYLIE**

FROM **TRUE, THE MAN'S MAGAZINE**

Originally published in February 1962

t noontime last Valentine's Day a pretty teller at the People's National Bank of Washington, in Seattle, started to take a drink from a water fountain, then changed her mind. "The fountain's full of plaster dust and paint chips again," she told the group at the lunch table a few minutes later. "What's going on around here anyway?"

All during that week the bank's employees had noticed a gentle but persistent rain of plaster dust that seemed to be sprinkling down from hairline cracks in the ceiling. The bank is close to Boeing Field, and huge jet planes roar overhead at frequent intervals. Some of the employees attributed the cracks and the plaster dust to the planes. "They're shaking this building apart," one said.

But instead of being shaken apart, the bank was actually being blown open.

Reaching its climax that week was one of the most preposterous bank robberies of 1961, or any other year. The job took more than four months to accomplish, but it netted its lone amateur burglar more than $45,000 and, long before he had spent the money, a term in jail.

It was in October 1960 that Wells Van Steenbergh Jr., a tall, clean-cut, well-mannered, 25-year-old commercial flier, grounded by a slump in his business and hard pressed for cash, came up with the notion of robbing a bank. Many men in dire financial straits have toyed with this idea and put it aside, but Van Steenbergh seems to have had no second thoughts. He immediately got into his blue Renault and drove around Seattle to case the possibilities.

Soon he was reconnoitering a branch of the People's National Bank of Washington. The bank is surrounded by residential buildings and small industries. Busy in the daytime, the area is deserted after dark. Directly behind the bank is a driveway that serves the drive-in window; behind that is an embankment and a vacant lot. Van Steenbergh decided to go into the bank the hard way.

Although his previous earthmoving experience was nil, he began to dig a tunnel into the weed-strewn embankment. This would go under the driveway and, he hoped, into the bank. He dug steadily until he had burrowed about eight feet; then the tunnel caved in. But Van Steenbergh wasn't discouraged. Early the next day he was on the telephone, ordering timber from a lumberyard. After dark he was back on the job, re-digging his tunnel and shoring up the shaft with the ardor of a gold prospector who feels sure he has hit a rich vein.

Van Steenbergh became one of the hardest-working ditchdiggers in town. Night after night, while Seattle slept, he labored industriously. In the hours before dawn he hauled out the dirt on a board, camouflaged the tunnel entrance with brush and scraps of lumber, and went home to a hard-earned rest.

Weeks passed, and still Seattle police and the People's National remained unaware of Van Steenbergh's molelike assault. During the day, above the tunnel, tellers dispensed cash to drive-in customers; and by night as well as day police patrols made their appointed rounds, passing within a few feet of the tunnel entrance. Nobody noticed the blue Renault frequently parked nearby at night.

By Halloween, Van Steenbergh had burrowed 18 feet beneath the driveway and commenced slanting the shaft upward, expecting to strike the floor of the bank. Instead, he broke through into a crawl space, about four feet high, beneath the bank. Its function was to provide access to plumbing and electrical installations.

Exploring his grotto with a flashlight, Van Steenbergh discovered a ladder leading up to a steel plate. He pried up the plate and found himself staring into the bank's furnace room, directly adjacent to the vault. Wary of burglar alarms, Van Steenbergh did not venture further. He replaced the manhole lid and descended the ladder, noting that the cement foundation beneath the vault was about 18 inches thick.

In the crawl space, Van Steenbergh was able to sit snug and dry, and plan his attack on the vault overhead without fear of interruption. After chipping away with a chisel at the concrete, he concluded he needed heavier machinery. He inquired at a tool rental shop about the type of tools necessary to penetrate thick concrete. He was shown a power hammer and star drills and was assured they could do the job. That night he returned to the shop, jimmied a back door, and helped himself to the equipment.

There remained the small matter of obtaining electricity for the power hammer. But by this time Van Steenbergh was completely at home around the bank. He simply plugged his electric cord into a convenient outlet in the furnace room. From then on the People's National was supplying the electric current for its own burglary.

The first time Van Steenbergh set about breaching the foundation, the stolen power hammer gave off such a hair-raising clatter that he dropped it and fled, certain that police sirens would be converging from all directions. But not a soul showed up to ask what was going on.

Nevertheless, the nerves of the pilot-turned-burglar were so shaken by the experience that he shut down his tunnel work temporarily and flew east to visit relatives during the Christmas holidays.

By the time he returned he had decided not to risk the racket of the power hammer night after night;

> *Van Steenbergh plugged his cord into a convenient outlet. The bank was now supplying the electric current for its own burglary.*

the safer approach was to blast a hole right into the bank vault. So he telephoned a powder company and chatted with a man about the use of dynamite in blasting rock.

He was directed to a town about 60 miles south of the city, where he purchased 25 dollars' worth of nitroglycerin. He set up his private munitions dump not far from the bank, and then went to the public library to bone up on blasting techniques.

In mid-February Van Steenbergh started drilling holes in the bank's foundation for his dynamite charges. This made clouds of dust in his cavern, so the resourceful burglar borrowed a garden hose from an adjoining utility room and sprinkled the dust in tidy fashion.

Deciding the time had come to shoot the works, he spread the dynamite liberally around his drill holes, lit a fuse, and retired to the furnace room to await results. The booming explosion shook the People's National from stem to stern, but took out only about five inches of concrete.

It was again enough, however, to scare the daylights out of Van Steenbergh, and he fled, feeling certain that the next day somebody in the bank would notice that strange things were happening. True, tellers, bookkeepers, and vice presidents began to complain about dust and plaster cracks turning up mysteriously in the walls and ceilings. A search for the cause

was organized, but the search party went up instead of down.

Mounting to the second floor, the group finally decided that a large paper cutter whose thumps could be heard throughout the bank were to blame, and there was also the theory that the vibrations of jets overhead might be causing the damage. But no action was taken. At close of business on Friday, February 17, the massive steel door of the vault was swung shut and its timers set for Monday morning. No qualms were felt over the fact that the vault contained approximately $150,000.

About 11 p.m. Van Steenbergh ventured back beneath the bank, drilled more holes into the base of the vault, stuffed them with dynamite, spread another layer underneath them and, after setting a fuse, scrambled out of the tunnel.

At 1:40 a.m. the nitroglycerin let go with a detonation that nearly lifted the People's National off its foundations. Van Steenbergh, sure that the concussion waves must have set off every alarm in the bank, whizzed away in his Renault. The muffled boom had indeed reached several neighborhood residents.

Just before midnight on Saturday, Van Steenbergh was back in his tunnel. Squirming through the explosion's debris, he gazed rapturously at a hole in the vault floor big enough for him to crawl through. By a fantastic stroke of luck, the hole had been blown dead center in the vault without triggering any alarms.

Clambering up, Van Steenbergh began prying drawers open with a screwdriver. For the rest of the night he made trip after trip through the tunnel, loading the Renault with bank notes and heavy bags of coin. At dawn he drove away with more than $45,000 and buried most of it in his woodland munitions dump. Sunday night, he returned to the scene of the crime to destroy any evidence that might connect him with the robbery, then made his way out of the tunnel for the last time.

At 8:45 Monday morning, the People's National discovered it had been divested of a goodly portion of its liquid assets. Amazed by the painstaking tunneling and blasting, police immediately assumed that professionals were involved and began dragnetting the city for known burglars. The FBI moved in with mine detectors and other electronic equipment. State police combed the area for clues.

If ever there was a time for a successful robber to lie low, this was it. But Van Steenbergh saw things differently. In downtown Seattle with stolen cash, he put down $1,000 to buy a station wagon.

As must have occurred to nearly everybody in Seattle except Van Steenbergh, the FBI and police were keeping close tabs on all large cash transactions. Serial numbers on the stolen bills that the amateur safecracker handed over for the station wagon were found to match those from the burgled vault. Early the next morning FBI agents were deployed around Van Steenbergh's home, and not long afterward he was sentenced to 20 years in prison.

The young man who bungled the almost perfect crime will be out of circulation a good deal longer than the money he stole in his subterranean treasure hunt.

Beyond Tragedy

*My father taught me how to handle death
with grace and courage. Years later,
his example still gives me comfort.*

BY **KATHLEEN KENNEDY TOWNSEND**

Originally published in November 2008

Death has been ever-present in my life. I was named for my aunt Kathleen, who died in a plane crash three years before I was born. My brother Joe was named for our uncle Joe, who had been killed in World War II, as had Kathleen's husband, Billy Hartington. My parents, Robert and Ethel, often talked about these three young people, each dead before the age of 30.

My aunt Kik was beautiful, lively, and giving. She had gone to England during the war to help and to be with the man she loved. My uncle Joe was smart, athletic, brave. They were in my thoughts daily. We prayed for them by name at every Sunday Mass, at the daily Mass we attended during the summers, and during nightly prayers. So while I didn't know my aunt and uncles, remembering them and honoring their memory was part of our daily ritual. I knew from the youngest age that death would take the vivacious and the brave. Immunity was not possible.

When I was just four years old, my mother's parents were killed in

Kathleen and dad Robert F. Kennedy, circa 1964.

Kathleen's aunts Eunice, Pat, and Jean, along with her father and her uncle John, during JFK's campaign for the Senate, September 1952.

a plane crash. Now death was even more present. I had known my grandparents, George and Ann. I had hugged them, sat on their laps, and visited their home in Greenwich, Connecticut, over Christmas. I saw vividly how sad my mother became. I have a memory of my father carrying her up and down the stairs because she was so brokenhearted that she could barely walk. I probably conflated that memory with the birth of my brother David.

Still, the fragility that death bred remains fixed in my consciousness.

My grandparents' names were added to Joe's and Kik's as family members we should pray for.

Then my uncle, President John F. Kennedy, was killed when I was 12. A few years later, another uncle of mine, George Skakel Jr.—my mother's brother—and one of my father's best friends, Dean Markham, were killed in a plane crash. Dean and his wife, Susie, were our neighbors. They had five children. They carpooled with us. Nine months later, George's wife, the mother of my four cousins, choked on a piece of food and died. My four orphaned cousins were sent to live with an aunt and uncle.

My father was killed in June 1968 when I was 16 and the oldest of ten children. My youngest sister was born in December of that year.

While we were in college, one of my best friends committed suicide.

For my 25th birthday, I asked for a skull and got one. I admit that when I opened that present, the guests at the party, who'd been expecting some lovely trinket, I am sure—bath salts or a beautiful bowl—were shocked. There was momentary silence.

❖ ❖ ❖

In college, a close friend told me that she had never been to a funeral. In the late 1950s and early '60s, her experience wasn't unique for people our age. The baby boomers grew up with death as a distant thought. But not me. A friend with whom I'd bought a car—a Volkswagen, for $200—was beaten senseless by thugs in 1971 and stayed in a coma

for 30 years before he died. My brother David died of a drug overdose; my brother Michael in a freak skiing accident. My cousin John and his wife and sister-in-law died in a plane crash just before my sister Rory's wedding.

Many of these deaths are not news to you. They're part of the public record.

I was named for my aunt Kathleen, who died three years before I was born.

———

What remains a mystery is how people cope. How do we go on?

The most straightforward answer I can give is: the same way that generations before have gone on. We acknowledge the pain and the loss. We develop rituals—religious services, music, funerals and wakes—where friends gather, hug one another, cry together, and share stories and laughs. And we remember.

I don't like the saying "Time

heals all wounds." It is not true. Years later, people can still be terribly sad and miss their mother, father, child, sibling, friend. Scars remain unhealed.

A decade after my uncle Joe and my aunt Kathleen died, my grandfather Joseph Kennedy wrote a letter to a friend whose son had died after brain surgery. Here's what he said:

Dear Jack,

There are no words to dispel your feelings at this time, and there is no time that will ever dispel them. Nor is it any easier the second time than it was the first. And yet I cannot share your grief, because no one could share mine.

When one of your children goes out of your life, you think of what he might have done with a few more years and you wonder what you are going to do with the rest of yours.

You never really accept it; you just go through the motions.

Then one day, because there is a world to be lived in, you find yourself a part of it again, trying to accomplish something

—something that he did not have time enough to do.

And, perhaps, that is the reason for it all. I hope so.

Sincerely,

Joe

I often hear people express sympathy for my losses, how difficult it must be to be in the public eye—to have all these tragedies happen on the world stage.

In fact, I think it is a blessing. Remember how I mentioned that my college friend had died? For a few years, his mother and I would write to each other. But then the letters slowed, and finally stopped.

I would see his friends, and we would talk about the wonderful Andrew Wojciehowski—his love of Billie Holiday, his brilliance, his leadership in helping me build a fireplace in my mother's home. But then our mutual friends graduated and went their separate ways. Now seldom do we reconnect. And when we do, we talk not about the past but about the present and the future. I remember Andrew in my heart, but it's a solitary memory, not shared.

In contrast, people all over the world know my father and uncle. Their legacies are large. There are monuments, libraries, universities, hospitals, highways, an airport. Their speeches are quoted. Authors have written books, documentaries, and dramatizations. Hardly a day passes that I don't meet someone who hasn't been touched by them, literally. A woman tells me she saw my father in Buffalo when he visited that city, or a man from Dubuque tells me how my father stepped out of the crowd to shake his hand.

Presidents and prime ministers from other countries tell me how my father welcomed them to his office in Washington when they were foreign students. I hear how he helped a sick child, set up a scholarship program, raised money for an urban park. Because of John and Robert Kennedy, someone became a teacher or a social worker, joined the Peace Corps or the war on poverty, or entered politics.

I feel that their spirit lives. It

Joseph P. Kennedy Jr., who died in World War II.

lives in the work of so many who still think of these two remarkable brothers. It lives in the stories that are told, in the work that these men started—work that continues. The good is not interred with their bones, but springs forth in a variety of ways.

They were fortunate. President Kennedy, when asked what happiness was, quoted the ancient Greek definition of happiness as "the full use of your powers along lines of excellence." These two had large talents, and they were able to use them. Most satisfyingly, they

A young generation of Kennedys with the 35th president in Hyannis Port, Massachusetts, August 1963. Kathleen holds her baby brother Christopher at far left.

used their talents for good. The belief that they lived a life of purpose permeates my memory.

❖ ❖ ❖

The loss of one of America's most beloved presidents—my uncle John Kennedy—to a brutal murder when I was 12 remains one of our nation's pivotal moments to this day. The memory is etched forever in the minds of those old enough to remember where they were when they heard that the president had been shot.

I was in music class at my school, the Convent of the Sacred Heart in Bethesda, Maryland, when Mother Mahaney came to tell me the news. Immediately I went home, where already many of my parents' friends had gathered. My normally loud and laughing home was now hushed.

I went upstairs to my parents' room and discussed the tragedy with a close friend of my father's, Dave Hackett. How on earth could this have happened? Wasn't my uncle fighting the good fights—against Communism and for civil

> *Because of John and Robert Kennedy, someone became a teacher or a social worker, joined the Peace Corps, or entered politics.*

rights, against poverty and for a more peaceful world? He had inspired millions of young people around the globe with his call to service. How could his own public service not have been protected? Where was the God we prayed to every day to protect Uncle John in his leadership? Did God know

this had happened? Did he care?

On the day that President Kennedy was buried, my father gave me a note he had just written. He was devastated. He had spent most of the time trying to comfort Aunt Jackie and working out the vast logistics, protocol, and transition in the wake of his brother's death. But what he wrote to me did not convey fear, anger, or bitterness. He did not speak of revenge. He focused on the future:

Dear Kathleen,

You seemed to understand that Jack died and was buried today. As the oldest of the Kennedy grandchildren, you have a particular responsibility now—a special responsibility to John [my cousin] and Joe [my brother]. Be kind to others and work for your country.
Love,
Daddy

Can you imagine, in your own moment of horrendous loss, reminding your child—and reminding yourself, really—to turn outward, not inward, to perform works of kindness and not of anger or revenge? It still stops my breath to think of my father stealing away on that chaotic, dreadful day for a quiet half minute at his desk to make sure I would have this message with me always. He entrusted me with his sense of duty to family and to country.

Over the next few months, my father spent many nights alone in his room. He read *The Greek Way* by the German-born educator and classicist Edith Hamilton. He read Aeschylus and Shakespeare in an effort to deal with the enormity of his loss and the greatness of his grief. Those readings put him in touch with the traditions that don't sugarcoat death, that don't diminish pain and loss and horror. The worst confronts us, and the question for each of us is, How do we respond?

The day that Martin Luther King Jr. was killed, my father was on his way to deliver a speech in Indianapolis during his campaign for president. He received word of Dr. King's murder and then word from Mayor Richard Lugar that he should not come to give the speech, as it was too dangerous downtown and the mayor could not guarantee his safety.

The mayor was not being unreasonable. Across the country, cities were about to break out in angry desperation and rioting as the awful news began to spread.

But my father believed that he had to go. His campaign was about reconciliation; he could not refuse to go. On his way there, he scribbled a few notes to himself.

Standing on the back of a flatbed truck, my father addressed the crowd and told them about Dr. King's death. They had not yet heard the news. After their gasps of grief and lost hope, he delivered a speech that, sadly, still resonates today (as my father also said to the crowd that day, "I had a member of my family killed … he was killed by a white man"):

"My favorite poet was Aeschylus. He once wrote, 'Even

Senator John F. Kennedy, left, with Robert in McLean, Virginia. "Their spirit lives in the work of many," says Kathleen.

in our sleep, pain which we cannot forget falls drop by drop upon the heart until, in our own despair, against our will comes wisdom through the awful grace of God.'

"What we need in the United States is not division. What we need in the United States is not hatred; what we need is not violence or lawlessness—but love and wisdom

I often heard, around our house, that Kennedys don't cry.

and compassion toward one another, and a feeling of justice for those who still suffer in our country whether they be white or whether they be black.

"So I ask you tonight to return home, to say a prayer for the family of Martin Luther King. But more importantly, to say a prayer for our own country, which all of us love— a prayer for understanding and compassion."

While riots broke out in more

than 100 cities that night, there were none in Indianapolis. A black assistant chief of police said that the senator and his family could have slept outside all night and remained unharmed. My father had reached people with his own understanding of suffering and pain and with what had been his clear determination to .rve and to help. His actions gave his words credibility.

❖   ❖   ❖

After my father was killed, I went to work on a Navajo reservation in Rough Rock, Arizona. I tutored in English, planted pistachio trees, and helped build a science center out of adobe brick. I had a sense of responsibility. I wanted to work. And over the next few years, I helped my mother take care of my younger brothers and sisters.

I had learned how to deal with death by watching my father's example. He had kept involved in public life. He had reached out to those who suffer. He had grasped the notion that suffering can be a path to wisdom, can be cathartic, a cleansing of the soul. And, all the time, he insisted to his own children that we try our best, do our best. He wanted to make sure that we had a sense of responsibility. To those who had been given much, much was expected.

I don't recall pity. We weren't expected to feel sorry for ourselves. Just the opposite. I often heard, around our house, that Kennedys don't cry.

I saw that my mother made an effort to be cheerful, to fill our house with activity and a sense that life must go on. That is, not to diminish the loss, which was horrific, but to affirm our duty to his memory and to the living.

Just as we honored those who had died, it was also wise to remember that we must live for those who were still with us. Our sadness didn't give us an excuse for endless solitude, for retreat from life's challenges. As Mother Jones, the great union activist of the early 20th century, put it: "Pray for the dead and fight like hell for the living."

I was attracted to the notion that I needed to put my energy into those who were still on earth. There were ten other children to care for. To retreat into a real recognition of death would have deserted those who were still living—who still needed us now.

There was not much solace in this. But the call to live for the living was compelling.

❖ ❖ ❖

My experience with my father's death is unique. But there are aspects of it that shed light on other situations.

When I was lieutenant governor of Maryland, I attended funerals for police, firefighters, and soldiers. Just as my father had, these men and women had died in the line of duty. They had given their lives so that we could all be safer, freer, and at peace. Our lives are better because of their dedication. The state of Maryland arranged their funerals with great solemnity, pomp, and circumstance. On a regular basis, their sacrifice was honored. The government and philanthropic individuals made a sustained effort to gather the families of these heroes together. It was important to let the families know that the sacrifice of

The author with her uncle Senator Edward M. Kennedy during her gubernatorial campaign in Maryland, October 2002.

their loved ones was appreciated.

Still, these stories are the exception. Most of us die in relative obscurity, as do those we love. We aren't afforded opportunities to talk about our parents or friends. We don't have annual ceremonies to remember them or to discuss the contributions they made to those around them, to remember their many dreams or to revive the spirit they embodied. We suffer their loss alone.

One of my daughters hates funerals. She really prefers not to go, even if they are for people she loved. I seldom succeed in convincing her to go.

But I wish I could. I find that funerals are a way to affirm a life, to acknowledge to myself and to the greater community that this person was important to me.

In his great poem "When Lilacs Last in the Dooryard Bloom'd," Walt Whitman wrote eloquently of how he wanted to break the twig of a lilac so that he could cover the coffin with the perfumed flower. That gesture speaks to the need we have to say to the deceased: "I love you, I care for you, I want to bless you. You are in my heart."

Giving Comfort

I have a set of lessons learned about how to console those who have suffered a loss, based on my own personal experience and observation over the years.

First, go to the funeral. Thirty years ago, Mayor Richard Lee of New Haven, Connecticut, told me that he always went to funerals. It's there that you see people, he said, and that they see you. It's there that you mingle with families, listen to them talk, and lend your full support. I had never heard that advice stated so explicitly, but he was exactly right. Death opens an enormous hole in the heart. A funeral service brings together those who can help fill that hole.

> *Most of us die in relative obscurity, as do those we love. We suffer their loss alone.*

Second, call or write your friend when someone close to her or him has died. It is remarkable how few people actually reach out in tough times. Perhaps they don't know what to say; perhaps they think the person would prefer to be left alone. It is better to try and be rejected than to never try at all. Your friend can always resist the effort—not answer the phone, not open the letter. But it is hard to imagine anyone not appreciating it.

Third, never say "You will get over it." People rarely do. The death of a loved one rips us apart, shakes us up, hurts terribly.

So my fourth tip is to embrace the person who suffers. I think of the kiss my mother would give me when I would scrape my knee or cut my finger. Her act of love was more healing than any antiseptic.

Make it clear in the letter or phone call to your friend that she or he is wonderful. The outstretched arm, the warm embrace, the freshly baked cookies, or the fragrant flowers do not replace the life. Not by any means.

But they do say to the grieving friend, "You are loved. You are cherished."

25 Jokes That Make You Sound like a Genius

If you want to find out how it feels to sound smart, try out some of these wisecracks.

—

BY **ANDY SIMMONS**

Originally published in September 2014

The smartest joke I ever heard was so clever, I didn't get it. Here it is: "Counting in binary is as easy as 01 10 11." I still don't get it, but I tell it all the time so I sound smart. These gags, held in high esteem among the literati, are best told with a smug smile.

1. What do you get when you cross a joke with a rhetorical question?

2. A pun, a play on words, and a limerick walk into a bar. No joke.

3. Oh, man! A hyperbole *totally* ripped into this bar and destroyed everything!

4. This sentence contains exactly threeee erors.

5. Knock, knock.
   Who's there?
   To.
   To who?
   No, to whom.

❖ ❖ ❖

Nothing has scrambled more brains than the sight of numerals waiting to be added, subtracted, divided, multiplied, or fractioned. See if you can tell these digit-laden jokes without stumbling.

6. Q: How do mathematicians scold their children?
   A: "If I've told you n times, I've told you n+1 times ..."

7. A mathematician wanders back home at 3 a.m. and proceeds to get an earful from his wife.
   "You're late!" she yells. "You said you'd be home by 11:45!"
   "Actually," the mathematician replies coolly, "I said I'd be home by a quarter of 12."

8. Did you hear about the mathematician who's afraid of negative numbers? He will stop at nothing to avoid them.

9. A recent finding by statisticians shows that the average human has one breast and one testicle.

❖ ❖ ❖

Musicians are looked upon as highly cultured. Leach off their reputation with these:

10. Why did Beethoven get rid of his chickens? All they said was, "Bach, Bach, Bach ..."

11. C, E-flat, and G walk into a bar.

The bartender shows them the door and says, "Sorry, we don't serve minors."

12. A sign at a music shop: "Gone Chopin. Bach in a minuet."

13. Q: What was Beethoven's favorite fruit?
A: BA-NA-NA-NAAAAAA!

❖ ❖ ❖

Telling these science-y gags screams "Behold! I am that person who did not blow up my chemistry class."

14. A photon is going through airport security. The TSA agent asks if he has any luggage. The photon says, "No, I'm traveling light."

15. What did the DNA say to the other DNA? "Do these genes make me look fat?"

16. The bartender says, "We don't serve time travelers in here."
A time traveler walks into a bar.

17. Did you hear about the suicidal homeopath? He took 1/50th of the recommended dose.

❖ ❖ ❖

Religion is fraught with roiling self-doubt and unwavering faith.

Show you're well aware of the issues by sharing these jests.

18. A ship, sailing past a remote island, spots a man who has been stranded there for several years. The captain goes ashore to rescue the man and notices three huts.
"What's the first hut for?" he asks.
"That's my house," says the castaway.
"What's the second hut for?"
"That's my church."
"And the third hut?"
"Oh, that?" sniffs the castaway. "That's the church I used to go to."

19. What did the Buddhist say to the hot dog vendor? "Make me one with everything."

20. A man is talking to God. "God, how long is a million years?"
God answers, "To me, it's about a minute."
"God, how much is a million dollars?"
"To me, it's a penny."
"God, may I have a penny?"
"Wait a minute."

❖ ❖ ❖

Is it your hope to impress upon people that you've been around the globe a few times? Trot out these worldly gags:

21. If you jumped off the bridge in Paris, you'd be in Seine.

22. Your mama is so classless, she could be a Marxist utopia.

23. A German walks into a bar and asks for a martini. The bartender asks, "Dry?"

The German replies, "Nein, just one."

24. René Descartes walks into a bar. The bartender says, "Would you like a beer?"

Descartes replies, "I think not," and promptly disappears.

25. Did you hear about the weekly poker game with Vasco da Gama, Christopher Columbus, Leif Erikson, and Francisco Pizarro? They can never seem to beat the Straights of Magellan.

The Sweet Uses of Solitude

It's separateness that enriches togetherness—or is it the other way around?

———

BY **JOAN MILLS**

Originally published in June 1970

ometimes it's best to be in company— sometimes better yet to be alone. I believe in both, and when I am surfeited with one, I feel compelled to the other. My pleasures come point-counterpoint.

Whenever I am locked into a series of days with a friend or relative—beloved, yes, but who will not, will not, let go—panic rises in me. "I must write a letter," I say, fleeing to my room. The other stands outside my door, relentlessly relaying the news about Berlioz,

urban renewal, corn cures, her analysis. I claw the sheets, or hang out the window, panting.

Or I am too much alone. No one comes near. No friend is at home to answer my call or hear me knock, and I need human contact. I go to market and engage the vegetable man in a discussion of his broccoli; I take the car to the gas station where I am called "dearie" and feel wanted.

In the ordinary rhythm of my life, it's easy to balance society and solitude. At the far side of every week spent in great part by myself, there is a weekend overflowing with friends and family. When enough of that is quite enough, Monday comes. Then everyone is gone but me.

On Monday mornings, I wander through unpeopled rooms, listening to the large, soft silence, giving myself over to being all alone. It is like a return to having a very private place in which to know oneself, and grow.

Children make such retreats for themselves. A towering old pine stands between woods and meadow near our house. Among its branches, in green obscurity, our two sons longed to build a deck of boards now weathered black. I imagine— for I never violated that privacy to see—that they created fanciful adventures there, or sprawled, lax and dreamy, breathing the summer air, sorting sounds, coming to friendly terms with bugs, and brooding upon the stately drift of clouds.

The loved place of my own childhood was a packing box. A piano had come in it; then it was painted and installed under a tree. No adult cared to take the long walk through burs and dusty grass to where it sat. No other child lived near enough to spy upon, envy, or ask to share its alluring privacy.

Daylight sank through leaves and entered the box by a window my father had cut and I had curtained with thumbtacked squares of chintz. The door was scaled to my size, open often to the sun or shut against the occasional leak of rain down the layers of golden willow.

A quilt within was wadded into lumps that fitted me—its calico pattern dimmed by an overprint of jam and chocolate, pollen smudges, crayon streaks, and berry stains. It was a lived-in quilt, and tucked into its hollows were many comforts: a rag doll floppily amenable to any scheme of mine, a pair of high heels to wear when I read adult literature, pebbles of satisfying shapes, a magnifying glass that made ants look alarming, and a harmonica that in the house drove my mother mad because I mostly kept it in my mouth and breathed two-notedly through it, in and out, absorbed in other things.

In the packing box, I was free to think about whatever pleased or puzzled me, which was considerable. I hummed homemade tunes, read books soft-spined from loving use. I arranged bouquets of bluets or buttercups in season, and chewed ruminatively on the sweet centers of clover blossoms. I solaced myself for what I did not have by imagining I had it—and thereby learned how little I needed to be happy. Every scent or sound or touch of air or prick of thought lightly reverberated, and added to the sum of me and all I knew.

My children have outgrown their secret, special places—and certainly so have I. But the feel of what those hidey-holes meant to us lingers, incorporated into the privacy we keep intact within ourselves. Even in company, we can withdraw to that when the need is on us: how often have I, deep in my thoughts, been unaware of the blathering of television, the boys racketing up and down the stairs, the girl squealing into the telephone.

Sometimes we move by only a little out of the immediacy of persons. I linger at the window that frames my favorite view or go out to look for mushrooms I daren't pick and eat. My husband skis for the sake of experience enjoyed alone and comes home happy for warmth and sociability. Our daughter takes to her car, the boys to their rooms. Each, in his own time, returns to be with people.

To be with people.

"I cannot bear to be lonely," I say, and it is true. My heart thrives upon the talk—and silences—by which we communicate with a near but always separate and different other. I like to close the distance with a touch of the hand; it reassures me. But I was a solitary child, and the habit of solitude is strong in me, too. I'm grateful that once a year or so my husband grants me a reserve of privacy by taking the children and himself away for a few days.

When they have gone, I neaten the house at once. The setting must be serene for the weightless, ruleless, easeful hours that are mine to spend. Beyond the tidying, I make no plans. That's the glory part.

No one knows if I am up and functioning, or if I am shamelessly snoring at noon. I can type at midnight, and nobody comes to glare and mutter. No one bangs on the bathroom door when I linger long in the tub, turning the hot water on and off with my toes and sloshing deliciously. No critic comments upon my working at crewel through the supper hour and dining much later by the flickering light of the late show.

Ah, my friends, it is grand. Alone, but not lonely, I postulate philosophies, explore my soul, and in the modesty of solitude, expose my love and angers, wishes and disappointments. I examine each, and put it in its place. Alone, I redefine my appreciation of the people with whom I live. I remember which child it is that keeps me womanly company when I cook, which it is that has displayed an unexpected tenderness or gallantry. I grin at discovering a boy's snorkeling gear hung beside the bathtub, reminding me that I am not the only one who lives here or, indeed, the only one prone to act out fantasies. Luxuriating in a bed to myself, I think of how companionable it is at other times to have somebody to talk to in the dark.

Time passes. I begin to mind being alone. Not much, at first, but some. Then more. "Well," I think, "maybe I should bake a pie for when they come home." And I do.

Then, suddenly, here they are, filling the house with greetings, belongings, souvenirs, and bags of laundry. They scatter the pieces of my privacy like dust upon the wind. It's all right. "I'm glad you're back," I say honestly. "I've been missing you."

"I missed you, too," someone says, bending to sniff the pie.

It's separateness that sweetens togetherness—or is it the other way around?

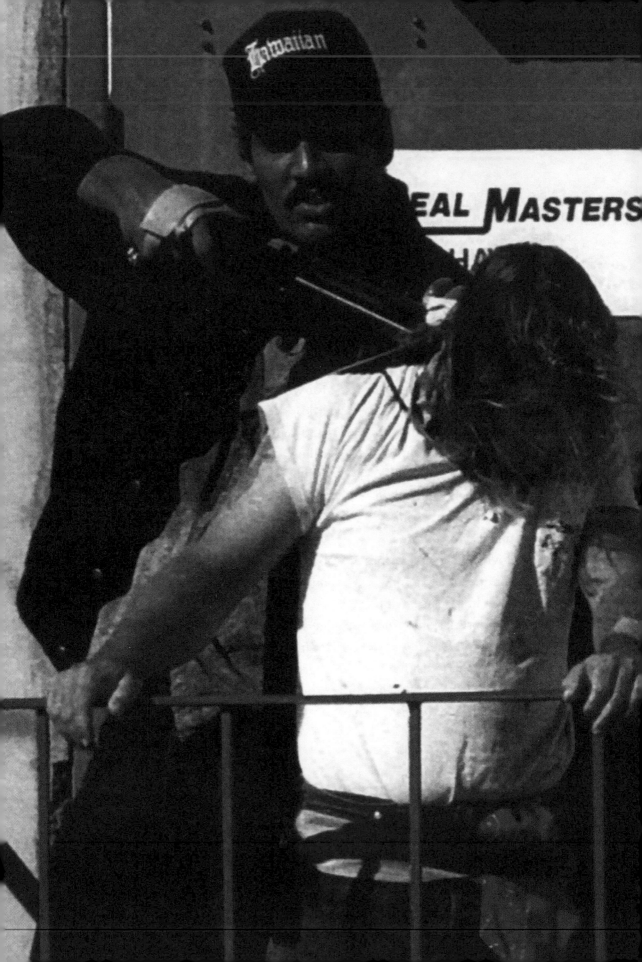

Alone with a Madman

With the barrel of a shotgun taped to the young man's neck, the countdown began.

———

BY WILLIAM M. HENDRYX

Originally published in March 1997

I t was going to be another glorious day in Hawaii. Wearing faded jeans and a white T-shirt, Tom McNeil, 30, slipped behind the wheel of his pickup and headed for Seal Masters of Hawaii, a concrete restoration company, where he worked as a specialist in waterproofing.

As he drove to the industrial enclave six miles west of Waikiki, Tom let his mind drift back to the lovely candlelight dinner his girlfriend, Sherri Davidson, had prepared for him the night before. McNeil had been attracted to the 26-year-old office manager at Seal Masters right from the start, and recently they had even started to talk about getting married.

At about the same time McNeil was setting out for work, Dick Spies, 64, arrived at the office and started a pot of coffee. Minutes later, Spies, vice president of Seal Masters, was joined by Guy George, also a vice president, and two workmen.

At about 6:50 a.m., Spies heard the heavy metal entrance door slam shut. He glanced down the hall, expecting to see Tom McNeil. Instead, a mountain of a man, wearing a dark jacket and long black shorts, filled the doorway. He held a semiautomatic shotgun, leveled waist-high.

"Hi, guys!" the man said, flashing a bitter, sardonic grin.

"Remember me?"

Dick Spies instantly recognized John Miranda.

"Good God, John," Spies said, struggling to keep his voice under control. "What are you doing?"

"Getting even!" the 28-year-old Hawaiian-Puerto Rican said. "This place is prejudiced against the brothers! Everyone drop to the floor, facedown!"

Miranda flung a phone at Spies and ordered him to call the company president. Spies punched in the number, then Miranda snatched back the phone. He demanded $20,000 in cash from the president—money, he claimed, for mistreated Hawaiians.

Forced on the Floor

Normally, Tom McNeil would have gone directly to his job site, but he had told Spies he would stop by the office to discuss their newest project. Just after 7 a.m. that Tuesday, February 6, 1996, McNeil started up the steel exterior stairs that led from the parking lot to the second-floor office of Seal Masters. *Oh, no,* he thought, noticing a

familiar car in the lot. *Not that guy again!*

McNeil was generally an easygoing, nonjudgmental guy, but John Miranda was one of the biggest troublemakers he'd ever encountered. A known drug abuser, Miranda had been in and out of trouble with the police. He had worked at Seal Masters off and on for approximately four years and

Using Guy George as a shield, he pointed the gun over the man's head and fired one blast.

always seemed to have a beef with someone. At six feet five inches tall and more than 240 pounds, he especially liked to intimidate smaller guys.

McNeil walked down the hall to Spies's office and was surprised to find the door closed. He heard muffled voices and knocked twice before the door eased open. Miranda's massive frame blocked any view of the room. His dark eyes were glassy, betraying the likely use of cocaine or methamphetamines. The round black opening of the shotgun muzzle was pointed at McNeil's chest.

"Get your butt in here, Tom!" Miranda growled.

Minutes later Miranda ordered the men to go to the owner's two-room office suite a few steps down the hall. *Thank God Sherri's not here yet*, McNeil thought. The outer office of the suite was hers.

Miranda forced them to lie on the floor, then ordered one of the workmen to bind their hands behind them with duct tape.

Just then, footsteps sounded on the metal stairs outside. Miranda grabbed the door. It was almost 8 a.m., the time Sherri Davidson reported for work.

Oh, God, no! McNeil thought.

Shattering Blast

Several years earlier, Davidson had accepted a job offer at Seal Masters and moved from her native Texas to Hawaii, the place of her dreams. One day Tom McNeil walked into her office. It wasn't exactly love at first sight, but the more she got to know the gentle young man with honest blue eyes, the deeper her feelings ran.

When Davidson got to the office that morning, she found the main door locked. *What's going on here?* she wondered. *Why is the door still closed up?*

While she looked for her keys, the door swung open, and Miranda pointed the shotgun at her throat. His eyes darted like a caged animal's. "Get the hell out of here, Sherri," he snarled.

Davidson clambered down the stairs. Moments later, the heavy steel door crashed open and Miranda stepped out. Using Guy George as a shield, he pointed the gun over the man's head and fired one blast into the cloudless sky. "I've got hostages!" he yelled. Then he ducked back inside, taking George with him.

The distinct smell of cordite from the gun blast hung heavy in the air. *Has George been shot?* McNeil wondered. *Or Sherri?*

A moment later, Miranda pushed

George back into Davidson's office and shot out the window behind her desk. Then he pointed the muzzle toward George. "You messed with me too long, man," he ranted. "You don't give a damn about the brothers!"

Miranda pulled the trigger. The blast ripped into George's right calf, splattering blood and flesh over Davidson's desk and the surrounding walls. George screamed in pain and collapsed.

On the floor in the next room, bound like a sheep headed for slaughter, McNeil had never felt more powerless in his life. *Guy is dead,* McNeil thought. *And we're next!*

Taped to the Gun

At 9:10 a.m., Miranda spoke with a local radio station, hoping to state his case to the public. The station manager decided not to broadcast the conversation, but to pass along details to the police.

The disc jockey asked Miranda, "Man, what happened to cause you to do this?"

"I don't know," Miranda answered. "I guess just stress, you know?"

"Now, you're not going to do anything weird here, right?" the DJ asked.

"Believe me," said Miranda, "those people are going to die. I sure ain't going back to prison."

The conversation continued for several minutes, but when Miranda discovered his words were not being broadcast, he slammed down the phone. "All right," he yelled to the hostages. "We're going to the bathroom!"

He's taking us in there to kill us! McNeil thought.

Miranda left Guy George, who couldn't move, and Dick Spies behind. He marched McNeil and the two workmen to the nearby bathroom and forced them to lie on the floor. *This is it!* McNeil thought, every muscle tensed. But to his surprise, Miranda entered a stall and relieved himself. McNeil tried to get his hands out of the tape, but it still held. Running or fighting would be impossible.

Around 9:30 Miranda forced the trio back to Davidson's office.

Guy George, one of the hostages, slips out of an office window and drops 12 feet to the ground, leaving a swath of blood on the side of the building.

George was gone! He had crawled to the window Miranda had shot out and dropped 12 feet to the ground.

Miranda erupted. He grabbed McNeil and jabbed the shotgun hard against the base of his neck. "Tape it on!" he commanded one of the hostages. "Nice and tight!"

Avoiding McNeil's eyes, his coworker wrapped silver two-inch tape around McNeil's neck several times, then made several wraps around the muzzle of the shotgun.

"Now, wrap some around my hand and the trigger," Miranda demanded. "If the cops shoot me, Tom's going down too!" Reluctantly, the workman wrapped tape around Miranda's right hand, binding it to the gun's trigger guard.

The cold steel barrel of the shotgun pressed against McNeil's head. *I'm a dead man!* he thought.

Miranda ordered Spies to hand over his keys and told him to stay put on the floor. "The rest of us are going to take a ride in Dick's truck," Miranda announced. He paraded the three men out the door and down the stairs, holding McNeil. "Don't try anything or he's dead!" he yelled out to the police.

The intersection just beyond Seal Masters was now closed off with patrol cars and heavily armed officers, including police negotiation team leader Lt. Karen Kaniho.

Concerned that his hostages weren't bound well enough, Miranda sent a workman back for more tape. The police, who had entered the building through a back door, grabbed the man and took him and Spies out to safety.

When the workman did not return, Miranda panicked. "Get back up the stairs!" he ordered McNeil and the remaining workman.

With the gun taped snugly to his neck, McNeil had no choice but to comply. But the other hostage saw his chance. He hurdled a four-foot retaining wall at the foot of the stairs and ran for his life.

Now Tom McNeil was all alone with the madman. At the top of the stairs, Miranda convulsed in a rage of swearing when he found the door locked. He was becoming more dangerous—and erratic.

Scanning the mass of police, media and spectators who had gathered below, Miranda grinned, apparently taking pleasure in being the center of attention. Then he muttered, "What the hell am I gonna do now?"

"You've got to give it up, John," McNeil said softly. "You're not a murderer, man."

What McNeil didn't know—what no one knew at the time—was that Miranda had killed his girlfriend just days before.

Deadly Pattern

Several hundred yards away, Sherri Davidson strained to see what was happening atop the stairway. The big guy with the gun had to be Miranda. But who was tied to the gun?

Nearby, a man held a pair of binoculars. "Could I borrow

those?" Davidson asked. She focused the lens. *It's Tom!*

Her knees buckled. "Please, God," she sobbed. "Save Tom for me!"

As noon approached, Miranda's bizarre behavior was showing a pattern Karen Kaniho recognized. He seemed intent on killing McNeil right before their eyes, which would force the police to shoot to stop

> ## "You've got to give it up, John," McNeil said softly. "You're not a murderer, man."

him. In police circles it's known as "suicide by cops."

Indeed, Miranda was following textbook signs of someone bent on self-destruction. First the subject announces his intent to die, and then he creates a confrontational posture with police. Five or six times Miranda marched his tethered victim up and down the stairs. "Go ahead, rush me!" he taunted. "I'm

going to blow him away, then you can blow me away!"

Kaniho took hope from the fact that negotiators had been communicating with Miranda for hours. He hadn't yet hurt McNeil, so the police still had a chance to save the hostage and take Miranda alive.

Like most of the men who worked in the field, McNeil carried a silent pager, one that pulsated when someone was calling. He and Davidson had worked out a secret code so she could buzz him during the day to signal "I'm thinking about you." Now she sent the message again and again. Miranda could not hear it, but McNeil knew Davidson was sending him her love and prayers.

By 2:30 p.m. one of the TV crews had let Davidson watch their monitor. Suddenly, a reporter interrupted the broadcast: "We've just received word that the gunman has started a 60-second countdown to the end!"

"God, no!" Davidson screamed, covering her ears from the expected blast.

Tom and Sherri McNeil are now married and living in Honolulu.

"Watch for crossfire!"

Lieutenant Kaniho's team offered the $20,000 to Miranda if he would remove the strapping from McNeil's neck. Miranda refused. He was becoming more frustrated and erratic as time wore on. After several more police attempts at negotiation, Miranda finally snapped.

"I'm just going to blow this guy's head off!" he screamed. "You've got 60 seconds, starting right now!"

Miranda jammed the gun against McNeil's neck. "Count, Tom! Count backward from 60!"

For seven grueling, tense hours now, McNeil had played the role of submissive hostage, trying to reason with Miranda, using his wits to keep him from going over the edge. But he would not count down to his own death.

Getting no response, Miranda began the count himself. "60, 59, 58 ..." The police braced to shoot Miranda. "Watch for crossfire!" they shouted at one another.

McNeil cocked his head to one side. His sweat had created slack in the tape, giving him a few inches of flexibility. He turned, looking over his left shoulder at his captor. "You don't have to do this, John," McNeil said softly, noting how Miranda was holding the gun. "You can still walk away."

"Don't look at me!" Miranda growled. "55, 54, 53 ..."

Kaniho and the negotiators tried to intervene. "The money's here, John," one yelled, holding up a wad of cash. "Stop counting and talk to us."

"It's too late!" said Miranda. "47, 46, 45 ..."

Dead or alive, McNeil decided, he'd go out fighting.

"24, 23, 22..."

McNeil leaned his head back against the hard steel muzzle. *Good, it's slightly to the right side,* he thought. Slowly, he eased his entire body to the left. "16, 15, 14..."

McNeil stiffened, his body screaming with adrenaline, his mind rehearsing each movement. *NOW!*

He darted hard to the left, dipped his left shoulder, and spun 180 degrees to face his captor—hair and flesh twisting under the tape. Miranda towered over him, but the look of surprise in his dark eyes said he'd lost control.

McNeil grabbed the gun barrel with his left hand and shoved it upward. *KA-BOOM!* The shot went past McNeil's ear.

Face-to-face, hand-to-hand, McNeil struggled for survival. *KA-BOOM!* The second shot bounced off the hot asphalt and deflected away.

McNeil dropped to one knee at Miranda's feet, giving the police a clear shot at the hulking man above. In the next instant, McNeil's ears rang with the sound of gunfire. *Pack! Pack! Pack! Pack!*

The bulky body of a fatally wounded John Miranda collapsed to the pavement. McNeil kneeled at his assailant's side, the gun still lashed to his neck.

❖ ❖ ❖

The body of Miranda's girlfriend, Sherry Lynn Holmes, was found in a wooded area on March 29, 1996. She had last been seen two days before the hostage incident. The medical examiner fixed the cause of death as asphyxia caused by strangulation.

Guy George underwent surgery on his leg and began a painful recovery. Tom McNeil was treated for mild dehydration. Six days after his countdown to death, surrounded by friends, he and Sherri Davidson married.

"She was with me through every moment of that ordeal," says McNeil. "I wanted to give her that same commitment, to be at her side for the rest of our lives."

"I Died at 10:52 A.M."

*For 23 minutes, the author's heart stopped,
and with it all signs of life.
This is what he experienced.*

———

BY **VICTOR D. SOLOW**

Originally published in October 1974

When I left home with my wife last March 23 to go for a ten-minute jog, I did not know that I would be gone for two weeks. My trip was the one that all of us must make eventually, from which only a rare few return. In my case a series of events occurred so extraordinarily timed to allow my eventual survival that words like "luck" or "coincidence" no longer seem applicable.

It was a beautiful Saturday morning. We had jogged and were driving back home to Mamaroncck, New York, along the Boston Post Road. It was 10:52 a.m. I had just stopped at a red light, opposite a gas station. My long, strange trip was about to start, and I must now use my wife's words to describe what happened for the next few minutes:

"Victor turned to me and said, 'Oh, Lucy, I...' Then, as swiftly as the expiration of a breath, he seemed simply to settle down in his seat with all his weight. His head remained erect, his eyes opened wide, like someone utterly astonished. I knew instantly he could no longer hear or see me.

"I pulled on the emergency

brake, pleading with him to hang on, shouting for help. The light changed and traffic moved around my car. No one noticed me. My husband's color had now turned gray-green; his mouth hung open, but his eyes continued seemingly to view an astounding scene. I frantically tried to pull him to the other seat so I could drive him to the hospital. Then my cries for help attracted Frank Colangelo, proprietor of the gas station, who telephoned the police."

WHEN SECONDS COUNT. It was now 10:55—three minutes had elapsed since my heart arrest. A first-aid manual reads, "When breathing and heartbeat stop and are not artificially started, death is inevitable. Therefore, artificial resuscitation must be started immediately. Seconds count." Time was running out. In another 60 seconds my brain cells could start to die.

Now came the first of the coincidences: Before police headquarters could radio the emergency call, Officer James Donnellan, cruising along the Boston Post Road, arrived at the intersection where our car seemed stalled. Checking me for pulse and respiration, and finding neither, he pulled me from the car with the help of Mr. Colangelo, and immediately started to perform cardiopulmonary resuscitation.

In the meantime, the police alert had reached Officer Michael Sena, who chanced to be cruising just half a mile from the scene. He reached me in less than half a minute. From his car Sena yanked an oxygen tank and an apparatus with a mask that is used to force air into the lungs. Within seconds he had the mask over my face. Donnellan continued with heart massage.

Sena later told me, "I was sure we were just going through the motions. I would have bet my job that you were gone."

Police headquarters also alerted the emergency rescue squad via a high-pitched radio signal on the small alert devices all squad members carry on their belts. When his warning signal went off, Tom McCann, volunteer firefighter and trained emergency medical technician, was conducting a fire inspection. He looked up and saw Officers Donnellan and Sena working on a "body" less than 50 yards away. McCann made the right connection and raced over, arriving just ten seconds after his alarm sounded.

"I tried the carotid pulse—you had no pulse," McCann later said. "There was no breathing. Your eyes were open, and your pupils were dilated—a bad sign!" Dilated pupils indicate that blood is not reaching the brain. It can mean that death has occurred.

IT WAS 10:56. McCann, who weighs 270 pounds, began to give me a no-nonsense heart massage.

PERFECT TIMING. The strange coincidences continued. The emergency squad warning beeper went off at the exact moment when Peter Brehmer, Ronald Capasso, Chip Rigano, and Richard and Paul Torpey were meeting at the firehouse to change shifts. A moment later and they would have left. The ambulance was right there. Everybody piled in. Manned by five trained first-aid technicians, the ambulance arrived three minutes later.

IT WAS 10:59. When I was being moved into the ambulance, United Hospital in Port Chester, six miles distant, was radioed. The hospital called a "Code 99" over its loudspeaker system, signaling all available personnel into the Emergency Room. Here, an ideal combination of specialists was available when I arrived; two internists, two surgeons, two technicians from the cardiology department, two respiratory therapists, and four nurses were waiting. Dr. Harold Roth later said: "The patient at that point was dead by available standards. There was no measurable pulse, he was not breathing, and he appeared to have no vital signs whatever."

11:10 A.M. A cardiac monitor was attached, a tube supplying pure oxygen was placed in my windpipe, intravenous injections were started. An electric-shock apparatus was then attached to my chest.

11:14. The first electric shock was powerful enough to lift my body inches off the operating table. But there was no result; my heart still showed no activity.

11:15. A second electric shock was administered—a final try. Twenty-three minutes had elapsed since my heart had stopped. Now, excitement exploded around the operating table as an irregular heart rhythm suddenly showed on the monitor. To everyone's amazement, I sat bolt upright and started to get off the table. I had to be restrained.

"THERE... AND BACK." Sometime later I was aware that my eyes were open. But I was still part of another world. It seemed that by chance I had been given this human body and it was difficult to wear. Dr. Roth later related: "I came to see you in the Coronary Care Unit. You were perfectly conscious. I asked how you felt, and your response was: 'I feel like I've been there and I've come back.' It was true: You were there and now you were back."

A hard time followed. I could not connect with the world around me. Was I really here now, or was it an illusion? Was that other condition of being I had just experienced the reality, or was that the illusion? I would lie there and observe my body with suspicion and amazement. It seemed to be doing things of its own volition and I was a visitor within. How strange to see my hand reach out for something. Eating, drinking, watching people had a dreamlike, slow-motion quality as if seen through a veil.

During those first few days I was two people. My absentmindedness and strange detachment gave the doctors pause. Perhaps the brain had been damaged after all. Their concern is reflected in hospital records:

"Retrograde amnesia and difficulty with subsequent current events was recognized ... The neurologist felt prognosis was rather guarded regarding future good judgment ..."

On the sixth day there was a sudden change. When I woke up, the world around me no longer seemed so peculiar. Something in me had decided to complete the return trip. From that day on, recovery was rapid. Eight days later

I was discharged from the hospital.

QUESTIONS. Now family, friends, and strangers began to ask what "death was like." Could I remember what had happened during those 23 minutes when my heart and breathing stopped? I found that the experience could not easily be communicated.

Later, feeling and thinking my way back into the experience, I discovered why I could not make it a simple recital of events: When I left my body I also left all sensory human tools behind with which we perceive the world we take for real. But I found that I now knew certain things about my place in this our world and my relationship to that other reality. My knowing was not through my brain but with another part of me that I cannot explain.

TRANSCENDENCE. For me, the moment of transition from life to death—what else can one call it?—was easy. There was no time for fear, pain or thought. There was no chance "to see my whole life before me," as others have related. The last impression I can recall lasted a brief instant. I was moving at high speed toward a net of great luminosity. The strands and knots where the luminous lines intersected were vibrating with a tremendous cold energy. The grid appeared as a barrier that would prevent further travel. I did not want to move through the grid. For a brief moment my speed appeared to slow down. Then I was in the grid. The instant I made contact with it, the vibrant luminosity increased to a blinding intensity, which drained, absorbed, and transformed me at the same time. There was no pain. The sensation was neither pleasant nor unpleasant but completely consuming. The nature of everything had changed. Words only vaguely approximate the experience from this instant on.

The grid was like a transformer, an energy converter transporting me through form and into formlessness, beyond time and space. Now I was not in a place, nor even in a dimension, but rather in a condition of being. This new "I" was not the I that I knew, but rather a distilled essence of it, yet something vaguely familiar, something I had always known that was buried under a superstructure of personal fears, hopes, wants, and needs. This "I" had no connection to ego. It was final, unchangeable, indivisible, indestructible pure spirit. While completely unique and individual as a fingerprint, "I" was, at the same time, part of some infinite, harmonious, and ordered whole. I had been there before.

The condition "I" was in was pervaded by a sense of great stillness and deep quiet. Yet there was also a sense of something momentous about to be revealed, a further change. But there is nothing further to tell except of my sudden return to the operating table.

I would like to repeat that these experiences outside the dimensions of our known reality did not "happen" as if I were on some sort of a voyage I could recollect. Rather, I discovered them afterward, rooted in my consciousness as a kind of unquestionable knowing. Being of a somewhat skeptical turn of mind, I am willing to grant the possibility that this is a leftover of some subtle form of brain damage. I know,

however, that since my return from that other condition of being, many of my attitudes toward our world have changed and continue to change, almost by themselves. A recurrent nostalgia remains for that other reality, that condition of indescribable stillness and quiet where the "I" is part of a harmonious whole. The memory softens the old drives for possession, approval and success.

POSTSCRIPT. I have just returned from a pleasant, slow, 1½-mile jog. I am sitting in our garden writing. Overhead a huge dogwood moves gently in a mild southerly breeze. Two small children, holding hands, walk down the street absorbed in their own world.

I am glad I am in the here and now. But I know that this marvelous place of sun and wind, flowers, children, and lovers, this murderous place of evil, ugliness, and pain, is only one of many realities through which I must travel to distant and unknown destinations. For the time being, I belong to the world and it belongs to me.

What I Learned from Hemingway

A budding writer is taught more about life than about letters.

BY **W. J. LEDERER**

Originally published in March 1962

Twenty years ago I was stationed on a U.S. Navy river gunboat at Chungking, China. I was only a junior-grade lieutenant, but in a modest way I was suddenly famous. At a Chinese "blind auction," I had bid on a large sealed wooden box, the contents of which were unknown. It was heavy as stone; everyone was certain it was filled with rocks, for the auctioneer was renowned for his practical jokes.

I had bid $30. When the auctioneer pointed to me and shouted "Sold!" someone whispered, "Another American sucker!" But when I opened the box, there were groans of envy and frustration. Inside were two cases of whiskey, a precious item in wartime Chungking.

A clerk from the British consulate offered me $30 for one bottle. I received other rich offers, but I refused them all. It was almost time for me to be transferred, and I planned to throw a big farewell party.

Ernest Hemingway peruses a page of his writing, circa 1944.

It was at this time that Ernest Hemingway came to Chungking. Like many others, he suffered from what we called Szechuan drought —a great thirst for alcohol when none was available. One day he came down to my gunboat, the USS *Tutuila*. "I hear you have two cases of booze," he said.

"Yup."

"What'll you take for six bottles?"

"Sorry, sir, but they're not for sale. I'm saving them all for a brawl when I receive orders to get the heck out of here."

Hemingway took out a fat roll of money. "I'll give you anything you want for a half-dozen bottles," he said.

"Anything?"

"You name the price."

I thought this over. "OK. I'll swap you six bottles for six lessons on how to become a writer."

"That's steep," he said. "Hell, man, it took me years to learn my trade."

"And it took me years of getting ripped off at auctions before I struck my bonanza."

Hemingway grinned. "It's a bargain."

I handed him the six bottles. During the next five days he gave me five lessons. He was a superb teacher. Also, he had a knack for making jokes. Frequently I kidded him back, especially about the whiskey. "You know, Mr. Hemingway, my taking a chance at

> ### At a "blind auction," I had bid on a large sealed wooden box, contents still unknown.

that auction sure has paid off. First, I fooled that auctioneer. And how I scroggled the other customers who were too chicken to bid! And now for six bottles of whiskey I'm getting the hard-earned literary secrets of the best writer in America."

He winked. "You're a shrewd trader. What I want to know is, just how many of those other bottles have you been tippling in private?"

"I haven't opened a one," I said.

"I'm saving every drop for my big party."

"Son, I want to give you some personal advice. Never delay kissing a pretty girl or opening a bottle of whiskey. Both should be investigated as quickly as possible."

Hemingway had to leave Chungking earlier than expected. I went to the airport with him, in order to collect my sixth lesson.

"I haven't forgotten it," he said. "I'm going to give it to you right now."

The plane's engines were roaring, and he put his head close to mine. "Bill," he said, "before you can write about people, you must be a civilized man. To be civilized, you must have two things: compassion and ability to roll with the punches. Never laugh at a guy who has had bad luck. And if you have bad luck, don't fight it; roll with it—and bounce back."

"I can't see why that's important for a writer," I interrupted, not quite understanding him.

"It's vital to anything you want in life," he said slowly.

Porters were loading the luggage, and Hemingway started toward the aircraft. On the way he turned and shouted, "Friend, you'd better sample that liquor before sending out invitations to that big wingding!"

A few minutes later the plane was in the air. When I got back to where the liquor was stowed, I opened a bottle. Then another and another. All were filled with tea. The auctioneer had swindled me after all!

Hemingway must have known this from the first day. But he never said so, never laughed at me, and he kept his part of the bargain cheerfully. Now I knew what he meant by being a civilized man.

Early to Bed and Late to Rise...

There are some mornings when it just doesn't pay to get out of bed—such as Monday through Friday.

—

BY **DON HEROLD**

Originally published in August 1965

've decided that getting up and going to work is just a form of nervousness, so I keep calm and stay in bed. It takes arrogance and courage, but I stay right there until I get some work done. Then I may go down to my office and play.

When I say play, I mean dictating letters, answering the telephone, holding "conferences" and doing those other office chores that most people call work.

One of the reasons I stay adamantly in bed in the a.m. is that I am an unusually energetic person, without a lazy bone in my body, and my natural impulses are to leap up, shave and dress in a jiffy, rush to the office, and start the day busily, achieving practically nothing. Instead I force myself to start what I consider real work at seven o'clock or eight, or whenever I wake up, and to stay at it and finish it before I waste any pep on the useless, unimportant movements of rising and getting to an office, or distracting myself with the morning paper and the morning mail.

I never look at my mail until afternoon. Looking at the mail first thing in the morning is nothing but sheer boyish curiosity, mixed with a certain amount of laziness. A man who attends to his morning mail in the morning is letting other people decide how he is to spend his day. (I've observed over the years that most people accomplish little more every day than getting up and going to work.)

I tell myself that my work is somewhat mental, and that a person can come nearer to being 100 percent mental in bed than anywhere else. His galluses don't chafe, his shoes don't hurt, the angle of the chair does not annoy him, he does not have to figure what to do with his arms or legs. If he has a brain, he's practically nothing but brain ... in bed.

Another advantage is that bed is the one place in the world where other people leave a man alone. People somehow regard bedrooms as sacred territory and do not, as a rule, crash in uninvited.

Furthermore, people feel that a normal man in bed fairly late in the morning must be sick, perhaps with something infectious. Let 'em think so!

Ruskin was grasping for a seclusion similar to that which bed gives when, upon entering on a serious spell of work, he sent out cards reading: "Mr. J. Ruskin is about to begin a work of great importance and therefore begs that in reference to calls and correspondence you will consider him dead for the next two months."

Mark Twain was the patron saint of all bed workers. He was a sensationally sensible man, and he saw no point in getting up to write.

A more recent advocate of bed work was Winston Churchill, who remained in bed until late in the a.m., went to bed again after lunch and again later in the day. Thanks to this conservation of energy, he lived into his hearty 90s.

Another famous bed worker was Rossini, the composer. Once, while composing an opera in bed, he dropped one of the arias on the floor and it slid some distance away. Instead of getting up to retrieve it, he merely wrote a new aria.

It is said Voltaire did most of his scribbling in bed, and that Disraeli wrote some of his greatest speeches while stretched out on the floor. And lawyer Louis Nizer says, "I prefer to work from a reclining position. Even my office chair tilts, and a hidden footrest permits me to recline sufficiently, without offending my client's notion of dignity. I have found justification for my lazy posture in medical journals that suggest that it takes strain off the heart and increases stamina as well as thinking powers."

My own theory is that an office is one of the least efficient inventions of modern man, and that it should be stayed out of as much as possible. If housewives only knew how most executive husbands fritter away their days, their awe of "father at the office" would become one more shattered schoolgirl illusion. Most men get more real work done on their trips and vacations than they do all the rest of the year. My regimen of relaxation brings all sorts of shame on my head. I am called a laggard, a bum, an escapist; I've also been accused of suffering from habitual hangovers. Perhaps I may even be accused of working for the Associated Mattress Manufacturers of America: If they can get everybody to spend 25 percent more time in bed, it will eventually boost mattress sales 25 percent. That's all right with me. What's good for the Associated Mattress Manufacturers is good for the country.

How to Be True to You

Give wisely and carry a big stick.

—

BY **SCOTT RUSSELL SANDERS**
FROM THE BOOK **HUNTING FOR HOPE**

Originally published in June 2000

knew a man, a very tall and spare and gentle man, for several years before I found out that he visited prisoners in our county jail, week in and week out, for decades. He would write letters for them, carry messages, fetch clothing or books. But mainly he just offered himself. He didn't preach to them, didn't pick and choose between the likable and the nasty, didn't look for any return on his kindness. All that mattered was that they were in trouble.

Why did he spend time with outcasts when he could have been golfing or watching TV?

"I go in case everyone else has given up on them," he told me once. "I never give up."

Never giving up is a trait we honor in athletes, in soldiers, in survivors of disaster, in patients recovering from severe injuries. If you struggle bravely against overwhelming odds, you're liable to end up on the evening news. But in less flashy, less newsworthy forms, fidelity to a mission or a person or an occupation shows up in countless lives all around us.

It shows up in parents who will not quit loving their daughter even after she dyes her hair purple and tattoos her belly and runs off with a rock band. It shows up in couples who choose to mend their marriages instead of filing for divorce. It shows up in volunteers at the hospital or library or women's shelter or soup kitchen. It shows up in unsung people everywhere who do their jobs well, not because the supervisor is watching or because they are paid gobs of money, but because they know their work matters.

> *Fidelity to a mission shows up at hospitals, libraries, women's shelters and soup kitchens— in unsung people everywhere.*

When my son Jesse was in sixth grade, his teacher was diagnosed with breast cancer. She told the children about the disease, about the surgery and therapy, and about her hopes for recovery. Jesse came home deeply impressed that she had trusted them with her news. She could have stayed home for the rest of the year on medical leave, but as soon as the mastectomy

healed, she began going in to school one afternoon a week, then two, then a full day, then two days and three.

When a parent worried aloud that she might be risking her health for the sake of the children, the teacher scoffed, "Oh, heavens no! They're my best medicine." Besides, these children would only be in sixth grade once, she said, and she meant to help them all she could while she had the chance.

The therapy must have worked, because ten years later she's going strong. When I see her around town, she always asks about Jesse. Is he still so funny, so bright, so excited about learning? He is, I tell her, and she beams.

A cause needn't be grand, it needn't impress a crowd to be worthy of our commitment. I have a friend who built houses Monday through Friday for people who could pay him and then built other houses for free on Saturday with Habitat for Humanity. A neighbor makes herself available to international students and their families, unriddling for them the puzzles of living in this new place. Other neighbors coach soccer, visit the sick, give rides to the housebound, tutor dropouts, teach adults to read. I could multiply these examples a hundredfold without ever leaving my county. Most likely you could do the same. Any community worth living in must have a web of people faithful to good work and to one another, or that community would fall apart.

To say that fidelity is common is not to say it's easy, painless, or free. It costs energy and time, maybe a lifetime.

And every firm yes we say requires many a firm no. One Sunday I was talking with the man who visited prisoners in jail, when a young woman approached to ask if he would join the board of a new peace group she was organizing. In a rush of words she told him why the cause was crucial, why the time was ripe, why she absolutely needed his leadership. Knowing this man's sympathies, I figured he would agree to serve. But after listening to her plea, he gazed at her soberly for a moment, then said, "That certainly

is a vital concern, worthy of all your passion. But it is not my concern."

The challenge for all of us is to find those few causes that are peculiarly our own—those to which we are clearly called—and then to embrace them with all our heart. By remaining faithful to a calling, we can create the conditions for finding a purpose and a pattern in our days.

If you imagine trying to solve all the world's problems at once, though, you're likely to quit before you finish rolling up your sleeves. But If you stake out your own workable territory, if you settle on a manageable number of causes, then you might accomplish a great deal, all the while trusting that others elsewhere are working faithfully in their own places.

I Once Was Lost

Orphaned and abandoned, Antwone Fisher thought he was alone in the world—until his heart led him home.

—

BY **ANTWONE QUENTON FISHER**
FROM THE BOOK **FINDING FISH**

Originally published in July 2001

began writing the story of my life when I was just a security guard at Sony Pictures Entertainment in Los Angeles. It was my first screenplay, so I labored long and hard on it, writing 41 drafts in all.

Then, in a wildly dramatic outcome, I learned that the story was bought by Twentieth Century Fox. Denzel Washington would direct the film and probably act in it as well.

If all of this seemed so incredible—even too good to be true—it's because my life, up to that point, had been one excruciating struggle.

As a foster child growing up in Cleveland, I'd suffered abuse, neglect, and mind-numbing despair. On top of that, I'd never known my real parents or my next of kin.

What little I did know about my family included the fact that my father, Edward Elkins, had died before I was born. And that my mother's name was Eva Fisher. But when I tried to locate her, I'd had no luck.

The hole in my heart, I thought,

The author with his wife, LaNette, and daughter, Indigo. "I used to be suspicious of happiness. Not anymore," he says.

would never be healed. Then came the day when, searching for my father's relatives, I finally struck gold.

The woman's voice on the other end of the phone was warm. "Hello?"

"Hello," I said nervously. "My name is Antwone Fisher. I'm calling long distance from Los Angeles ... Uh, is this Annette Elkins?" I'd more or less picked her name at random from the Cleveland telephone book.

"Yes?" she replied.

"I'm looking for the family of an Edward Elkins, and I was wondering if you might have a relative by that name."

"I have a brother by that name," the woman said. "But he's been dead a long time." She paused. "Who is this?"

Softly I answered, "I ... I think I'm his son."

Another stretch of silence followed. Finally she said, "Well, if you are Edward's son, you have a big family."

In a whirl of disbelief, I told Annette my birth date, my mother's name, and that I had been raised as a ward of the state, mainly in a foster home in Glenville, a section of Cleveland. After my foster mother kicked me out at the age of 16, I'd bounced around in the world quite a bit. I'd served in the Navy, and now I was holding my own as a security guard in L.A.

After I had finished talking,

> *I began writing the story of my life when I was just a security guard at Sony Pictures Entertainment.*

Annette told me that if anybody in the Elkins family had known about me, they would have found me and brought me home as one of their own.

Holding back my tears, I listened as Annette filled me in on the family I'd been missing all my life. Incredibly, the Elkins family had lived two blocks away from where

I'd grown up. Annette said that her parents (my grandparents) had died some years earlier. Still living in Cleveland were her two sisters and two brothers. Another sister lived in Chicago.

Annette took my phone number, and then decided to give me the numbers of my aunts and uncles.

My aunts and uncles. I hung up, already feeling all kinds of new and unidentifiable sensations.

Shortly after that, the phone rang. It was my aunt Eda, calling from Chicago.

Within minutes I felt as if I'd known her for years. A teacher, Eda was articulate and well read, a lover of poets from Shakespeare to Edgar Allan Poe. "And your father, Eddie, was a wonderful writer," she said. "I'll never forget the letters and poems he sent home when he was in the Army."

I told Eda a little about my story, mentioning that I wrote poems as well. I even offered to send her some.

When she received them, Eda wrote back, amazed at how much my writing reminded her of my

The author's father, Edward Elkins, as a young man in Cleveland, Ohio.

father's. During our next phone call, she asked about the possibility of my visiting Cleveland to meet the family.

"I'm new on my job and won't have any vacation for a while," I replied. "I hope I can come next summer."

She assured me that everyone was happy about the prospect of meeting me. They would just have to be patient, she said. Then, shortly before Thanksgiving, Eda surprised me with an invitation to come for the holiday. The family, she said, wanted to contribute to the cost of my plane ticket.

The author, center, with some of his strongest supporters: from left, wife LaNette and daughter Indigo; social worker Patricia Nees Klanac; teacher Brenda Profit; and Navy mentor Lawrence Akiona.

I asked my supervisor about taking time off from work and told him my story. When he gave his OK, I made the ten-day trip.

Each moment, each encounter, was happier and more poignant than the last. All the Elkinses were attractive and tall, with unusual colored eyes—greens, silvers, browns. And everyone said how much I looked like my father.

The love and happiness I felt coming toward me and flowing out of me was like a powerful cleansing. That Thanksgiving I was the guest of honor as we ate turkey and gravy, stuffing, cranberries, sweet potatoes, and all kinds of desserts.

I was given a picture of my father, Eddie. In uniform at age

19, he looked ready to take on the world. His smile could light up the night sky.

My head was still spinning from all of this when I stayed over one night at the home of my half-sister Pamela. Early the next morning she and my other half-sister, Renee, walked right into my room and sat on the bed, waking me up.

I was surprised to see them there. I'd never had sisters before, so I thought this must be what sisters do.

Pamela began urgently, "Spi called." She was referring to our uncle Spinoza.

Then Renee interjected, "He thinks they found your mother."

I got dressed. In the car, Spi recounted how his wife had had the idea to call a longtime family friend, Jess Fisher. Jess, a retired construction worker, did have the same last name as mine. "So I just called him," Spi said, "and asked him if he knew anybody named Eva Fisher."

Eva Fisher, as it turned out, was his sister.

We went to meet Jess, a short, strong-looking man. "I'm glad to meet you," I said to the first relative on my mother's side.

"You can call me Jess. Or, you can call me Fish," he said, grinning.

"You can call me Fish," I replied, smiling back.

We rode together for a while, my two uncles and I. Then Jess parked in front of a housing project. My

Holding back my tears, I listened as Annette filled me in on the family I'd been missing.

heart beat rapidly as we approached the door.

I had prepared a script in my mind for what I needed to say to my mother. It had been painfully written over the 33 years of my life. I would ask: Why didn't you come for me? Didn't you ever wonder about me? What I was doing, or if I was even still alive?

She would hear me say, I dreamed about you every day,

what you looked like, your voice, even your scent. Didn't you miss me at all?

I would let her know that I'd taken care of myself all my life, that I'd never been in trouble with the law. I've made my way through some terrible times, I'd say. And I've become a good man, a good person.

But then the door opened, and I walked into a dimly lit apartment with shabby furniture. Turning, I saw a frail woman who looked too old to be my mother. Her hair was uncombed. She wore nightclothes.

Jess said to his sister, "This is Antwone Quenton Fisher." She made the connection and started to moan, losing her footing, holding on to a chair. "Oh, God, please ... Oh God. I thought it was Eddie. Oh, Lord!"

I went to her and put my arms around her. I tried to look at her to say that it was all right, but she turned her face away in awful shame. And when I released her, she hurried out of the room, crying.

I later learned that my mother had tried to get a man to marry her so she could come for me, and take care of me in an environment that would satisfy social services. "But there just wasn't enough love there" was her reason it didn't work out.

After giving birth to me, my mother had gone on to bear four other children. Like me, all of them grew up as wards of the state. Over the years, for various reasons, my

> *I had prepared a script in my mind for what I needed to say to my mother. It had been painfully written over the 33 years of my life.*

mother had been hospitalized, incarcerated, and on probation.

Though my road had been long and hard, I finally understood that my mother's had been longer and harder.

She had faced poverty, loneliness, and rejection. Where the hurt of abandonment had lived inside me, now there was only compassion.

I had not cried in Cleveland. But on the plane back to L.A. my protective shield came down and I could no longer dam up the tears.

I had found out the truth about my parents, so different from what I had imagined. They were human and flawed, like me. But I loved them and forgave them. Though I was just a security guard at the time, when I came back to L.A. I felt like a very rich man.

Here's where my life turned into a wild and different kind of adventure. After I'd told my supervisor my story—because I needed time off to meet my family—he had been moved enough to tell others about me. By the time I got back to work, many producers on the Sony lot had heard about me, and several production entities began courting me.

They all wanted to make a movie about my life. But there was a catch: They wanted an established screenwriter to tell my story. Whenever I suggested myself, I was politely dismissed.

I may have been inexperienced in deal-making for movies, but I knew enough not to sell myself short. No one had to give me permission to write. So, under the tutelage of a producer who believed in me—a man by the name of Todd Black—I wrote my own screenplay until I got it right.

Today, I keep in touch with my relatives. I'm also a husband and the father of a little girl. When Indigo is older, she'll know the story of my childhood. And she'll understand why, after spending so long finding a family, it's difficult for me to be separated from her or her mother for even one night.

Credits and Acknowledgments

"Where Success Comes From" by Arthur Gordon, *Reader's Digest*, June 1960
    Illustrations on page 1, 5 by Reader's Digest

"An Electric Nightmare" by John Robben, *Reader's Digest*, June 1973
    Illustration on page 11 by Reader's Digest

"Anybody Want to Buy a $2,300 Dog?" by Robert de Roos, *Reader's Digest*, October 1958
    Illustration on page 12 by Reader's Digest

"Terror in the Night" by Dave Shiflett, *Reader's Digest*, September 1991

"My Bad Genes" by Michael Ian Black from the book *Naval Gazing* by Michael Ian Black, Copyright © 2016 by Hot Schwartz Productions, Inc., published by Gallery Books, a division of Simon & Schuster, Inc.; *Reader's Digest*, February 2017
    Illustration on page 22 by Marcos Chin

"A Soldier's Story" by Robert Hodierne, *Reader's Digest*, May 2002
    Photograph on pages 30-31/back cover courtesy Robert Hodierne

"Tear Down This Wall" by Peter Robinson from the book *Tear Down This Wall: How Ronald Reagan Changed My Life*, Copyright © 2003 by Peter Robinson, published by HarperCollins Publishers; *Reader's Digest*, February 2004
    Photograph on pages 36-37 by Mike Sargent/AFP via Getty Images

"The Night I Met Einstein" by Jerome Weidman, *Reader's Digest*, November 1955
    Photograph on page 38 by The LIFE Picture Collection/Shutterstock

"Awake Through a Brain Operation" by Annette Anselmo, *Reader's Digest*, July 1964

"My Fight with Jack Dempsey" by Paul Gallico, *Reader's Digest*, July 1954
    Illustration on page 53 by Reader's Digest

"So Long, Duck" by Virginia Bennett Moore, *Reader's Digest*, April 1970
    Illustration on page 57 by Reader's Digest

"The Case of the Swaggering Smuggler" by Richard & Joyce Wolkomir, *Reader's Digest*, May 1994
    Illustrations on page 63, 64, 69 by Reader's Digest

"The Greatest Quotes Never Said" by Ralph Keyes from the book *Nice Guys Finish Seventh*, Copyright © 1992 by Ralph Keyes, published by HarperCollins Publishers; *Reader's Digest*, June 1993
    Illustrations on pages 73, 74, 77 by Michael Witte

"My Father's Music" by Wayne Kalyn, *Reader's Digest*, August 1991

"There's a Tidal Wave Loose in Here!" by Lawrence Elliott, *Reader's Digest*, July 1960
    Illustrations on pages 82, 91 by Reader's Digest

"Bit by the Fitbit" by David Sedaris from *The New Yorker* and currently published in the book *Calypso*, Copyright © 2018 by David Sedaris, published by Back Bay Books/Little, Brown and Company; *Reader's Digest*, June 2015
    Illustration on page 93 by John Cuneo

"1,000 Men and a Baby" by Lawrence Elliott, *Reader's Digest*, December 1994
    Illustration on page 103 by Reader's Digest

"The Kidnapping of Christine Aragao" by Malcolm McConnell, *Reader's Digest*, February 2001

"Princess Power" by Ashley Lewis, *Reader's Digest*, February 2018
    Photograph on page 112/front cover by Mike McGregor

"Call of the Wild" by Penny Porter, *Reader's Digest*, February 1997
Photograph on page 121 (cat) by Tom Rosenthal/ Superstock; Ron Dahlquist/ Superstock

"How We Kept Mother's Day" by Stephen Leacock from the book *The Leacock Roundabout*, Copyright © 1926 by Dodd, Mead & Co.; *Reader's Digest*, May 1950

"A Life in Buttons" by Karen Grissinger from *Country Woman* (February/ March 2017); *Reader's Digest*, July/August 2020
Illustration on page 124 by Maria Amador for Reader's Digest

"Deadly Cargo" by Christopher Davis, *Reader's Digest*, July 2001
Illustration on page 130 by Tom Christopher; photograph by Jon Muresan

"The Funniest Football Game Ever Played" by O. K. Armstrong, *Reader's Digest*, October 1955
Illustration on page 134 by Reader's Digest

"Killer Connection" by Ann Rule, *Reader's Digest*, October 2004
Photographs on page 141 by Kevin Horan; pages 143, 144 (right), 147, 148 (left), 152 (victims) courtesy Anne Rule; page 144 (Ted Bundy) by Bettman/Getty

Images; page 148 (right) by Eric Gay/AP Photo; page 152 (Green River) by Matthew McVay; page 154 by Anthony P. Bolante/ Reuters; page 155 by Elaine Thompson/Shutterstock

"'You Two Must Meet!'" by Cornelia Otis Skinner, *Reader's Digest*, August 1961

"The Will to Live" by Gail Cameron Wescott, *Reader's Digest*, March 2004
Photograph on pages 160, 165 courtesy Greg and Laura Manning

"Well, This Is Awkward" by Jessica Hagy, *Reader's Digest*, March 2014
Illustration on page 167 by Steve Wacksman

"I Hunted Down the Woman Who Stole My Life" by Anita Bartholomew, *Reader's Digest*, January 2008
Photograph on page 170 by Erik Butler; page 173 by San Francisco Chronicle/ Getty Images; page 174 Paul Chinn/San Francisco Chronicle/Getty Images; illustration on page 176 by Jason Lee

"My Mother Barked like a Seal" by Jeanmarie Coogan from *Ladies' Home Journal* (May 1962), Copyright © 1962 by Jeanmarie Coogan; *Reader's Digest*, May 1994

"50 Seconds from Death"

by Robert Kiener, *Reader's Digest*, June 2017
Photograph on page 183 by Fly Fast/Getty Images; pages 186-187 by Robin O'Neill/ViralHog; page 188/front cover by West Australian Newspapers Limited

"America's 10 Funniest Jokes" by Andy Simmons, *Reader's Digest*, June 2009
Illustration on page 191 by Drew Friedman

"A Dog like No Other" by Peter Muilenburg, *Reader's Digest*, June 1998
Illustration on page 203 by William Low

"The Book That Changed My Life" by Rick Bragg, *Reader's Digest*, May 2010
Illustration on page 204 by Jason Holley; photograph on page 211 Bettmann/Getty Images

"'Twas the Night After Christmas..." by Corey Ford, *Reader's Digest*, January 1960
Illustration on page 215 by Reader's Digest

"'I Never Forgot You'" by Marina Lopes from *The Washington Post Magazine* (February 6, 2019), Copyright © 2019 by Washington Post; *Reader's Digest*, International Edition, 2020
Photographs on pages 216/back cover, 223 courtesy of the author; page

220 by Shutterstock

"The Almost-Perfect Kidnapping" by Joseph P. Blank, *Reader's Digest*, June 1971

"Bad Puns Are How Eye Roll" by Peter Rubin from *Wired* (September 29, 2016), Copyright © 2016 by Condé Nast; *Reader's Digest*, November 2017
　Photograph on page 235/back cover by Lapina/Shutterstock; page 236 by Ryan Young

"My Journey to Moscow" by Ed Sullivan, *Reader's Digest*, March 1960
　Photograph on page 240 by Hulton Archive/Getty Images

"Almost Ready to Do My Taxes!" by Emma Rathbone from *The New York Times* (March 12, 2016), Copyright © 2016 by Emma Rathbone; *Reader's Digest*, April 2017

"The Case of the Blasted Bank" by Evan McLeod Wylie from *True, The Man's Magazine* (November 1962), Copyright © 1962 by Fawcett Publications, Inc.; *Reader's Digest*, February 1962
　Illustration on page 254 by Reader's Digest

"Beyond Tragedy" by Kathleen Kennedy Townsend, *Reader's Digest*, November 2008
　Photograph on pages 256 courtesy Elizabeth Kuhner Archives; page 258 Yale Joel/The LIFE Picture Collection/Shutterstock; page 261 by Hulton Archive/Getty Images; page 262 public domain; page 265 Paul Schutzer/The LIFE Picture Collection/Shutterstock; 268 by Roberto Borea/AP

"25 Jokes That Make You Sound like a Genius" by Andy Simmons, *Reader's Digest*, September 2014
　Illustrations on page 270, 273 by Steve Wacksman

"The Sweet Uses of Solitude" by Joan Mills, *Reader's Digest*, June 1970

"Alone with a Madman" by William M. Hendryx, *Reader's Digest*, March 1997
　Photographs on page 278, 283, 286 by Lum/The Honolulu Advertiser

"'I Died at 10:52 A.M.'" by Victor D. Solow, *Reader's Digest*, October 1974

"What I Learned from Hemingway" by W. J. Lederer, *Reader's Digest*, March 1962
　Photograph on page 294 by Hulton Deutsch/Getty Images

"Early to Bed and Late to Rise..." by Don Herold, *Reader's Digest*, August 1965
　Illustration on page 298 by Reader's Digest

"How to Be True to You" by Scott Russell Sanders from the book *Hunting for Hope*, Copyright © 1998 by Scott Russell Sanders, published by Beacon Press; *Reader's Digest*, June 2000

"I Once Was Lost" by Antwone Quenton Fisher from the book *Finding Fish*, Copyright © 2001 by Antwone Quenton Fisher and Mim Eichler Rivas, published by William Morrow/HarperCollins Publishers; *Reader's Digest*, July 2001
　Photographs on page 304/back cover and 308 by Stephanie Diani; page 307 courtesy of the author

Photograph of dog on front cover: Tatyana Consaul/Getty Images

Photograph of barn on front cover: arinahabich/Getty Images